Table of Contents

```
   SAS statements
   do j=1 to 10;
      SAS statements
   end;
      SAS statements
end;
```

The DATA step below computes the value of a one-year investment that earns 7.5% annual interest, compounded monthly.

```
data work.earn;
   Capital=2000;
   do month=1 to 12;
      Interest=capital*(.075/12);
      capital+interest;
   end;
run;
```

Let's assume the same amount of capital is to be added to the investment each year for 20 years. The new program must perform the calculation for each month during each of the 20 years. To do this, you can include the monthly calculations within another DO loop that executes 20 times.

```
data work.earn;
   do year=1 to 20;
      Capital+2000;
      do month=1 to 12;
         Interest=capital*(.075/12);
         capital+interest;
      end;
   end;
run;
```

During each iteration of the outside DO loop, an additional 2,000 is added to the capital, and the nested DO loop executes twelve times.

```
data work.earn;
   do year=1 to 20;
      Capital+2000;
      do month=1 to 12;
         Interest=capital*(.075/12);
         capital+interest;
      end;
   end;
run;
```

Remember, in order for nested DO loops to execute correctly, you must assign a unique index-variable name in each iterative DO statement.

```
data work.earn;
  do year=1 to 20;
    Capital+2000;
    do month=1 to 12;
      Interest=capital*(.075/12);
      capital+interest;
    end;
  end;
run;
```

end each DO loop with an END statement.

```
data work.earn;
  do year=1 to 20;
    Capital+2000;
    do month=1 to 12;
      Interest=capital*(.075/12);
      capital+interest;
    end;
  end;
run;
```

It is easier to manage nested DO loops if you indent the statements in each DO loop as shown above.

Mixing Input Styles

Evaluating your raw data and choosing the most appropriate input style is a very important task. You have already worked with three input styles for reading raw data.

Input Styles and the Types of Information They Read

Input Style	Reads
Column	standard data values in fixed fields
Formatted	standard and nonstandard data values in fixed fields

List   data values that are not arranged in fixed fields, but are separated by blanks or other delimiters

With some file layouts, you might need to mix input styles in the same INPUT statement in order to read the data correctly.

Look at the raw data file below and think about how to combine input styles to read these values.

Raw Data Showing Mixed Input Styles

```
1---+----10---+----20---+----30---+----40-
209-20-3721 07JAN78 41,983 SALES 2896
223-96-8933 03MAY86 27,356 EDUCATION 2344
232-18-3485 17AUG81 33,167 MARKETING 2674
251-25-9392 08SEP84 34,033 RESEARCH 2956
```

Column input is an appropriate choice for the first field because the values can be read as standard character values and are located in fixed columns.

The next two fields are also located in fixed columns, but the values require an informat. So, formatted input is a good choice here.

Values in the fourth field begin in column 28 but do not end in the same column. List input is appropriate here, but notice that some values are longer than eight characters. You need to use the : format modifier with an informat to read these values.

The last field does not always begin or end in the same column, so list input is the best input style for those values.

Input Styles to Read the Raw Data

Field Description	Starting Column	Field Width	Data Type	Input Style
Social Security #	1	11	character	column
Date of Hire	13	7	date	formatted
Annual Salary	21	6	numeric	formatted
Department	28	5 to 9	character	list

Phone Extension	??	4	character	list

The INPUT statement to read the data should look like this:


```
data sasuser.mixedstyles;
  infile rawdata.dat;
  input SSN $ 1-11 @13 HireDate date7.
     @21 Salary comma6. Department : $9. Phone $;
run;
proc print data=sasuser.mixedstyles;
run;
```

When you submit the PRINT procedure, the output displays values for each variable.

Output Created by PROC PRINT

Obs	SSN	HireDate	Salary	Department	Phone
1	209-20-3721	6581	41983	SALES	2896
2	223-96-8933	9619	27356	EDUCATION	2344
3	232-18-3485	7899	33167	MARKETING	2674
4	251-25-9392	9017	34033	RESEARCH	2956

Group Processing Using the BY Statement

Like the CLASS statement, the BY statement specifies variables to use for categorizing observations.

General form, BY statement:

BY *variable(s)*;

where *variable(s)* specifies category variables for group processing.

But BY and CLASS differ in two key ways:

Unlike CLASS processing, BY processing requires that your data already be sorted or indexed in the order of the BY variables. Unless data set observations are already sorted, you will need to run the SORT procedure before using PROC MEANS with any BY group.

⚠ Be careful when sorting data sets to enable group processing. If you don't specify an output data set by using the OUT= option, PROC SORT will overwrite your initial data set with the newly sorted observations.

BY group results have a layout that is different from the layout of CLASS group results. Note that the BY statement in the program below creates four small tables; a CLASS statement would produce a single large table.

```
proc sort data=clinic.heart out=work.heartsort;
   by survive sex;
run;
proc means data=work.heartsort maxdec=1;
   var arterial heart cardiac urinary;
   by survive sex;
run;
```

BY Groups Created by PROC MEANS

The MEANS Procedure

Survive=DIED Sex=1

Variable	N	Mean	Std Dev	Minimum	Maximum
Arterial	4	92.5	10.5	83.0	103.0
Heart	4	111.0	53.4	54.0	183.0
Cardiac	4	176.8	75.2	95.0	260.0
Urinary	4	98.0	186.1	0.0	377.0

Survive=DIED Sex=2

Variable	N	Mean	Std Dev	Minimum	Maximum
Arterial	6	94.2	27.3	72.0	145.0
Heart	6	103.7	16.7	81.0	130.0
Cardiac	6	318.3	102.6	156.0	424.0
Urinary	6	100.3	155.7	0.0	405.0

Survive=SURV Sex=1

Variable	N	Mean	Std Dev	Minimum	Maximum
Arterial	5	77.2	12.2	61.0	88.0
Heart	5	109.0	32.0	77.0	149.0
Cardiac	5	298.0	139.8	66.0	410.0
Urinary	5	100.8	60.2	44.0	200.0

Survive=SURV Sex=2

Variable	N	Mean	Std Dev	Minimum	Maximum
Arterial	5	78.8	6.8	72.0	87.0
Heart	5	100.0	13.4	84.0	111.0
Cardiac	5	330.2	87.0	256.0	471.0
Urinary	5	111.2	152.4	12.0	377.0

Because it doesn't require a sorting step, the CLASS statement is easier to use than the BY statement. However, BY group processing can be more efficient when your categories might contain many levels.

Chapter 9: Producing HTML Output

Using ODS statements, how many types of output can you generate at once?

1 (only HTML output)

2

3

as many as you want

Correct answer: d

You can generate any number of output types as long as you open the ODS destination for each type of output you want to create.

If ODS is set to its default settings in the SAS windowing environment for Microsoft Windows and UNIX, , what types of output are created by the code below?

```
ods html file='c:\myhtml.htm';
ods pdf file='c:\mypdf.pdf';
```

HTML and PDF

PDF only

HTML, PDF, and listing

No output is created because ODS is closed by default.

Correct answer: b

HTML output is created by default in the SAS windowing environment for Microsoft Windows and UNIX, so these statements create HTML and PDF output.

In the SAS windowing environment for Microsoft Windows and UNIX, what is the purpose of closing the HTML destination in the code shown below?

```
ods html close;
ods rtf ... ;
```

It conserves system resources.

It simplifies your program.

It makes your program compatible with other hardware platforms.

It makes your program compatible with previous versions of SAS.

Correct answer: a

By default, in the SAS windowing environment for Microsoft Windows and UNIX, SAS programs produce HTML output. If you want only RTF output, it's a good idea to close the HTML destination before creating RTF output, as an open destination uses system resources.

When the code shown below is run, what will the file **D:\Output\body.html** contain?

```
ods html body='d:\output\body.html';
proc print data=work.alpha;
run;
proc print data=work.beta;
run;
ods html close;
```

The PROC PRINT output for Work.Alpha.

The PROC PRINT output for Work.Beta.

The PROC PRINT output for both Work.Alpha and Work.Beta.

Nothing. No output will be written to **D:\Output\body.html**.

Correct answer: c

When multiple procedures are run while HTML output is open, procedure output is appended to the same body file.

When the code shown below is run, what file will be referenced by the links in
D:\Output\contents.html?

```
ods html body='d:\output\body.html'
        contents='d:\output\contents.html'
        frame='d:\output\frame.html';
```

D:\Output\body.html

D:\Output\contents.html

D:\Output\frame.html

There are no links from the file **D:\Output\contents.html**.

Correct answer: a

The CONTENTS= option creates a table of contents containing links to the body file,
D:\Output\body.html.

The table of contents created by the CONTENTS= option contains a numbered heading for

each procedure.

each procedure that creates output.

each procedure and DATA step.

each HTML file created by your program.

Correct answer: b

The table of contents contains a numbered heading for each procedure that creates output.

When the code shown below is run, what will the file **D:\Output\frame.html** display?

```
ods html body='d:\output\body.html'
      contents='d:\output\contents.html'
      frame='d:\output\frame.html';
```

The file **D:\Output\contents.html**.

The file **D:\Output\frame.html**.

The files **D:\Output\contents.html** and **D:\Output\body.html**.

It displays no other files.

Correct answer: c

The FRAME= option creates an HTML file that integrates the table of contents and the body file.

What is the purpose of the URL= suboptions shown below?

```
ods html body='d:\output\body.html' (url='body.html')
      contents='d:\output\contents.html'
      (url='contents.html')
      frame='d:\output\frame.html';
```

To create absolute link addresses for loading the files from a server.

To create relative link addresses for loading the files from a server.

To allow HTML files to be loaded from a local drive.

To send HTML output to two locations.

Correct answer: b

Specifying the URL= suboption in the file specification provides a URL that ODS uses in the links it creates. Specifying a simple (one name) URL creates a relative link address to the file.

Which ODS HTML option was used in creating the following table?

XisError: altImageDescription Element Should Not Be Blank.

Obs	Sex	Age	Height	Weight	ActLevel
1	M	27	72	168	HIGH
2	F	34	66	152	HIGH
3	F	31	61	123	LOW

format=brown

format='brown'

style=brown.

style='brown'

Correct answer: c

You can change the appearance of HTML output by using the STYLE= option in the ODS HTML statement. The style name doesn't need quotation marks.

What is the purpose of the PATH= option?

```
ods html path='d:\output' (url=none)
     body='body.html'
     contents='contents.html'
     frame='frame.html';
```

It creates absolute link addresses for loading HTML files from a server.

It creates relative link addresses for loading HTML files from a server.

It allows HTML files to be loaded from a local drive.

It specifies the location of HTML file output.

Correct answer: d

You use the PATH= option to specify the location for HTML files to be stored. When you use the PATH= option, you don't need to specify the full path name for the body, contents, or frame files.

Chapter 8: Producing Descriptive Statistics

The default statistics produced by the MEANS procedure are n, mean, minimum, maximum, and...

median

range

standard deviation

standard error of the mean.

Correct answer: c

By default, the MEANS procedure produces the n, mean, minimum, maximum, and standard deviation.

Which statement will limit a PROC MEANS analysis to the variables Boarded, Transfer, and Deplane?

by boarded transfer deplane;

class boarded transfer deplane;

output boarded transfer deplane;

var boarded transfer deplane;

Correct answer: d

To specify the variables that PROC MEANS analyzes, add a VAR statement and list the variable names.

The data set Survey.Health includes the following variables. Which is a poor candidate for PROC MEANS analysis?

IDnum

Age

Height

Weight

Correct answer: a

Unlike Age, Height, or·Weight, the values of IDnum are unlikely to yield any useful statistics.

Which of the following statements is true regarding BY group processing?

BY variables must be either indexed or sorted.

Summary statistics are computed for BY variables.

BY group processing is preferred when you are categorizing data that contains few variables.

BY group processing overwrites your data set with the newly grouped observations.

Correct answer: a

Unlike CLASS processing, BY group processing requires that your data already be indexed or sorted in the order of the BY variables. You might need to run the SORT procedure before using PROC MEANS with a BY group.

Which group processing statement produced the PROC MEANS output shown below?

XisError: altImageDescription Element Should Not Be Blank.

The MEANS Procedure

Survive	Sex	N Obs	Variable	N	Mean	Std Dev	Minimum	Maximum
DIED	1	4	Arterial	4	92.5000000	10.4721854	83.0000000	103.0000000
			Heart	4	111.0000000	53.4103610	54.0000000	183.0000000
			Cardiac	4	176.7500000	75.2257713	95.0000000	260.0000000
			Urinary	4	98.0000000	186.1343601	0	377.0000000
	2	6	Arterial	6	94.1666667	27.3160514	72.0000000	145.0000000
			Heart	6	103.6666667	16.6573307	81.0000000	130.0000000
			Cardiac	6	318.3333333	102.6034437	156.0000000	424.0000000
			Urinary	6	100.3333333	155.7134120	0	405.0000000
SURV	1	5	Arterial	5	77.2000000	12.1942609	61.0000000	88.0000000
			Heart	5	109.0000000	31.9687347	77.0000000	149.0000000
			Cardiac	5	298.0000000	139.8499196	66.0000000	410.0000000
			Urinary	5	100.8000000	60.1722527	44.0000000	200.0000000
	2	5	Arterial	5	78.8000000	6.8337398	72.0000000	87.0000000
			Heart	5	100.0000000	13.3790882	84.0000000	111.0000000
			Cardiac	5	330.2000000	86.9839066	256.0000000	471.0000000
			Urinary	5	111.2000000	152.4096454	12.0000000	377.0000000

class sex survive;

class survive sex;

by sex survive;

by survive sex;

Correct answer: b

A CLASS statement produces a single large table, whereas BY group processing creates a series of small tables. The order of the variables in the CLASS statement determines their order in the output table.

Which program can be used to create the following output?

XisError: altImageDescription Element Should Not Be Blank.

Sex	N Obs	Variable	N	Mean	Std Dev	Minimum	Maximum
F	11	Age	11	48.9090909	13.3075508	16.0000000	63.0000000
		Height	11	63.9090909	2.1191765	61.0000000	68.0000000
		Weight	11	150.4545455	18.4464828	102.0000000	168.0000000
M	9	Age	9	44.0000000	12.3895117	15.0000000	54.0000000
		Height	9	70.6666667	2.6457513	66.0000000	75.0000000
		Weight	9	204.2222222	30.2893454	140.0000000	240.0000000

```
proc means data=clinic.diabetes;
  var age height weight;
  class sex;
  output out=work.sum_gender
    mean=AvgAge AvgHeight AvgWeight;
run;
```

```
proc summary data=clinic.diabetes print;
  var age height weight; class sex;
  output out=work.sum_gender
    mean=AvgAge AvgHeight AvgWeight;
run;
```

```
proc means data=clinic.diabetes noprint;
  var age height weight;
  class sex;
  output out=work.sum_gender
    mean=AvgAge AvgHeight AvgWeight;
run;
```

Both a and b.

Correct answer: d

You can use either PROC MEANS or PROC SUMMARY to create the table. Adding a PRINT option to the PROC SUMMARY statement produces the same report as if you used PROC MEANS.

By default, PROC FREQ creates a table of frequencies and percentages for which data set variables?

character variables

numeric variables

both character and numeric variables

none: variables must always be specified

Correct answer: c

By default, PROC FREQ creates a table for all variables in a data set.

Frequency distributions work best with variables that contain

continuous values.

numeric values. .

categorical values.

unique values.

Correct answer: c

Both continuous values and unique values can result in lengthy, meaningless tables. Frequency distributions work best with categorical values.

Which PROC FREQ step produced this two-way table?

XisError: altImageDescription Element Should Not Be Blank.

The FREQ Procedure

Frequency Percent Row Pct Col Pct	Table of Weight by Height			
		Height		
Weight	< 5'5"	5'5-10"	> 5'10"	Total
< 140	2	0	0	2
	10.00	0.00	0.00	10.00
	100.00	0.00	0.00	
	28.57	0.00	0.00	
140-180	5	5	0	10
	25.00	25.00	0.00	50.00
	50.00	50.00	0.00	
	71.43	62.50	0.00	
> 180	0	3	5	8
	0.00	15.00	25.00	40.00
	0.00	37.50	62.50	
	0.00	37.50	100.00	
Total	7	8	5	20
	35.00	40.00	25.00	100.00

```
proc freq data=clinic.diabetes;
   tables height weight;
   format height htfmt. weight wtfmt.;
run;



proc freq data=clinic.diabetes;
   tables weight height;
   format weight wtfmt. height htfmt.;
run;



proc freq data=clinic.diabetes;
   tables height*weight;
   format height htfmt. weight wtfmt.;
run;



proc freq data=clinic.diabetes;
   tables weight*height;
   format weight wtfmt. height htfmt.;
run;
```

Correct answer: d

An asterisk is used to join the variables in a two-way TABLES statement. The first variable forms the table rows. The second variable forms the table columns.

Which PROC FREQ step produced this table?

XisError: altImageDescription Element Should Not Be Blank.

The FREQ Procedure

Percent	Table of Sex by Weight			
		Weight		
Sex	< 140	140-180	> 180	Total
F	10.00	45.00	0.00	55.00
M	0.00	5.00	40.00	45.00
Total	2	10	8	20
	10.00	50.00	40.00	100.00

```
proc freq data=clinic.diabetes;
  tables sex weight / list;
  format weight wtfmt.;
run;



proc freq data=clinic.diabetes;
  tables sex*weight / nocol;
  format weight wtfmt.;
run;



proc freq data=clinic.diabetes;
  tables sex weight / norow nocol;
  format weight wtfmt.;
run;



proc freq data=clinic.diabetes;
  tables sex*weight / nofreq norow nocol;
  format weight wtfmt.;
run;
```

Correct answer: d

An asterisk is used to join the variables in crosstabulation tables. The only results shown in this table are cell percentages. The NOFREQ option suppresses cell frequencies, the NOROW option suppresses row percentages, and the NOCOL option suppresses column percentages.

Using Line Pointer Controls

You know that as SAS reads raw data values, it keeps track of its position with an input pointer. You have used column pointer controls and column specifications to determine the column placement of the input pointer.

Input Statements for Column Specifications and Column Pointer Controls

Column Specifications   **input Name $ 1-12 Age 15-16 Gender $ 18;**

Column Pointer Controls   **input Name $12. @15 Age 2. @18 Gender $1.;**

But you can also position the input pointer on a specific record by using a line pointer control in the INPUT statement.

INPUT Statement and Raw Data File Admit

input #2 Name $ 1-12 Age 15-16 Gender $ 18;

```
       Raw Data File Admit
    ┌─────────────────────────┐
    │1---+----10---+----      │
    │S. Thompson    37 M      │
    │L. Rochester   31 F      │
    │M. Sabatello   43 M      │
    └─────────────────────────┘
```

There are two types of line pointer controls.

The forward slash (/) specifies a line location that is relative to the current one.

The #*n* specifies the absolute number of the line to which you want to move the pointer.

First we'll look at the forward slash (/). Later in the chapter, you'll learn how to use the #*n*, and you will see how these two controls can be combined.

Identifying Observations

You've learned how to remove the Obs column altogether. As another alternative, you can use one or more variables to replace the Obs column in the output.

Using the ID Statement

To specify which variables should replace the Obs column, use the ID statement. This technique is particularly useful when observations are too long to print on one line.

General form, ID statement:

ID *variable(s)*;

where *variable(s)* specifies one or more variables to print instead of the observation number at the beginning of each row of the report.

Example

To replace the Obs column and identify observations based on an employee's ID number and last name, you can submit the following program.

```
proc print data=sales.reps;
   id idnum lastname;
run;
```

This is HTML output from the program:

HTML Output

IDnum	LastName	FirstName	City	State	Sex	JobCode	Salary	Birth	Hired	HomePhone
1269	CASTON	FRANKLIN	STAMFORD	CT	M	NA1	41690.00	06MAY60	01DEC80	203/781-3335
1935	FERNANDEZ	KATRINA	BRIDGEPORT	CT		NA2	51081.00	31MAR42	19OCT69	203/675-2962
1417	NEWKIRK	WILLIAM	PATERSON	NJ	,	NA2	52270.00	30JUN52	10MAR77	201/732-6611
1839	NORRIS	DIANE	NEW YORK	YN	F	NA1	43433.00	02DEC58	06JUL81	718/384-1767
1111	RHODES	JEREMY	PRINCETON	NJ	M	NA1	40586.00	17JUL61	03NOV80	201/812-1837
1352	RIVERS	SIMON	NEW YORK	NY	M	NA2	5379.80	05DEC48	19OCT74	718/383-3345
1332	STEPHENSON	ADAM	BRIDGEPORT	CT	M	NA1	42178.00	20SEP58	07JUN79	203/675-1497
1443	WELLS	AGNES	STAMFORD	CT	F	NA1	422.74	20NOV56	01SEP79	203/781-5546

In LISTING output, the IDnum and LastName columns are repeated for each observation that is printed on more than one line.

LISTING Output

```
 IDnum   LastName    FirstName     City       State    Sex    JobCode

  1269   CASTON      FRANKLIN     STAMFORD      CT       M       NA1
  1935   FERNANDEZ   KATRINA      BRIDGEPO      CT               NA2
  1417   NEWKIRK     WILLIAM      PATERSON      NJ       ,       NA2
  1839   NORRIS      DIANE        NEW YORK      NY       F       NA1
  1111   RHODES      JEREMY       PRINCETO      NJ       M       NA1
  1352   RIVERS      SIMON        NEW YORK      NY       M       NA2
  1332   STEPHENS    ADAM         BRIDGEPO      CT       M       NA1
  1443   WELLS       AGNES        STAMFORD      CT       F       NA1


 IDnum   LastName     Salary      Birth       Hired       HomePhone

  1269   CASTON      41690.00    06MAY60     01DEC80     203/781-3335
  1935   FERNANDEZ   51081.00    31MAR42     19OCT69     203/675-2962
  1417   NEWKIRK     52270.00    30JUN52     10MAR77     201/732-6611
  1839   NORRIS      43433.00    02DEC58     06JUL81     718/384-1767
  1111   RHODES      40586.00    17JUL61     03NOV80     201/812-1837
  1352   RIVERS       5379.80    05DEC48     19OCT74     718/383-3345
  1332   STEPHENS    42178.00    20SEP58     07JUN79     203/675-1497
  1443   WELLS         422.74    20NOV56     01SEP79     203/781-5546
```

If a variable in the ID statement also appears in the VAR statement, the output contains two columns for that variable. In the example below, the variable IDnum appears twice.

```
proc print data=sales.reps;
   id idnum lastname;
   var idnum sex jobcode salary;
run;
```

IDNUM Output

IDnum	LastName	IDnum	Sex	JobCode	Salary
1269	CASTON	1269	M	NA1	41690.00
1935	FERNANDEZ	1935		NA2	51081.00
1417	NEWKIRK	1417	,	NA2	52270.00
1839	NORRIS	1839	F	NA1	43433.00
1111	RHODES	1111	M	NA1	40586.00
1352	RIVERS	1352	M	NA2	5379.80
1332	STEPHENSON	1332	M	NA1	42178.00
1443	WELLS	1443	F	NA1	422.74

Selecting Observations

By default, a PROC PRINT step lists all the observations in a data set. You can control which observations are printed by adding a WHERE statement to your PROC PRINT step. There should be only one WHERE statement in a step. If multiple WHERE statements are issued, only the last statement is processed.

General form, WHERE statement:

WHERE *where-expression*;

where *where-expression* specifies a condition for selecting observations. The *where-expression* can be any valid SAS expression.

For example, the following WHERE statement selects only observations for which the value of Age is greater than 30:

```
proc print data=clinic.admit;
   var age height weight fee;
   where age>30;
run;
```

Here is the procedure output from the PROC PRINT step with the WHERE statement:

PROC PRINT Output with WHERE Statement

Obs	Age	Height	Weight	Fee
2	34	66	152	124.80
3	31	61	123	149.75
4	43	63	137	149.75
5	51	71	158	124.80
7	32	67	151	149.75
8	35	70	173	149.75
9	34	73	154	124.80
10	49	64	172	124.80
11	44	66	140	149.75
14	40	69	163	124.80
15	47	72	173	124.80
16	60	71	191	149.75
17	43	65	123	124.80
20	41	67	141	149.75
21	54	71	183	149.75

Specifying WHERE Expressions

In the WHERE statement you can specify any variable in the SAS data set, not just the variables that are specified in the VAR statement. The WHERE statement works for both character and numeric variables. To specify a condition based on the value of a character variable, you must

enclose the value in quotation marks

write the value with lowercase, uppercase, or mixed case letters exactly as it appears in the data set.

You use the following comparison operators to express a condition in the WHERE statement:

Comparison Operators in a WHERE Statement

Symbol	Meaning	Example

= or eq	equal to	**where name='Jones, C.';**
^= or ne	not equal to	**where temp ne 212;**
> or gt	greater than	**where income>20000;**
< or lt	less than	**where partno lt "BG05";**
>= or ge	greater than or equal to	**where id>='1543';**
<= or le	less than or equal to	**where pulse le 85;**

You can learn more about valid SAS expressions in <u>Creating SAS Data Sets from External Files</u>.

Using the CONTAINS Operator

The CONTAINS operator selects observations that include the specified substring. The symbol for the CONTAINS operator is **?**. You can use either the CONTAINS keyword or the symbol in your code, as shown below.

where firstname CONTAINS 'Jon';
where firstname ? 'Jon';

Specifying Compound WHERE Expressions

You can also use WHERE statements to select observations that meet multiple conditions. To link a sequence of expressions into compound expressions, you use logical operators, including the following:

Compound WHERE Expression Operators

Operator   Meaning

AND #38   and, both. If both expressions are true, then the compound expression is true.

OR | or, either. If either expression is true, then the compound expression is true.

Examples of WHERE Statements

You can use compound expressions like these in your WHERE statements:

```
where age<=55 and pulse>75;
where area='A' or region='S';
where ID>'1050' and state='NC';
```

When you test for multiple values of the same variable, you specify the variable name in each expression:

```
where actlevel='LOW' or actlevel='MOD';
where fee=124.80 or fee=178.20;
```

You can use the IN operator as a convenient alternative:

```
where actlevel in ('LOW','MOD');
where fee in (124.80,178.20);
```

To control the way compound expressions are evaluated, you can use parentheses (expressions in parentheses are evaluated first):

```
where (age<=55 and pulse>75) or area='A';
where age<=55 and (pulse>75 or area='A');
```

Referencing SAS Files

Two-Level Names

To reference a permanent SAS data set in your SAS programs, you use a two-level name consisting of the library name and the filename, or data set name:

libref.filename

In the two-level name, *libref* is the name of the SAS data library that contains the file, and *filename* is the name of the file, or data set. A period separates the libref and filename.

Two-Level SAS Name

For example, suppose we want to create a new permanent sas library named Clinic. In our sample program, Clinic.Admit is the two-level name for the SAS data set Admit, which is stored in the library named Clinic. Notice that the LIBNAME statement is used to define the libref, Clinic, and to give SAS the physical location of the data files.

```
libname clinic 'c:\Users\Name\sasuser';
data clinic.admit2;
  set clinic.admit;
  weight =round(weight);
run;
```

Two-Level Name Clinic.Admit

Referencing Temporary SAS Files

To reference temporary SAS files, you can specify the default libref Work, a period, and the filename. For example, the two-level name Work.Test references the SAS data set named *Test* that is stored in the temporary SAS library Work.

Two-Level Temporary SAS Library Work.Test

Alternatively, you can use a one-level name (the *filename* only) to reference a file in a temporary SAS library. When you specify a one-level name, the default libref Work is assumed. For example, the one-level name Test also references the SAS data set named Test that is stored in the temporary SAS library Work.

One-Level Temporary SAS Library Test

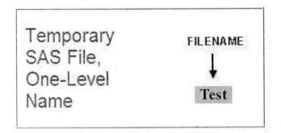

Referencing Permanent SAS Files

You can see that Clinic.Admit and Clinic.Admit2 are permanent SAS data sets because the library name is Clinic, not Work.

Referencing Permanent SAS Files

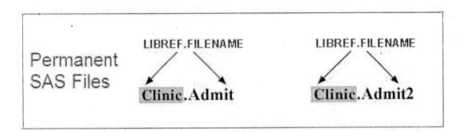

So, referencing a SAS file in any library except Work indicates that the SAS file is stored permanently. For example, when our sample program creates Clinic.Admit2, it stores the new Admit2 data set permanently in the SAS library Clinic.

Rules for SAS Names

These rules apply only to the filename portion of a SAS data set name. A libref can have a length of only eight characters.

SAS data set names and variable names

    can be 1 to 32 characters long

    must begin with a letter (A-Z, either uppercase or lowercase) or an underscore (_)

    can continue with any combination of numbers, letters, or underscores.

These are examples of valid data set names and variable names:

Payroll

LABDATA1995_1997

_EstimatedTaxPayments3

Chapter Quiz

Select the best answer for each question. After completing the quiz, you can check your answers using the answer key in the appendix.

Which program creates the output shown below?

Output 1

```
Raw Data File Furnture
1---+----10---+----20---+----30---+
310 oak    pedestal table 329.99
311 maple  pedestal table 369.99
312 brass  floor    lamp   79.99
313 glass  table    lamp   59.99
314 oak    rocking  chair 153.99
```

Output 2

StockNum	Finish	Style	Item	TotalPrice
310	oak	pedestal	table	329.99
311	maple	pedestal	table	699.98
312	brass	floor	lamp	779.97
313	glass	table	lamp	839.96

```
data test2;
   infile furnture;
   input StockNum $ 1-3 Finish $ 5-9 Style $ 11-18
       Item $ 20-24 Price 26-31;
   if finish='oak' then delete;
   retain TotPrice 100;
   totalprice+price;
   drop price;
run;
proc print data=test2 noobs;
run;
```

```
data test2;
   infile furnture;
   input StockNum $ 1-3 Finish $ 5-9 Style $ 11-18
```

```
         Item $ 20-24 Price 26-31;
      if finish='oak' and price<200 then delete;
      TotalPrice+price;
   run;
   proc print data=test2 noobs;
   run;




   data test2(drop=price);
      infile furnture;
      input StockNum $ 1-3 Finish $ 5-9 Style $ 11-18
         Item $ 20-24 Price 26-31;
      if finish='oak' and price<200 then delete;
      TotalPrice+price;
   run;
   proc print data=test2 noobs;
   run;




   data test2;
      infile furnture;
      input StockNum $ 1-3 Finish $ 5-9 Style $ 11-18
         Item $ 20-24 Price 26-31;
      if finish=oak and price<200 then delete price;
      TotalPrice+price;
   run;
   proc print data=test2 noobs;
   run;
```

How is the variable Amount labeled and formatted in the PROC PRINT output?

```
data credit;
   infile creddata;
   input Account $ 1-5 Name $ 7-25 Type $ 27
         Transact $ 29-35 Amount 37-50;
   label amount='Amount of Loan';
   format amount dollar12.2;
run;
proc print data=credit label;
   label amount='Total Amount Loaned';
   format amount comma10.;
run;
```

label Amount of Loan, format DOLLAR12.2

label Total Amount Loaned, format COMMA10.

label Amount, default format

The PROC PRINT step does not execute because two labels and two formats are assigned to the same variable.

Consider the IF-THEN statement shown below. When the statement is executed, which expression is evaluated first?

```
if finlexam>=95
  and (research='A' or
     (project='A' and present='A'))
  then Grade='A+';
```

finlexam>=95

research='A'

project='A' and present='A'

research='A' or
(project='A' and present='A')

Consider the small raw data file and program shown below. What is the value of Count after the fourth record is read?

```
data work.newnums;
  infile numbers;
  input Tens 2-3;
  Count+tens;
run;
```

XisError: altImageDescription Element Should Not Be Blank.

```
1---+----10
 10
 20

 40
 50
```

missing

0

30

70

Now consider the revised program below. What is the value of Count after the third observation is read?

```
data work.newnums;
   infile numbers;
   input Tens 2-3;
   retain Count 100;
   count+tens;
run;
```

XisError: altImageDescription Element Should Not Be Blank.

```
1---+----10
  10
  20

  40
  50
```

missing

0

100

130

For the observation shown below, what is the result of the IF-THEN statements?

Status	Type	Count	Action	Control
Ok	3	12	E	Go

```
if status='OK' and type=3
   then Count+1;
if status='S' or action='E'
   then Control='Stop';
```

Count = 12   Control = Go

Count = 13   Control = Stop

Count = 12   Control = Stop

Count = 13   Control = Go

Which of the following can determine the length of a new variable?

the length of the variable's first reference in the DATA step

the assignment statement

the LENGTH statement

all of the above

Which set of statements is equivalent to the code shown below?


```
if code='1' then Type='Fixed';
if code='2' then Type='Variable';
if code^='1' and code^='2' then Type='Unknown';
```


```
if code='1' then Type='Fixed';
else if code='2' then Type='Variable';
else Type='Unknown';
```


```
 if code='1' then Type='Fixed';
if code='2' then Type='Variable';
else Type='Unknown';
```


```
if code='1' then type='Fixed';
else code='2' and type='Variable';
else type='Unknown';
```

```
if code='1' and type='Fixed';
then code='2' and type='Variable';
else type='Unknown';
```

What is the length of the variable Type, as created in the DATA step below?

```
data finance.newloan;
  set finance.records;
  TotLoan+payment;
  if code='1' then Type='Fixed';
  else Type='Variable';
  length type $ 10;
run;
```

    5

    8

    10

    it depends on the first value of Type

Which program contains an error?

```
data clinic.stress(drop=timemin timesec);
  infile tests;
  input ID $ 1-4 Name $ 6-25 RestHR 27-29 MaxHR 31-33
     RecHR 35-37 TimeMin 39-40 TimeSec 42-43
     Tolerance $ 45;
  TotalTime=(timemin*60)+timesec;
  SumSec+totaltime;
run;
```

```
proc print data=clinic.stress;
  label totaltime='Total Duration of Test';
  format timemin 5.2;
  drop sumsec;
run;
```

```
proc print data=clinic.stress(keep=totaltime timemin);
  label totaltime='Total Duration of Test';
  format timemin 5.2;
run;
```

```
data clinic.stress;
   infile tests;
   input ID $ 1-4 Name $ 6-25 RestHR 27-29 MaxHR 31-33
      RecHR 35-37 TimeMin 39-40 TimeSec 42-43
      Tolerance $ 45;
   TotalTime=(timemin*60)+timesec;
   keep id totaltime tolerance;
run;
```

Match-Merge Processing

Overview

The match-merging examples in this chapter are straightforward. However, match-merging can be more complex, depending on your data and on the output data set that you want to create. To predict the results of match-merges correctly, you need to understand how the DATA step performs match-merges.

When you submit a DATA step, it is processed in two phases:

the compilation phase, in which SAS checks the syntax of the SAS statements and compiles them (translates them into machine code). During this phase, SAS also sets up descriptor information for the output data set and creates the program data vector (PDV), an area of memory where SAS holds one observation at a time.

Match-Merge Processing: Compilation Phase

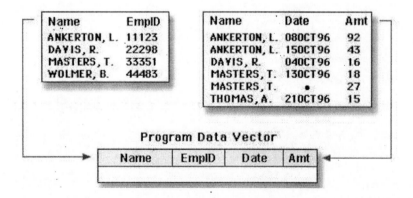

the execution phase, in which the DATA step reads data and executes any subsequent programming statements. When the DATA step executes, data values are read into the appropriate variables in the program data vector. From here, the variables are written to the output data set as a single observation.

Match-Merge Processing: Execution Phase

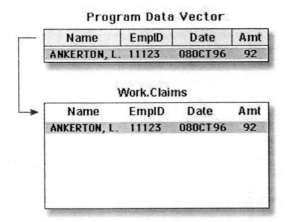

The following pages cover DATA step processing in greater detail. In those pages, you learn

how the DATA step sets up the new output data set

what happens when variables in different data sets have the same name

how the DATA step matches observations in input data sets

what happens when observations don't match

how missing values are handled.

The Compilation Phase: Setting Up the New Data Set

To prepare to merge data sets, SAS

reads the descriptor portions of the data sets that are listed in the MERGE statement

reads the rest of the DATA step program

creates the program data vector (PDV) for the merged data set

assigns a tracking pointer to each data set that is listed in the MERGE statement.

If variables that have the same name appear in more than one data set, the variable from the first data set that contains the variable (in the order listed in the MERGE statement) determines the length of the variable.

The Compilation Phase: Setting Up the New Data Set

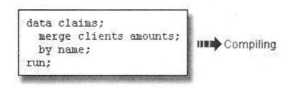

```
data claims;
   merge clients amounts;
   by name;
run;
```
⇒ Compiling

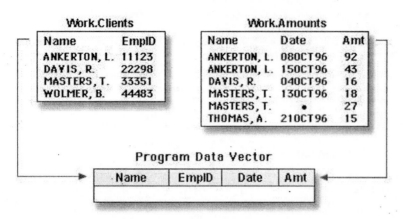

The illustration above shows match-merging during the compilation phase. After reading the descriptor portions of the data sets Clients and Amounts, SAS

> creates a program data vector for the new Claims data set. The program data vector contains all variables from the two data sets. Note that although Name appears in both input data sets, it appears in the program data vector only once.

> assigns tracking pointers to Clients and Amounts.

The Execution Phase: Match-Merging Observations

After compiling the DATA step, SAS sequentially match-merges observations by moving the pointers down each observation of each data set and checking to see whether the BY values match.

> If *Yes*, the observations are read into the PDV in the order in which the data sets appear in the MERGE statement. Values of any same-named variable are overwritten by values of the same-named variable in subsequent data sets. SAS writes the combined observation to the new data set and retains the values in the PDV until the BY value changes in all the data sets.

> *The Execution Phase: Match-Merging Observations*

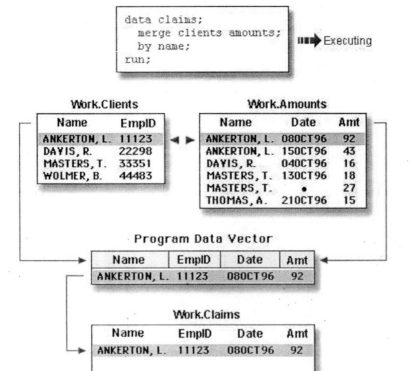

If *No*, SAS determines which BY value comes first and reads the observation that contains this value into the PDV. Then the contents of the PDV are written

The Execution Phase: PDV

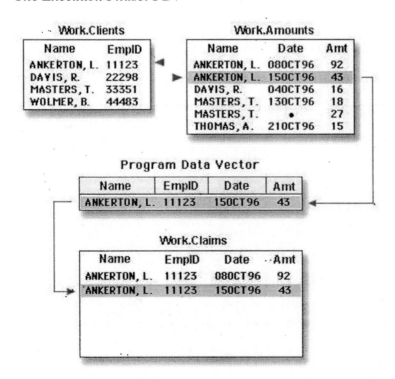

When the BY value changes in all the input data sets, the PDV is initialized to missing.

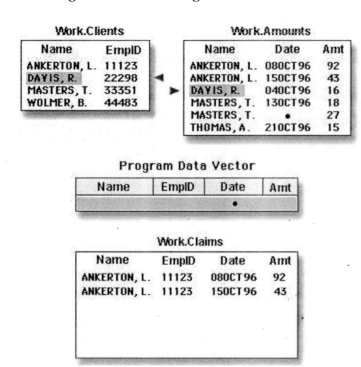

The DATA step merge continues to process every observation in each data set until it has processed all observations in all data sets.

Handling Unmatched Observations and Missing Values

By default, all observations that are read into the PDV, including observations that have missing data and no matching BY values, are written to the output data set. (If you specify a subsetting IF statement to select observations, then only those that meet the IF condition are written.)

If an observation contains missing values for a variable, then the observation in the output data set contains the missing values as well. Observations that have missing values for the BY variable appear at the top of the output data set because missing values sort first in ascending order.

Handling Unmatched Observations and Missing Values

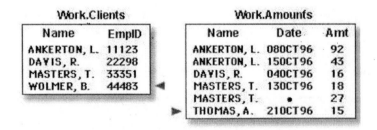

If an input data set doesn't have a matching BY value, then the observation in the output data set contains missing values for the variables that are unique to that input data set.

Handling Unmatched Observations and Missing Values: Unique Missing Values

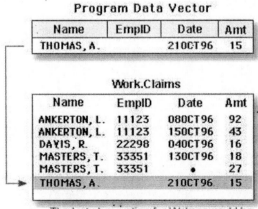

The last observation for Wolmer would be added after the Thomas observation.

Chapter Quiz

Select the best answer for each question. After completing the quiz, you can check your answers using the answer key in the appendix.

Which of the following is *not* created during the compilation phase?

   the data set descriptor

   the first observation

   the program data vector

   the _N_ and _ERROR_ automatic variables

During the compilation phase, SAS scans each statement in the DATA step, looking for syntax errors. Which of the following is *not* considered a syntax error?

   incorrect values and formats

   invalid options or variable names

   missing or invalid punctuation

   missing or misspelled keywords

Unless otherwise directed, the DATA step executes...

   once for each compilation phase.

   once for each DATA step statement.

   once for each record in the input file.

   once for each variable in the input file.

At the beginning of the execution phase, the value of _N_ is **1**, the value of _ERROR_ is **0**, and the values of the remaining variables are set to:

   0

   1

   undefined

   missing

Suppose you run a program that causes three DATA step errors. What is the value of the automatic variable _ERROR_ when the observation that contains the third error is processed?

   0

1

2

3

Which of the following actions occurs at the beginning of an iteration of the DATA step?

The automatic variables _N_ and _ERROR_ are incremented by one.

The DATA step stops execution.

The descriptor portion of the data set is written.

The values of variables created in programming statements are re-set to missing in the program data vector.

Look carefully at the DATA step shown below. Based on the INPUT statement, in what order will the variables be stored in the new data set?

```
data perm.update;
   infile invent;
   input IDnum $ Item $ 1-13 Instock 21-22
       BackOrd 24-25;
   Total=instock+backord;
run;
```

IDnum Item InStock BackOrd Total

Item IDnum InStock BackOrd Total

Total IDnum Item InStock BackOrd

Total Item IDnum InStock BackOrd

If SAS cannot interpret syntax errors, then...

data set variables will contain missing values.

the DATA step does not compile.

the DATA step still compiles, but it does not execute.

the DATA step still compiles and executes.

What is wrong with this program?

```
data perm.update;
   infile invent
   input Item $ 1-13 IDnum $ 15-19 Instock 21-22
         BackOrd 24-25;
   total=instock+backord;
run;
```

missing semicolon on second line

missing semicolon on third line

incorrect order of variables

incorrect variable type

Look carefully at this section of a SAS session log. Based on the note, what was the most likely problem with the DATA step?

```
NOTE: Invalid data for IDnum in line 7 15-19.
RULE: ----+----1----+----2----+----3----+----4
7          Bird Feeder LG088 3 20
Item=Bird Feeder IDnum=. InStock=3 BackOrd=20
Total=23 _ERROR_=1 _N_=1
```

A keyword was misspelled in the DATA step.

A semicolon was missing from the INFILE statement.

A variable was misspelled in the INPUT statement.

A dollar sign was missing in the INPUT statement.

Overview

Introduction

To list the information in a data set, you can create a report with a PROC PRINT step. Then you can enhance the report with additional statements and options to create reports like those shown below.

PROC PRINT

Basic Report

Column Totals

Sorting and Labels

Selected Observations and Variables

Objectives

In this chapter, you learn to

specify SAS data sets to print

select variables and observations to print

sort data by the values of one or more variables

specify column totals for numeric variables

double space LISTING output

add titles and footnotes to procedure output

assign descriptive labels to variables

apply formats to the values of variables.

Converting Data with Functions

Introduction to Converting Data

Suppose you are asked to complete a number of modifications to the data set Hrd.Temp. The first modification is to create a new variable that contains the salary of temporary employees. Examining the data set, you realize that one of the variables needed to calculate salaries is the character variable PayRate. To complete the calculation, you need to convert PayRate from character to numeric.

City	State	Zip	Phone	StartDate	EndDate	PayRate	Days	Hours
CARY	NC	27513	6224549	14567	14621	10	11	88
CARY	NC	27513	6223251	14524	14565	8	25	200
CHAPEL HILL	NC	27514	9974749	14570	14608	40	26	208

```
data hrd.newtemp;
  set hrd.temp;
  Salary=payrate*hours;
run;
```

In such cases, you should use the INPUT function before attempting the calculation. The INPUT function converts character data values to numeric values. The PUT function converts numeric data values to character values. Both functions are discussed in this section.

Potential Problems of Omitting INPUT or PUT

What happens if you skip the INPUT function or the PUT function when converting data?

SAS will detect the mismatched variables and will try an automatic character-to-numeric or numeric-to-character conversion. However, this process doesn't always work. Suppose each value of PayRate begins with a dollar sign ($). When SAS tries to automatically convert the values of PayRate to numeric values, the dollar sign blocks the process. The values cannot be converted to numeric values. Similar problems can occur with automatic numeric-to-character conversion.

Therefore, it is *always* best to include INPUT and PUT functions in your programs to avoid data type mismatches and circumvent automatic conversion.

Automatic Character-to-Numeric Conversion

Let's begin with the automatic conversion of character values to numeric values.

By default, if you reference a character variable in a numeric context such as an arithmetic operation, SAS tries to convert the variable values to numeric. For example, in the DATA step below, the character variable PayRate appears in a numeric context. It is multiplied by the numeric variable Hours to create a new variable named Salary.

```
data hrd.newtemp;
  set hrd.temp;
  Salary=payrate*hours;
run;
```

When this step executes, SAS automatically attempts to convert the character values of PayRate to numeric values so that the calculation can occur. This conversion is completed by creating a temporary numeric value for each character value of PayRate. This temporary value is used in the calculation. The character values of PayRate are *not* replaced by numeric values.

Whenever data is automatically converted, a message is written to the SAS log stating that the conversion has occurred.

```
4          data hrd.newtemp;
5             set hrd.temp;
6             Salary=payrate*hours;
7          run;

NOTE: Character values have been converted
      to numeric values at the places given
      by: (Line):(Column).

      6:11

NOTE: The data set HRD.NEWTEMP has 40 observations
      and 19 variables.
NOTE: The data statement used 0.78 seconds.
```

When Automatic Conversion Occurs

Automatic character-to-numeric conversion occurs when a character value is

assigned to a previously defined numeric variable, such as the numeric variable Rate

Rate=payrate;

used in an arithmetic operation

Salary=payrate*hours;

compared to a numeric value, using a comparison operator

if payrate>=rate;

specified in a function that requires numeric arguments.

NewRate=sum(payrate,raise);

The automatic conversion

uses the *w.* informat, where *w* is the width of the character value that is being converted

produces a numeric missing value from any character value that does not conform to standard numeric notation (digits with an optional decimal point, leading sign or scientific notation).

Automatic Conversion of Character Variables

Character Value	automatic conversion	Numeric Value
12.47	→	12.47
-8.96	→	-8.96
1.243E1	→	12.43
1,742.64	→	.

Restriction for WHERE Expressions

The WHERE statement does *not* perform automatic conversions in comparisons. The simple program below demonstrates what happens when a WHERE expression encounters the wrong data type. The variable Number contains a numeric value, and the variable Character contains a character value, but the two WHERE statements specify the wrong data type.

```
data work.convtest;
  Number=4;
  Character='4';
run;
proc print data=work.convtest;
  where character=4;
run;
proc print data=work.convtest;
  where number='4';
run;
```

This mismatch of character and numeric variables and values prevents the program from processing the WHERE statements. Automatic conversion is not performed. Instead, the program stops, and error messages are written to the SAS log.

```
1        data work.convtest;
2            Number=4;
3            Character='4';
4        run;
NOTE: The data set Work.ConvTest has 1 observations and 2
      variables.

5        proc print data=work.convtest;
6            where character=4;
7        run;
ERROR: Where clause operator requires compatible variables.

NOTE: The SAS System stopped processing this step because
      of errors.

8        proc print data=work.convtest;
9            where number='4';
10       run;
ERROR: Where clause operator requires compatible variables.

NOTE: The SAS System stopped processing this step because
      of errors.
```

Explicit Character-to-Numeric Conversion

Using the INPUT Function

In order to avoid the problems we have seen, use the INPUT function to convert character data values to numeric values. To learn how to use this function, let's examine one of the data set modifications needed for Hrd.Temp. As mentioned earlier, you need to calculate employee salaries by multiplying the character variable PayRate by the numeric variable Hours.

SAS Data Set Hrd.Temp

City	State	Zip	Phone	StartDate	EndDate	PayRate	Days	Hours
CARY	NC	27513	6224549	14567	14621	10	11	88
CARY	NC	27513	6223251	14524	14565	8	25	200
CHAPEL HILL	NC	27514	9974749	14570	14608	40	26	208
RALEIGH	NC	27612	6970450	14516	14527	15	10	80

To calculate salaries, you write the following DATA step. It creates a new data set, Hrd.Newtemp, to contain the original data plus the new variable Salary.

data hrd.newtemp;

```
   set hrd.temp;
   Salary=payrate*hours;
run;
```

However, you know that submitting this DATA step would cause an automatic character-to-numeric conversion, because the character variable PayRate is used in a numeric context. You can explicitly convert the character values of PayRate to numeric values by using the INPUT function.

General form, INPUT function:

INPUT(*source,format*)

where

source indicates the character variable, constant, or expression to be converted to a numeric value

a numeric *informat* must also be specified, as in this example:

input(payrate,2.)

When choosing the informat, be sure to select a numeric informat that can read the form of the values.

Character Values and Associated Informats

Character Value	Informat
2115233	7.
2,115,233	COMMA9.

Example

Here's an example of the INPUT function:

Test=input(saletest,comma9.);

The function uses the numeric informat COMMA9. to read the values of the character variable SaleTest. Then the resulting numeric values are stored in the variable Test.

Now let's use the INPUT function to convert the character values of PayRate to numeric values.

You begin the function by specifying PayRate as the source.

Because PayRate has a length of 2, you choose the numeric informat 2. to read the values of the variable.

input(payrate,2.)

Finally, you add the function to the assignment statement in your DATA step.

```
data hrd.newtemp;
  set hrd.temp;
   Salary=input(payrate,2.)*hours;
run;
```

After the DATA step is executed, the new data set (which contains the variable Salary) is created.

SAS Data Set Hrd.Newtemp

City	State	Zip	Phone	StartDate	EndDate	PayRate	Days	Hours	BirthDate	Salary
CARY	NC	27513	6224549	14567	14621	10	11	88	7054	880
CARY	NC	27513	6223251	14524	14565	8	25	200	5757	1600

Notice that no conversion messages appear in the SAS log when you use the INPUT function.

SAS Log

```
13        data hrd.newtemp;
14          set hrd.temp;
15          Salary=input (payrate,2.) *hours;
16        run;

NOTE: The data set Hrd.Newtemp has 40 observations
      and 19 variables.
NOTE: The DATA statement used 0.55 seconds.
```

The form of the INPUT function is very similar to the form of the PUT function (which performs numeric-to-character conversions).

INPUT(*source,informat*)

PUT(*source,format*))

However, note that the INPUT function requires an informat, whereas the PUT function requires a format. To remember which function requires a format versus an informat, note that the INPUT function requires the informat.

Automatic Numeric-to-Character Conversion

The automatic conversion of numeric data to character data is very similar to character-to-numeric conversion. Numeric data values are converted to character values whenever they are used in a character context.

For example, the numeric values of the variable Site are converted to character values if you

assign the numeric value to a previously defined character variable, such as the character variable SiteCode: SiteCode=site;

use the numeric value with an operator that requires a character value, such as the concatenation operator: SiteCode=site||dept;

specify the numeric value in a function that requires character arguments, such as the SUBSTR function: Region=substr(site,1,4);

Specifically, SAS writes the numeric value with the BEST12. format, and the resulting character value is right-aligned. This conversion occurs before the value is assigned or used with any operator or function. Automatic numeric-to-character conversion can cause unexpected results. For example, suppose the original numeric value has fewer than 12 digits. The resulting character value will have leading blanks, which might cause problems when you perform an operation or function.

Automatic numeric-to-character conversion also causes a message to be written to the SAS log indicating that the conversion has occurred.

SAS Log

```
9     data hrd.newtemp;
10        set hrd.temp;
11          SiteCode=site;
12    run;

NOTE: Numeric values have been converted
      to character values at the
      places given by: (Line):(Column).

      11:13

NOTE: The data set HRD.NEWTEMP has 40 observations
      and 19 variables.
NOTE: The data statement used 1.06 seconds.
```

As we saw with the INPUT statement, it is best not to rely on automatic conversion. When you know that numeric data must be converted to character data, perform an explicit conversion by including a PUT function in your SAS program. We look at the PUT function in the next section.

Explicit Numeric-to-Character Conversion

You can use the PUT function to explicitly convert numeric data values to character data values.

Let's use this function to complete one of the modifications needed for the data set Hrd.Temp. Suppose you are asked to create a new character variable named Assignment that concatenates the values of the numeric variable Site and the character variable Dept. The new variable values must contain the value of Site followed by a slash (/) and then the value of Dept, for example, **26/DP**. The following figure shows selected variables from the Hrd.Temp data set.

SAS Data Set Hrd.Temp

Overtime	Job	Contact	Dept	Site
4	Word processing	Word Processor	DP	26
.	Filing, administrative duties	Admin. Asst.	PURH	57
.	Organizational dev. specialist	Consultant	PERS	34
.	Bookkeeping, word processing	Bookkeeper Asst.	BK	57

You write an assignment statement that contains the concatenation operator (||) to indicate that Site should be concatenated with Dept, using a slash as a separator. Note that the slash is enclosed in quotation marks. All character constants must be enclosed in quotation marks.

```
data hrd.newtemp;
   set hrd.temp;
   Assignment=site||'/'||dept;
run;
```

You know that submitting this DATA step will cause SAS to automatically convert the numeric values of Site to character values, because Site is used in a character context. The variable Site appears with the concatenation operator, which requires character values. To explicitly convert the numeric values of Site to character values, you must add the PUT function to your assignment statement.

General form, PUT function:

PUT(*source,format*)

where

source indicates the numeric variable, constant, or expression to be converted to a character value

a *format* matching the data type of the source must also be specified, as in this example:

put(site,2.)

The PUT function always returns a character string.

The PUT function returns the *source* written with a *format*.

The *format* must agree with the *source* in type.

Numeric formats right-align the result; character formats left-align the result.

If you use the PUT function to create a variable that has not been previously identified, it creates a character variable whose length is equal to the format width.

Because you are listing a numeric variable as the source, you must specify a numeric format.

Now that you know the general form of the PUT function, you can rewrite the assignment statement in your DATA step to explicitly convert the numeric values of Site to character values.

To perform this conversion, write the PUT function, specifying Site as the source. Because Site has a length of 2, choose 2. as the numeric format. After you add this PUT function to the assignment statement, the DATA step creates the new data set that contains Assignment.

```
data hrd.newtemp;
  set hrd.temp;
  Assignment=put(site,2.)||'/'||dept;
run;
```

SAS Data Set Hrd.Newtemp

Overtime	Job	Contact	Dept	Site	BirthDate	Assignment
4	Word processing	Word Processor	DP	26	7054	26/DP
.	Filing, administrative duties	Admin. Asst.	PURH	57	5757	57/PURH

Notice that no conversion messages appear in the SAS log when you use the PUT function.

SAS Log

```
13      data hrd.newtemp;
14          set hrd.temp;
15          Assignment=put(site,2.)||'/'||dept;
16      run;


NOTE: The data set Hrd.Newtemp has 40 observations
      and 19 variables.
NOTE: The DATA statement used 0.71 seconds.
```

Matching the Data Type

Remember that the format specified in the PUT function must match the data type of the source.

PUT(source,format)

So, to do an explicit numeric-to-character data conversion, you specify a numeric source and a numeric format. The form of the PUT function is very similar to the form of the INPUT function.

PUT(source,format)

INPUT(source,informat)

Note that the PUT function requires a format, whereas the INPUT function requires an informat. To remember which function requires a format versus an informat, note that the INPUT function requires the informat.

Creating Tables in List Format

Overview

When three or more variables are specified, the multiple levels of *n*-way tables can produce considerable output. Such bulky, often complex crosstabulations are often easier to read as a continuous list. Although this eliminates row and column frequencies and percents, the results are compact and clear.

The LIST option is not available when you also specify statistical options.

To generate list output for crosstabulations, add a slash (/) and the LIST option to the TABLES statement in your PROC FREQ step.

TABLES *variable-1 *variable-2 <* ... variable-n>* / **LIST;**

Example

Adding the LIST option to our Clinic.Diabetes program puts its frequencies in a simple, short table.

```
proc format;
   value wtfmt low-139='< 140'
          140-180='140-180'
          181-high='> 180';
   value htfmt low-64='< 5"5"'
          65-70='5"5-10"'
          71-high='> 5"10"';
run;
proc freq data=clinic.diabetes;
   tables sex*weight*height / list;
   format weight wtfmt. height htfmt.;
run;
```

Table Created by Using the LIST Option

Sex	Weight	Height	Frequency	Percent	Cumulative Frequency	Cumulative Percent
F	< 140	< 5'5"	2	10.00	2	10.00
F	140-180	< 5'5"	5	25.00	7	35.00
F	140-180	5'5-10"	4	20.00	11	55.00
M	140-180	5'5-10"	1	5.00	12	60.00
M	> 180	5'5-10"	3	15.00	15	75.00
M	> 180	> 5'10"	5	25.00	20	100.00

Changing the Table Format

Beginning in SAS®9, adding the CROSSLIST option to your TABLES statement displays crosstabulation tables in ODS column format. This option creates a table that has a table definition that you can customize by using the TEMPLATE procedure.

Notice the structure of the output that is produced by the program shown below.

```
proc format;
    value wtfmt low-139='< 140'
            140-180='140-180'
            181-high='> 180';
    value htfmt low-64='< 5"5"'
            65-70='5"5-10"'
            71-high='> 5"10"';
run;
proc freq data=clinic.diabetes;
    tables sex*weight*height / crosslist;
    format weight wtfmt. height htfmt.;
run;
```

Table Created by Using CROSSLIST Option: Sex=F

The FREQ Procedure

Table of Weight by Height					
Controlling for Sex=F					
Weight	Height	Frequency	Percent	Row Percent	Column Percent
< 140	< 5'5"	2	18.18	100.00	28.57
	5'5-10"	0	0.00	0.00	0.00
	> 5'10"	0	0.00	0.00	.
	Total	2	18.18	100.00	
140-180	< 5'5"	5	45.45	55.56	71.43
	5'5-10"	4	36.36	44.44	100.00
	> 5'10"	0	0.00	0.00	.
	Total	9	81.82	100.00	
> 180	< 5'5"	0	0.00	.	0.00
	5'5-10"	0	0.00	.	0.00
	> 5'10"	0	0.00	.	.
	Total	0	0.00	.	.
Total	< 5'5"	7	63.64		100.00
	5'5-10"	4	36.36		100.00
	> 5'10"	0	0.00		.
	Total	11	100.00		

Table Created by Using CROSSLIST Option: Sex=M

Table of Weight by Height

Controlling for Sex=M

Weight	Height	Frequency	Percent	Row Percent	Column Percent
< 140	< 5'5"	0	0.00	.	.
	5'5-10"	0	0.00	.	0.00
	> 5'10"	0	0.00	.	0.00
	Total	0	0.00	.	
140-180	< 5'5"	0	0.00	0.00	.
	5'5-10"	1	11.11	100.00	25.00
	> 5'10"	0	0.00	0.00	0.00
	Total	1	11.11	100.00	
> 180	< 5'5"	0	0.00	0.00	.
	5'5-10"	3	33.33	37.50	75.00
	> 5'10"	5	55.56	62.50	100.00
	Total	8	88.89	100.00	
Total	< 5'5"	0	0.00		.
	5'5-10"	4	44.44		100.00
	> 5'10"	5	55.56		100.00
	Total	9	100.00		

Suppressing Table Information

Another way to control the format of crosstabulations is to limit the output of the FREQ procedure to a few specific statistics. Remember that when crosstabulations are run, PROC FREQ produces tables with cells that contain:

cell frequency

cell percentage of total frequency

cell percentage of row frequency

cell percentage of column frequency.

You can use options to suppress any of these statistics. To control the depth of crosstabulation results, add any combination of the following options to the TABLES statement:

NOFREQ suppresses cell frequencies

NOPERCENT suppresses cell percentages

NOROW suppresses row percentages

NOCOL suppresses column percentages.

Example

Suppose you want to use only the percentages of Sex and Weight combinations in the data set Clinic.Diabetes. To block frequency counts and row and column percentages, add the NOFREQ, NOROW, and NOCOL options to your program's TABLES statement.

```
proc format;
   value wtfmt low-139='< 140'
           140-180='140-180'
           181-high='> 180';
run;
proc freq data=clinic.diabetes;
   tables sex*weight / nofreq norow nocol;
   format weight wtfmt.;
run;
```

Suppressing Table Information

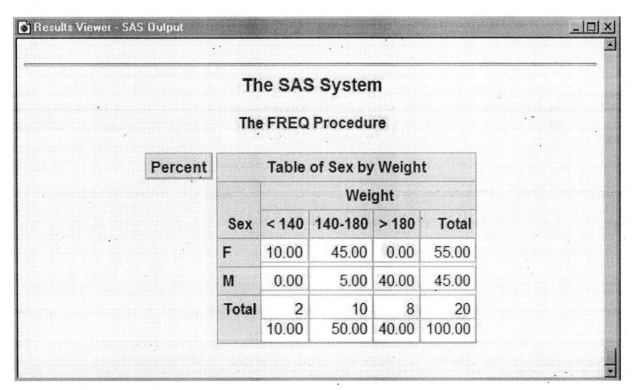

Notice that Percent is the only statistic that remains in the table's legend box.

Creating Samples

Because it performs iterative processing, a DO loop provides an easy way to draw sample observations from a data set. For example, suppose you would like to sample every tenth observation of the 5,000 observations in Factory.Widgets. Start with a simple DATA step:

```
data work.subset;
  set factory.widgets;
run;
```

You can create the sample data set by enclosing the SET statement in a DO loop. Use the start, stop, and increment values to select every tenth observation of the 5,000. Add the POINT= option to the SET statement, setting the POINT= option equal to the index variable that is used in the DO loop. (You learned about the POINT= option in Reading SAS Data Sets.)

```
data work.subset;
  do sample=10 to 5000 by 10;
    set factory.widgets point=sample;
  end;
run;
```

Remember that, in order to prevent continuous DATA step looping, you need to add a STOP statement when using the POINT= option. You also need to add an OUTPUT statement. Place the statement inside the DO loop to output each observation selected. (If the OUTPUT statement were placed after the DO loop, only the last observation would be written.)

```
data work.subset;
  do sample=10 to 5000 by 10;
    set factory.widgets point=sample;
    output;
  end;
  stop;
run;
```

When the program runs, the DATA step reads the observations in Factory.Widgets identified by the POINT= option. The values of the POINT= option are provided by the DO loop, which starts at **10** and goes to **5,000** in increments of 10. The data set Work.Subset contains 500 observations.

Overview

Introduction

If you read Creating List Reports, you learned to associate formats with variables either temporarily or permanently.

Variable and Format

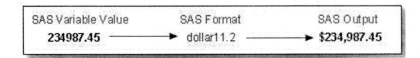

SAS Variable Value	SAS Format	SAS Output
234987.45 →	dollar11.2 →	$234,987.45

But sometimes you might want to create custom formats for displaying variable values. For example, you can format a product number so that it is displayed as descriptive text, as shown below.

Variable and Custom Format

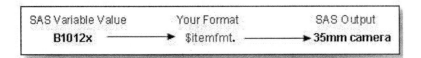

SAS Variable Value	Your Format	SAS Output
B1012x →	$itemfmt. →	35mm camera

Using the FORMAT procedure, you can define your own formats for variables. You can store your formats temporarily or permanently, and you can display a list of all your formats and descriptions of their values.

Objectives

In this chapter, you learn to

create your own formats for displaying variable values

permanently store the formats that you create

associate your formats with variables.

Reading Microsoft Excel Data

Overview

In addition to reading raw data files, SAS can also read Microsoft Excel data. Whether the input data source is a SAS data set, a raw data file, or a file from another application, you use the DATA step to create a SAS data set. The difference between reading these various types of input is in how you reference the data. To read in Excel data you use one of the following methods:

SAS/ACCESS LIBNAME statement

Import Wizard

Remember, the Base SAS LIBNAME statement associates a SAS name (libref) with a SAS DATA library by pointing to its physical location. But, the SAS/ACCESS LIBNAME statement associates a SAS name with an Excel workbook file by pointing to its location.

In doing so, the Excel workbook becomes a new library in SAS, and the worksheets in the workbook become the individual SAS data sets in that library.

The figure below illustrates the difference between how the two LIBNAME statements treat the data.

Comparing Libname Statements

The next figure shows how the DATA step is used with three types of input data.

Using the DATA step with Different Types of Output

Notice how the INFILE and INPUT statements are used in the DATA step for reading raw data, but the SET statement is used in the DATA step for reading in the Excel worksheets.

Running SAS with Microsoft Excel

You must have licensed SAS/ACCESS Interface to PC Files to use a SAS/ACCESS LIBNAME statement that references an Excel workbook.

If you are running SAS version 9.1 or earlier and want to read in Microsoft Excel data, you must use Microsoft Excel 2003 or earlier.

To read Microsoft Excel 2007 data you must be running SAS version 9.2 or later.

The examples in this section are based on SAS version 9.2 running with Microsoft Excel 2007.

Steps for Reading Excel Data

Let's look at the steps for reading in an Excel workbook file.

To read the Excel workbook file, the DATA step must provide the following instructions to SAS:

a libref to reference the Excel workbook to be read

the name and location (using another libref) of the new SAS data set

the name of the Excel worksheet that is to be read

The table below outlines the basic statements that are used in a program that reads Excel data and creates a SAS data set from an Excel worksheet. The PROC CONTENTS and PROC PRINT statements are not requirements for reading in Excel data and creating a SAS data set. However, these statements are useful for confirming that your Excel data has successfully been read into SAS.

Basic Steps for Reading Excel Data into a SAS Data Set

To do this...	Use this SAS statement...	Example
Reference an Excel workbook file	SAS/ACCESS LIBNAME statement	libname results **'c:\users\exercise.xlsx';**
Output the contents of the SAS Library	PROC CONTENTS	proc contents data=results._all_;
Execute the PROC CONTENTS statement	RUN statement	run;
Name and create a new SAS data set	DATA statement	data work.stress;
Read in an Excel worksheet (as the input data for the new SAS data set)	SET statement	set results.'ActLevel$'n;
Execute the DATA step	RUN statement	run;
View the contents of a particular data set	PROC PRINT	proc print data=stress;
Execute the PROC PRINT statement	RUN statement	run;

The SAS/ACCESS LIBNAME Statement

The general form of the SAS/ACCESS LIBNAME statement is as follows:

General form, SAS/ACCESS LIBNAME statement:

LIBNAME *libref 'location-of-Excel-workbook ' <options>*;

where

> *libref* is a name that you associate with an Excel workbook.

> *'location-of-Excel-workbook'* is the physical location of the Excel workbook.

Example:

libname results **'c:\users\exercise.xlsx';**

Referencing an Excel Workbook

Overview

This example uses data similar to the scenario used for the raw data in the previous section. The data shows the readings from exercise stress tests that have been performed on patients at a health clinic.

The stress test data is located in an Excel workbook named exercise.xlsx (shown below), which is stored in the location **c:\users**.

Excel Workbook

Work-sheets   **Cells formatted as dates**

Notice in the sample worksheet above that the date column is defined in Excel as dates. That is, if you right-click on the cells and select **Format Cells** (in Excel), the cells have a category of Date. SAS reads this data just as it is stored in Excel. If the date had been stored as text in Excel, then SAS would have read it as a character string.

To read in this workbook, you must first create a libref to point to the workbook's location:

libname results 'c:\users\exercise.xlsx';

The LIBNAME statement creates the libref **results**, which points to the Excel workbook exercise.xlsx. The workbook contains two worksheets, **tests** and **ActLevel**, which are now available in the new SAS library (results) as data sets.

After submitting the LIBNAME statement, you can look in the SAS Explorer window to see how SAS handles your Excel workbook. The Explorer window enables you to manage your files in the SAS windowing environment.

SAS Explorer Window

SAS Explorer Window

Each worksheet in the Excel workbook is treated as though it is a SAS data set.

Worksheet names appear with a dollar sign at the end of the name.

Name Literals

In the figure above, notice how the LIBNAME statement created a permanent library, **results**, which is the SAS name (libref) we gave to the workbook file and its location. The new library contains two SAS data sets, which accesses the data from the Excel worksheets. From this window you can browse the list of SAS libraries or display the descriptor portion of a SAS data set.

Notice that the Excel worksheet names have the special character ($) at the end. All Excel worksheets are designated this way. But remember, special characters such as these are not allowed in SAS data set names by default. So, in order for SAS to allow this character to be included in the data set name, you must assign a name literal to the data set name. A SAS name literal is a name token that is expressed as a string within quotation marks, followed by the uppercase or lowercase letter *n*. The name literal tells SAS to allow the special character ($) in the data set name.

Name Literal

Named Ranges

A named range is a range of cells within a worksheet that you define in Excel and assign a name to. In the example below, the worksheet contains a named range, tests_week_1, which SAS recognizes as a data set.

The named range, tests_week_1, and its parent worksheet, tests, will appear in the SAS Explorer window as separate data sets, except that the data set created from the named range will have no dollar sign ($) appended to its name.

For more information on named ranges, see your Microsoft Excel documentation.

Named Range

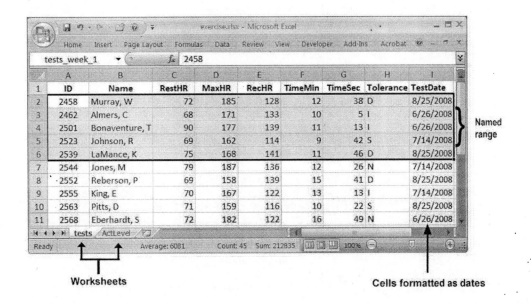

Using PROC CONTENTS

In addition to using the SAS explorer window to view library data, you can also use the CONTENTS procedure with the _ALL_ keyword to produce information about a data library and its contents. In the example below, PROC CONTENTS outputs summary information for the SAS data set tests, including data set name, variables, data types, and other summary information. This statement is useful for making sure that SAS successfully read in your Excel data before moving on to the DATA step.

proc contents data=results._all_;
run;

CONTENTS Procedure Output

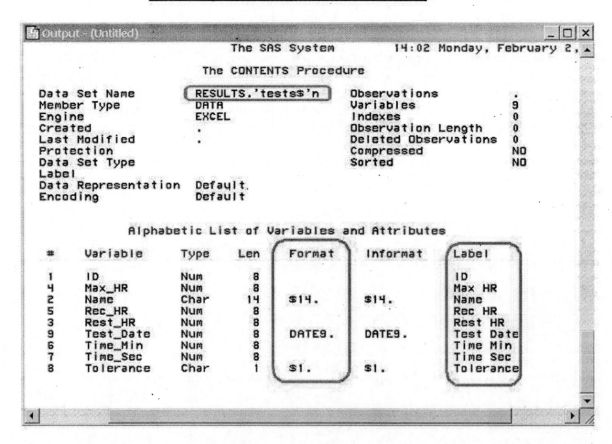

About the sample output above:

    The variables in the data set are pulled from the Excel column headings. SAS uses underscores to replace the spaces.

    The Excel dates in the Format column are converted to SAS dates with the default DATE9. format.

This is partial output. The ACTLEVEL data set would also be included in the PROC CONTENTS report.

Creating the DATA Step

You use the DATA statement to indicate the beginning of the DATA step and name the SAS data set to be created. Remember that the SAS data set name is a two-level name. For example, the two-level name results.Admit specifies that the data set Admit is stored in the permanent SAS library to which the libref results has been assigned.

When reading Excel data, use the SET statement to indicate which worksheet in the Excel file that you want to read. To read in the Excel file you write the DATA and SET statements as follows:

```
data work.stress;
  set results.'ActLevel$'n;
run;
```

In this example, the DATA statement tells SAS to name the new data set, stress, and store it in the temporary library WORK. The SET statement in the DATA step specifies the libref (reference to the Excel file) and the worksheet name as the input data.

You can use several statements in the DATA step to subset your data as needed. Here, the WHERE statement is used with a variable to include only those participants whose activity level is HIGH.

```
data work.stress;
  set results.'ActLevel$'n;
  where ActLevel='HIGH';
run;
```

The figure below shows the partial output for this DATA step in table format.

DATA Step Output

	ID	Age	Activity Level	Sex
1	2462	38	HIGH	F
2	2523	26	HIGH	M
3	2544	29	HIGH	M
4	2568	28	HIGH	M

Using PROC PRINT

After using the DATA step to read in the Excel data and create the SAS data set, you can use PROC PRINT to produce a report that displays the data set values.

You can also use the PRINT procedure to refer to a specific worksheet. Remember to use the name literal when referring to a specific Excel worksheet. In the example below, the first PRINT statement displays the data values for the new data set that was created in the DATA step. The second PRINT statement displays the contents of the Excel worksheet that was referenced by the LIBNAME statement.

```
proc print data=work.stress;
run;
proc print data=results.'ActLevel$'n;
run;
```

Disassociating a Libref

If SAS has a libref assigned to an Excel workbook, the workbook cannot be opened in Excel. To disassociate a libref, use a LIBNAME statement, specifying the libref and the CLEAR option.

```
libname results 'c:\users\exercise.xlsx';
  proc print data=results.'tests$'n;
run;

libname results clear;
```

SAS disconnects from the data source and closes any resources that are associated with that libref's connection.

Chapter 1: Base Programming

How many observations and variables does the data set below contain?

XisError: altImageDescription Element Should Not Be Blank.

Name	Sex	Age
Picker	M	32
Fletcher		28
Romano	F	.
Choi	M	42

3 observations, 4 variables

3 observations, 3 variables

4 observations, 3 variables

can't tell because some values are missing

Correct answer: c

Rows in the data set are called observations, and columns are called variables. Missing values don't affect the structure of the data set.

How many program steps are executed when the program below is processed?

```
data user.tables;
   infile jobs;
   input date name $ job $;
run;
proc sort data=user.tables;
   by name;
run;
proc print data=user.tables;
run;
```

three

four

five

six

Correct answer: a

When it encounters a DATA, PROC, or RUN statement, SAS stops reading statements and executes the previous step in the program. The program above contains one DATA step and two PROC steps, for a total of three program steps.

What type of variable is the variable AcctNum in the data set below?

XisError: altImageDescription Element Should Not Be Blank.

AcctNum	Gender
3456_1	M
2451_2	
Romano	F
Choi	M

numeric

character

can be either character or numeric

can't tell from the data shown

Correct answer: b

It must be a character variable, because the values contain letters and underscores, which are not valid characters for numeric values.

What type of variable is the variable Wear in the data set below, assuming that there is a missing value in the data set?

XisError: altImageDescription Element Should Not Be Blank.

Brand	Wear
Acme	43
Ajax	34
Atlas	.

numeric

character

can be either character or numeric

can't tell from the data shown

Correct answer: a

It must be a numeric variable, because the missing value is indicated by a period rather than by a blank.

Which of the following variable names is valid?

4BirthDate

$Cost

Items

Tax-Rate

Correct answer: c

Variable names follow the same rules as SAS data set names. They can be 1 to 32 characters long, must begin with a letter (A-Z, either uppercase or lowercase) or an underscore, and can continue with any combination of numerals, letters, or underscores.

Which of the following files is a permanent SAS file?

    Sashelp.PrdSale

    Sasuser.MySales

    Profits.Quarter1

    all of the above

Correct answer: d

To store a file permanently in a SAS data library, you assign it a libref other than the default Work. For example, by assigning the libref Profits to a SAS data library, you specify that files within the library are to be stored until you delete them. Therefore, SAS files in the Sashelp and Sasuser and Profits libraries are permanent files.

In a DATA step, how can you reference a temporary SAS data set named Forecast?

    Forecast

    Work.Forecast

    Sales.Forecast (after assigning the libref Sales)

    only a and b above

Correct answer: d

To reference a temporary SAS file in a DATA step or PROC step, you can specify the one-level name of the file (for example, Forecast) or the two-level name using the libref Work (for example, Work.Forecast).

What is the default length for the numeric variable Balance?

XisError: altImageDescription Element Should Not Be Blank.

Name	Balance
Adams	105.73
Geller	107.89
Martinez	97.45
Noble	182.50

    5

    6

    7

8

Correct answer: d

The numeric variable Balance has a default length of 8. Numeric values (no matter how many digits they contain) are stored in 8 bytes of storage unless you specify a different length.

How many statements does the following SAS program contain?

```
proc print data=new.prodsale
         label double;
   var state day price1 price2; where state='NC';
   label state='Name of State'; run;
```

three

four

five

six

Correct answer: c

The five statements are: 1) the PROC PRINT statement (two lines long); 2) the VAR statement; 3) the WHERE statement (on the same line as the VAR statement); 4) the LABEL statement; and 5) the RUN statement (on the same line as the LABEL statement).

What is a SAS library?

collection of SAS files, such as SAS data sets and catalogs

in some operating environments, a physical collection of SAS files

a group of SAS files in the same folder or directory.

all of the above

Correct answer: d

Every SAS file is stored in a SAS library, which is a collection of SAS files, such as SAS data sets and catalogs. In some operating environments, a SAS library is a physical collection of files. In others, the files are only logically related. In the Windows and UNIX environments, a SAS library is typically a group of SAS files in the same folder or directory.

Additional Features

In this section, you learned to read raw data by using an INPUT statement that uses column input. You also learned how to write to a raw data file by using the FILE statement with column input. However, column input is appropriate only in certain situations. When you use column input, your data must be

- standard character and numeric values. If the raw data file contains nonstandard values, then you need to use formatted input, another style of input. To learn about formatted input, see Reading SAS Data Sets.

- in fixed fields. That is, values for a particular variable must be in the same location in all records. If your raw data file contains values that are not in fixed fields, you need to use list input. To learn about list input, see Reading Free-Format Data.

Other forms of the INPUT statement enable you to read

- nonstandard data values such as hexadecimal, packed decimal, dates, and monetary values that contain dollar signs and commas

- free-format data (data that is not in fixed fields)

- implied decimal points

- variable-length data values

- variable-length records

- different record types.

Producing HTML Output

Overview

The Output Delivery System

Opening and Closing ODS Destinations

Creating HTML Output with Options

Creating HTML Output with a Table of Contents

Using Options to Specify Links and Paths

Changing the Appearance of HTML Output

Additional Features

Chapter Summary

Chapter Quiz

Using Conditional Clauses with the Iterative DO Statement

You have seen how the DO WHILE and DO UNTIL statements enable you to execute statements conditionally and how the iterative DO statement enables you to execute statements a set number of times, unconditionally.

DO WHILE(*expression*);
DO UNTIL(*expression*);
DO *index-variable=start* TO *stop* BY *increment*;

Now let's look at a form of the iterative DO statement that combines features of both conditional and unconditional execution of DO loops.

In this DATA step, the DO UNTIL statement determines how many years it takes (13) for an investment to reach $50,000.

```
data work.invest;
   do until(Capital>=50000);
     Year+1;
     capital+2000;
     capital+capital*.10;
   end;
run;
```

SAS Data Set Work.Invest

Capital	Year
53949.97	13

Suppose you also want to limit the number of years you invest your capital to 10 years. You can add the UNTIL or WHILE expression to an iterative DO statement to further control the number of iterations. This iterative DO statement enables you to execute the DO loop until Capital is greater than or equal to **50000** or until the DO loop executes ten times, whichever occurs first.

```
data work.invest;
   do year=1 to 10 until(Capital>=50000);
     capital+2000;
     capital+capital*.10;
   end;
   if year=11 then year=10;
run;
```

SAS Data Set Work.Invest

Capital	Year
35062.33	10

In this case, the DO loop stops executing after ten iterations, and the value of Capital never reaches **50000**. If you increase the amount added to Capital each year to **4000**, the DO loop stops executing after the eighth iteration when the value of Capital exceeds **50000**.

```
data work.invest;
  do year=1 to 10 until(Capital>=50000);
    capital+4000;
    capital+capital*.10;
  end;
  if year=11 then year=10;
run;
```

SAS Data Set Work.Invest

Capital	Year
50317.91	8

The UNTIL and WHILE specifications in an iterative DO statement function similarly to the DO UNTIL and DO WHILE statements. Both statements require a valid SAS expression enclosed in parentheses.

DO *index-variable=start* TO *stop* BY *increment* UNTIL(*expression*);

DO *index-variable=start* TO *stop* BY *increment* WHILE(*expression*);

The UNTIL expression is evaluated at the bottom of the DO loop, so the DO loop always executes at least once. The WHILE expression is evaluated before the execution of the DO loop. So, if the condition is initially false, the DO loop never executes.

ALL keyword ...

CHARACTER keyword ...

ERROR automatic variable

DATA step iterations and ...

functionality

initializing variables

PUT statement and

_N_ automatic variable

DATA step processing and ...

Chapter Quiz

Select the best answer for each question. After completing the quiz, check your answers using the answer key in the appendix

If you don't specify the LIBRARY= option, your formats are stored in Work.Formats, and they exist ...

> only for the current procedure.

> only for the current DATA step.

> only for the current SAS session.

> permanently.

Which of the following statements will store your formats in a permanent catalog?

```
libname library 'c:\sas\formats\lib';
proc format lib=library
    ...;
```

```
libname library 'c:\sas\formats\lib';
format lib=library
    ...;
```

```
library='c:\sas\formats\lib';
proc format library
    ...;
```

```
        library='c:\sas\formats\lib';
        proc library
            ...;
```

When creating a format with the VALUE statement, the new format's name

    cannot end with a number

    cannot end with a period

    cannot be the name of a SAS format, and...

    cannot be the name of a data set variable.

    must be at least two characters long.

    must be at least eight characters long.

    must begin with a dollar sign ($) if used with a character variable.

Which of the following FORMAT procedures is written correctly?

```
        proc format lib=library
            value colorfmt;
                1='Red'
                2='Green'
                3='Blue'
        run;
```

```
        proc format lib=library;
            value colorfmt
                1='Red'
                2='Green'
                3='Blue';
        run;
```

```
        proc format lib=library;
            value colorfmt;
                1='Red'
                2='Green'
                3='Blue'
        run;
```

```
        proc format lib=library;
```

```
        value colorfmt
            1='Red';
            2='Green';
            3='Blue';
        run;
```

Which of these is *false*? Ranges in the VALUE statement can specify...

a single value, such as **24** or **'S'**.

a range of numeric values, such as **0-1500**.

a range of character values, such as **'A'-'M'**.

a list of numeric and character values separated by commas, such as **90,'B',180,'D',270**.

How many characters can be used in a label?

40

96

200

256

Which keyword can be used to label missing numeric values as well as any values that are not specified in a range?

LOW

MISS

MISSING

OTHER

You can place the FORMAT statement in either a DATA step or a PROC step. What happens when you place it in a DATA step?

You temporarily associate the formats with variables.

You permanently associate the formats with variables.

You replace the original data with the format labels.

You make the formats available to other data sets.

The format JOBFMT was created in a FORMAT procedure. Which FORMAT statement will apply it to the variable JobTitle in the program output?

```
        format jobtitle jobfmt;



        format jobtitle jobfmt.;



        format jobtitle=jobfmt;



        format jobtitle='jobfmt';
```

Which keyword, when added to the PROC FORMAT statement, will display all the formats in your catalog?

CATALOG

LISTFMT

FMTCAT

FMTLIB

Processing a DATA Step That Creates One Observation per Header Record

During the compile phase, the variable type is flagged so that later it can be dropped. The value for Address and Total (SUM statement) are retained.

```
data perm.people (drop=type);
   infile census end=last;
   retain Address;
   input type $1. @;
   if type='H' then do;
      if _n_ > 1 then output;
      Total=0;
      input Address $3-17;
   end;
   else if type='P' then total+1;
   if last then output;
run;
```

```
>----+----10---+----

H 321 S. MAIN ST
P MARY E     21  F
P WILLIAM M 23  M
P SUSAN K     3  F
H 324 S. MAIN ST
```

		Retain	Drop	Retain
N	last	Address	type	Total
•	•			•

As the execution begins, _N_ is 1 and last is 0. Total is 0 because of the sum statement.

```
data perm.people (drop=type);
   infile census end=last;
   retain Address;
   input type $1. @;
   if type='H'then do;
      if _n_ > 1 then output;
      Total=0;
      input Address $3-17;
   end;
   else if type='P' then total+1;
   if last then output;
run;
```

```
>V---+----10---+----
H 321 S. MAIN ST
P MARY E      21 F
P WILLIAM M 23 M
P SUSAN K     3 F
H 324 S. MAIN ST
```

		Retain	Drop	Retain
N	last	Address	type	Total
1	0			0

Now the value for type is read, the condition type='H' is true, and therefore the statements in the DO group execute.

```
data perm.people (drop=type);
   infile census end=last;
   retain Address;
   input type $1. @;
   if type='H'then do;
      if _n_ > 1 then output;
      Total=0;
      input Address $3-17;
   end;
   else if type='P' then total+1;
   if last then output;
run;
```

```
>-V--+----10---+----
H 321 S. MAIN ST
P MARY E      21 F
P WILLIAM M 23 M
P SUSAN K.    3 F
H 324 S. MAIN ST
```

		Retain	Drop	Retain
N	last	Address	type	Total
1	0		H	0

The condition N>1 is not true, so the OUTPUT statement is not executed. However, Total is assigned the value of 0 and the value for Address is read.

```
data perm.people (drop=type);
   infile census end=last;
   retain Address;
   input type $1. @;
   if type='H'then do;
      if _n_ > 1 then output;
      Total=0;
      input Address $3-17;
   end;
   else if type='P' then total+1;
   if last then output;
run;
```

```
>----+----10---+--V-
H 321 S. MAIN ST
P MARY E      21 F
P WILLIAM M 23 M
P SUSAN K     3 F
H 324 S. MAIN ST
```

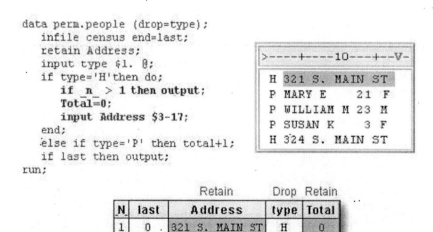

		Retain	Drop	Retain
N	last	Address	type	Total
1	0 .	321 S. MAIN ST	H	0

The END statement closes the DO group. The alternative condition expressed in the ELSE statement is not checked because the first condition, type='H', was true.

```
data perm.people (drop=type);
    infile census end=last;
    retain Address;
    input type $1. @;
    if type='H' then do;
        if _n_ > 1 then output;
        Total=0;
        input Address $3-17;
    end;
    else if type='P' then total+1;
    if last then output;
run;
```

The value of last is still **0**, so the OUTPUT statement is not executed. Control returns to the top of the DATA step.

```
data perm.people (drop=type);
    infile census end=last;
    retain Address;
    input type $1. @;
    if type='H' then do;
        if _n_ > 1 then output;
        Total=0;
        input Address $3-17;
    end;
    else if type='P' then total+1;
    if last then output;
run;
```

During the second iteration, the value of type is **'P'** and Total is incremented by 1. Again, the value of last is **0**, so control returns to the top of the DATA step.

```
data perm.people (drop=type);
    infile census end=last;
    retain Address;
    input type $1. @;
    if type='H' then do;
        if _n_ > 1 then output;
        Total=0;
        input Address $3-17;
    end;
    else if type='P' then total+1;
    if last then output;
run;
```

During the fifth iteration, the value of type is **'H'** and _N_ is greater than 1, so the values for Address and Total are written to the data set as the first observation.

```
data perm.people (drop=type);
    infile census end=last;
    retain Address;
    input type $1. @;
    if type='H'then do;
       if _n_ > 1 then output;
       Total=0;
       input Address $3-17;
    end;
    else if type='P' then total+1;
    if last then output;
run;
```

As the last record in the file is read, the variable last is set to **1**. Now that the condition for last is true, the values in the program data vector are written to the data set as the final observation.

```
data perm.people (drop=type);
    infile census end=last;
    retain Address;
    input type $1. @;
    if type='H'then do;
       if _n_ > 1 then output;
       Total=0;
       input Address $3-17;
    end;
    else if type='P' then total+1;
    if last then output;
run;
```

Reading Date and Time Values

Overview

How SAS Stores Date Values

How SAS Stores Time Values

More about SAS Date and Time Values

Chapter Quiz

Select the best answer for each question. After completing the quiz, check your answers using the answer key in the appendix.

Which SAS statement correctly uses column input to read the values in the raw data file below in this order: Address (4th field), SquareFeet (second field), Style (first field), Bedrooms (third field)?

```
1---+----10---+----20---+----30
2STORY 1810 4 SHEPPARD AVENUE
CONDO  1200 2 RAND  STREET
RANCH  1550 3 MARKET STREET
```

input Address 15-29 SquareFeet 8-11 Style 1-6
Bedrooms 13;

input $ 15-29 Address 8-11 SquareFeet $ 1-6 Style
13 Bedrooms;

input Address $ 15-29 SquareFeet 8-11 Style $ 1-6
Bedrooms 13;

input Address 15-29 $ SquareFeet 8-11 Style 1-6
$ Bedrooms 13;

Which is *not* an advantage of column input?

It can be used to read character variables that contain embedded blanks.

No placeholder is required for missing data.

Standard as well as nonstandard data values can be read.

Fields do not have to be separated by blanks or other delimiters.

Which is an example of standard numeric data?

-34.245

$24,234.25

1/2

50%

Formatted input can be used to read

standard free-format data

standard data in fixed fields

nonstandard data in fixed fields

both standard and nonstandard data in fixed fields

Which informat should you use to read the values in column 1-5?

```
1---+----10---+----20---+----30
2STORY 1810 4 SHEPPARD AVENUE
CONDO  1200 2 RAND STREET
RANCH  1550 3 MARKET STREET
```

w.

$w.

w.d

COMMAw.d

The COMMAw.d informat can be used to read which of the following values?

12,805

$177.95

18%

all of the above

Which INPUT statement correctly reads the values for ModelNumber (first field) after the values for Item (second field)? Both Item and ModelNumber are character variables.

```
1---+----10---+----20---+----30
DG345 CD PLAYER    $174.99
HJ756 VCR          $298.99
AS658 CAMCORDER $1,195.99
```

input +7 Item $9. @1 ModelNumber $5.;

input +6 Item $9. @1 ModelNumber $5.;

input @7 Item $9. +1 ModelNumber $5.;

input @7 Item $9 @1 ModelNumber 5.;

Which INPUT statement correctly reads the numeric values for Cost (third field)?

```
1---+----10---+----20---+----30
DG345 CD PLAYER    $174.99
HJ756 VCR          $298.99
AS658 CAMCORDER $1,195.99
```

input @17 Cost 7.2;

input @17 Cost 9.2.;

input @17 Cost comma7.;

input @17 Cost comma9.;

Which SAS statement correctly uses formatted input to read the values in this order: Item (first field), UnitCost (second field), Quantity (third field)?

```
1---+----10---+----20---+
ENVELOPE  $13.25 500
DISKETTES $29.50  10
BANDS      $2.50 600
RIBBON     $94.20  12
```

input @1 Item $9. +1 UnitCost comma6.
    @18 Quantity 3.;

input Item $9. @11 UnitCost comma6.
    @18 Quantity 3.;

input Item $9. +1 UnitCost comma6.
    @18 Quantity 3.;

all of the above

Which raw data file requires the PAD option in the INFILE statement in order to correctly read the data using either column input or formatted input?

```
1---+----10---+----20---+
JONES     M 48 128.6
LAVERNE   M 58 158
JAFFE     F 33 115.5
WILSON    M 28 130
```

```
1---+----10---+----20---+
JONES     M 48 128.6
LAVERNE   M 58 158.0
JAFFE     F 33 115.5
WILSON    M 28 130.0
```

```
1---+----10---+----20---+
JONES     M 48 128.6
LAVERNE   M 58    158
JAFFE     F 33 115.5
WILSON    M 28    130
```

```
1---+----10---+----20---+
    JONES      M 48 128.6
LAVERNE        M 58 158.0
    JAFFE      F 33 115.5
  WILSON       M 28 130.0
```

Setting System Options

Overview

If you create your procedure output as LISTING output, you can also control the appearance of your output by setting system options such as

  line size (the maximum width of the log and output)

  page size (the number of lines per printed page of output)

  the display of page numbers

  the display of date and time.

  The above options do not affect the appearance of HTML output.

All SAS system options have default settings that are used unless you specify otherwise. For example, page numbers are automatically displayed in LISTING output (unless your site modifies this default).

LISTING Output Showing Default Settings

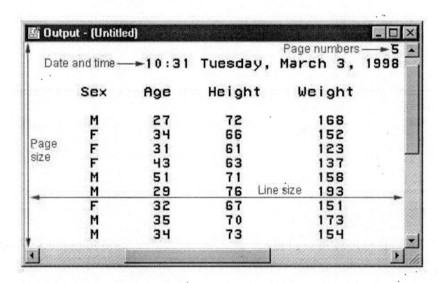

Changing System Options

To modify system options in your LISTING output, you submit an OPTIONS statement. You can place an OPTIONS statement anywhere in a SAS program to change the settings from that point onward. However, it is good programming practice to place OPTIONS statements outside of DATA or PROC steps so that your programs are easier to read and debug.

Because the OPTIONS statement is global, the settings remain in effect until you modify them, or until you end your SAS session.

General form, OPTIONS statement:

OPTIONS *options*;

where *options* specifies one or more system options to be changed. The available system options depend on your host operating system.

Example: DATE | NODATE and NUMBER | NONUMBER Options

By default, page numbers and dates appear with LISTING output. The following OPTIONS statement suppresses the printing of both page numbers and the date and time in LISTING output.

options nonumber nodate;

In the following example, the NONUMBER and NODATE system options suppress the display of page numbers and the date in the PROC PRINT output. Page numbers are not displayed in the PROC FREQ output, either, but the date does appear at the top of the PROC FREQ output since the DATE option was specified.

```
ods listing;
options nonumber nodate;
proc print data=sasuser.admit;
  var id sex age height weight;
  where age>=30;
run;
options date;
proc freq data=sasuser.diabetes;
  where fastgluc>=300;
  tables sex;
run;
proc print data=sasuser.diabetes;
run;
ods listing close;
```

PROC PRINT LISTING Output for sasuser.diabetes

```
                   The SAS System
Obs        ID     Sex     Age     Height     Weight
 2        2462     F       34       66         152
 3        2501     F       31       61         123
 4        2523     F       43       63         137
 5        2539     M       51       71         158
 7        2552     F       32       67         151
 8        2555     M       35       70         173
 9        2563     M       34       73         154
10        2568     F       49       64         172
11        2571     F       44       66         140
13        2574     M       30       69         147
14        2575     F       40       69         163
15        2578     M       47       72         173
16        2579     M       60       71         191
17        2584     F       43       65         123
20        2589     F       41       67         141
21        2595     M       54       71         183
```

PROC FREQ LISTING Output for sasuser.diabetes

```
                    The SAS System              11:11 Saturday, May 14, 2011

                    The FREQ Procedure

                                   Cumulative      Cumulative
Sex      Frequency     Percent     Frequency        Percent

F            2          25.00          2            25.00
M            6          75.00          8           100.00
```

PROC PRINT LISTING Output for sasuser.diabetes

```
                          The SAS System           11:03 Monday, May 16, 2011
                                                          Fast     Post
Obs     ID    Sex   Age   Height   Weight   Pulse   Gluc     Gluc
 1    2304    F     16     61       102      100     568      625
 2    1128    M     43     71       218       76     156      208
 3    4425    F     48     66       162       80     244      322
 4    1387    F     57     64       142       70     177      206
 5    9012    F     39     63       157       68     257      318
 6    6312    M     52     72       240       77     362      413
 7    5438    F     42     62       168       83     247      304
 8    3788    M     38     73       234       71     486      544
 9    9125    F     56     64       159       70     166      215
10    3438    M     15     66       140       67     492      547
11    1274    F     50     65       153       70     193      271
12    3347    M     53     70       193       78     271      313
13    2486    F     63     65       157       70     152      224
14    1129    F     48     61       137       69     267      319
15    9723    M     52     75       219       65     348      403
16    8653    M     49     68       185       79     259      311
17    4451    M     54     71       196       81     373      431
18    3279    M     40     70       213       82     447      504
19    4759    F     60     68       164       71     155      215
20    6488    F     59     64       154       75     362      409
```

PROC FREQ LISTING Output with Date and Still No Page Number

The FREQ Procedure

Sex	Frequency	Percent	Cumulative Frequency	Cumulative Percent
F	2	25.00	2	25.00
M	6	75.00	8	100.00

Example: PAGENO= Option

If you print page numbers, you can specify the beginning page number for your LISTING report by using the PAGENO= option. If you don't specify PAGENO=, output is numbered sequentially throughout your SAS session, starting with page 1.

In the following example, the output pages are numbered sequentially throughout the SAS session, beginning with number 3.

```
ods listing;
options nodate number pageno=3;
proc print data=hrd.funddrive;
run;
ods listing close;
```

Since SAS 9.3 does not creating LISTING output by default, the ODS LISTING statement was added to generate LISTING output.

LISTING Output with the PAGENO= Option Set

The SAS System   3

Obs	LastName	Qtr1	Qtr2	Qtr3	Qtr4
1	ADAMS	18	18	20	20
2	ALEXANDER	15	18	15	10
3	APPLE	25	25	25	25
4	ARTHUR	10	25	20	30
5	AVERY	15	15	15	15
6	BAREFOOT	20	20	20	20
7	BAUCOM	25	20	20	30
8	BLAIR	10	10	5	10
9	BLALOCK	5	10	10	15
10	BOSTIC	20	25	30	25
11	BRADLEY	12	16	14	18
12	BRADY	20	20	20	20
13	BROWN	18	18	18	18
14	BRYANT	16	18	20	18
15	BURNETTE	10	10	10	10
16	CHEUNG	30	30	30	30
17	LEHMAN	20	20	20	20
18	VALADEZ	14	18	40	25

Example: PAGESIZE= Option

The PAGESIZE= option (alias PS=) specifies how many lines each page of output contains. In the following example, each page of the output that the PRINT procedure produces contains 15 lines (including those used by the title, date, and so on).

```
options number date pagesize=15;
proc print data=sasuser.admit;
run;
```

LISTING Output with PAGESIZE= 15

```
                  The SAS System            13:23 Tuesday, April 12, 2011   17

 Obs    LastName    Qtr1      Qtr2      Qtr3      Qtr4

  12    BRADY        20        20        20        20
  13    BROWN        18        18        18        18
  14    BRYANT       16        18        20        18
  15    BURNETTE     10        10        10        10
  16    CHEUNG       30        30        30        30
  17    LEHMAN       20        20        20        20
  18    VALADEZ      14        18        40        25
```

Example: LINESIZE= Option

The LINESIZE= option (alias LS=) specifies the width of the print line for your procedure output and log. Observations that do not fit within the line size continue on a different line.

In the following example, the observations are longer than 64 characters, so the observations continue on a subsequent page.

```
ODS listing;
options number linesize=64;
proc print data=flights.europe;
run;
ODS listing close;
```

LISTING Output with the LINESIZE= Option Set, Page 1

```
                      The SAS System                    55
                                13:23 Tuesday, April 12, 2011

                                              Day
                    Non                        Of
 Obs Transferred  Revenue  Deplaned  Capacity Month  Revenue

  1      17          7        222       250      1    150634
  2       8          3        163       250      1    156804
  3      15          5        227       250      1    190098
  4      13          4        222       250      1    150634
  5      14          6        158       250      1    193930
  6      18          7        172       250      2    166470
  7       8          1        114       250      2    167772
  8       7          4        187       250      2    163248
```

LISTING Output with the LINESIZE= Option Set, Page 2

```
Obs Flight    Date Depart Orig Dest Miles Mail Freight Boarded

  9   821  09MAR99 14:56  LGA  LON  3442  219   368     203
 10   271  09MAR99 13:17  LGA  PAR  3635  357   282     159
 11   821  10MAR99  9:31  LGA  LON  3442  389   479     188
 12   271  10MAR99 11:40  LGA  PAR  3856  415   463     182
 13   622  03MAR99 12:19  LGA  FRA  3857  296   414     180
 14   821  03MAR99 14:56  LGA  LON  3442  448   282     151
 15   271  03MAR99 13:17  LGA  PAR  3635  352   351     147
 16   219  04MAR99  9:31  LGA  LON  3442  331   376     232
```

Handling Two-Digit Years: Year 2000 Compliance

If you use two-digit year values in your data lines, external files, or programming statements, you should consider another important system option, the YEARCUTOFF= option. This option specifies which 100-year span is used to interpret two-digit year values.

The Default 100 Year Span in SAS

All versions of SAS represent dates correctly from 1582 A.D. to 20,000 A.D. (Leap years, century, and fourth-century adjustments are made automatically. Leap seconds are ignored, and SAS does not adjust for Daylight Savings Time.) However, you should be aware of the YEARCUTOFF= value to ensure that you are properly interpreting two-digit years in data lines.

As with other system options, you specify the YEARCUTOFF= option in the OPTIONS statement:

options yearcutoff=1925;

How the YEARCUTOFF= Option Works

When a two-digit year value is read, SAS interprets it based on a 100-year span which starts with the YEARCUTOFF= value. The default value of YEARCUTOFF= is **1920**.

Default YEARCUTOFF= Date (1920)

`1920 ◄―100 years―► 2019`

Date Expressions and How They Are Interpreted

Date Expression   Interpreted As

12/07/41	12/07/1941
18Dec15	18Dec2015
04/15/30	04/15/1930
15Apr95	15Apr1995

However, you can override the default and change the value of YEARCUTOFF= to the first year of another 100-year span. For example, if you specify YEARCUTOFF=1950, then the 100-year span will be from 1950 to 2049.

options yearcutoff=1950;

Using YEARCUTOFF=1950, dates are interpreted as shown below:

Interpreting Dates When YEARCUTOFF=1950

Date Expressions and How They Are Interpreted

Date Expression	Interpreted As
12/07/41	12/07/2041
18Dec15	18Dec2015
04/15/30	04/15/2030
15Apr95	15Apr1995

How Four-Digit Years Are Handled

Remember, the value of the YEARCUTOFF= system option affects only two-digit year values. A date value that contains a four-digit year value will be interpreted correctly even if it does not fall within the 100-year span set by the YEARCUTOFF= system option.

You can learn more about reading date values in Reading Date and Time Values.

Using System Options to Specify Observations

You've seen how to use SAS system options to change the appearance of output and interpret two-digit year values. You can also use the FIRSTOBS= and OBS= system options to specify the observations to process from SAS data sets.

You can specify either or both of these options as needed. That is, you can use

FIRSTOBS= to start processing at a specific observation

OBS= to stop processing after a specific observation

FIRSTOBS= and OBS= together to process a specific group of observations.

General form, FIRSTOBS= and OBS= options in an OPTIONS statement:

FIRSTOBS=n

OBS=n

where n is a positive integer. For FIRSTOBS=, n specifies the number of the *first* observation to process. For OBS=, n specifies the number of the *last* observation to process. By default, FIRSTOBS=1. The default value for OBS= is MAX, which is the largest signed, eight-byte integer that is representable in your operating environment. The number can vary depending on your operating system.

XisError: altImageDescription Element Should Not Be Blank. ⚠ Each of these options applies to every input data set that is used in a program or a SAS process.

Examples: FIRSTOBS= and OBS= Options

The data set clinic.heart contains 20 observations. If you specify FIRSTOBS=10, SAS reads the 10th observation of the data set first and reads through the last observation (for a total of 11 observations).

```
options firstobs=10;
proc print data=sasuser.heart;
run;
```

The PROC PRINT step produces the following output:

PROC PRINT Output with FIRSTOBS=10

Obs	Patient	Sex	Survive	Shock	Arterial	Heart	Cardiac	Urinary
10	509	2	SURV	OTHER	79	84	256	90
11	742	1	DIED	HYPOVOL	100	54	135	0
12	609	2	DIED	NONSHOCK	93	101	260	90
13	318	2	DIED	OTHER	72	81	410	405
14	412	1	SURV	BACTER	61	87	296	44
15	601	1	DIED	BACTER	84	101	260	377
16	402	1	SURV	CARDIO	88	137	312	75
17	98	2	SURV	CARDIO	84	87	260	377
18	4	1	SURV	HYPOVOL	81	149	406	200
19	50	2	SURV	HYPOVOL	72	111	332	12
20	2	2	DIED	OTHER	101	114	424	97

If you specify OBS=10 instead, SAS reads through the 10th observation, in this case for a total of 10 observations. (Notice that FIRSTOBS= has been reset to the default value.)

```
options firstobs=1 obs=10;
proc print data=sasuser.heart;
run;
```

Now the PROC PRINT step produces this output:

PROC PRINT Output with FIRSTOBS=1 and Obs=10

The SAS System

Obs	Patient	Sex	Survive	Shock	Arterial	Heart	Cardiac	Urinary
1	203	1	SURV	NONSHOCK	88	95	66	110
2	54	1	DIED	HYPOVOL	83	183	95	0
3	664	2	SURV	CARDIO	72	111	332	12
4	210	2	DIED	BACTER	74	97	369	0
5	101	2	DIED	NEURO	80	130	291	0
6	102	2	SURV	OTHER	87	107	471	65
7	529	1	DIED	CARDIO	103	106	217	15
8	524	2	DIED	CARDIO	145	99	156	10
9	426	1	SURV	OTHER	68	77	410	75
10	509	2	SURV	OTHER	79	84	256	90

Combining FIRSTOBS= and OBS= processes observations in the middle of the data set. For example, the following program processes only observations 10 through 15, for a total of 6 observations:

```
options firstobs=10 obs=15;
proc print data=sasuser.heart;
run;
```

Here is the output:

PROC PRINT Output with FIRSTOBS=10 and Obs=15

The SAS System

Obs	Patient	Sex	Survive	Shock	Arterial	Heart	Cardiac	Urinary
10	509	2	SURV	OTHER	79	84	256	90
11	742	1	DIED	HYPOVOL	100	54	135	0
12	609	2	DIED	NONSHOCK	93	101	260	90
13	318	2	DIED	OTHER	72	81	410	405
14	412	1	SURV	BACTER	61	87	296	44
15	601	1	DIED	BACTER	84	101	260	377

To reset the number of the last observation to process, you can specify OBS=MAX in the OPTIONS statement.

```
options obs=max;
```

This instructs any subsequent SAS programs in the SAS session to process through the last observation in the data set being read.

Using FIRSTOBS= and OBS= for Specific Data Sets

As you saw above, using the FIRSTOBS= or OBS= system options determines the first or last observation, respectively, that is read for all steps for the duration of your current SAS session or until you change the setting. However, you may want to

override these options for a given data set

apply these options to a specific data set only.

To affect any single file, you can use FIRSTOBS= or OBS= as data set options instead of as system options. You specify the data set option in parentheses immediately following the input data set name.

A FIRSTOBS= or OBS= specification from a data set option overrides the corresponding FIRSTOBS= or OBS= system option.

Example: FIRSTOBS= and OBS= as Data Set Options

As shown in the last example below, this program processes only observations 10 through 15, for a total of 6 observations:

```
options firstobs=10 obs=15;
proc print data=sasuser.heart;
run;
```

You can create the same output by specifying FIRSTOBS= and OBS= as data set options, as follows. The data set options override the system options for this instance only.

```
options firstobs=10 obs=15;
proc print data=sasuser.heart(firstobs=10 obs=15);
run;
```

To specify FIRSTOBS= or OBS= for this program only, you could omit the OPTIONS statement altogether and simply use the data set options.

The SAS System Options Window

You can also set system options by using the SAS System Options window. The changed options are reset to the defaults at the end of your SAS session.

To view the SAS System Options window, select **Tools** ➡ **Options** ➡ **System**.

The SAS System Options Window

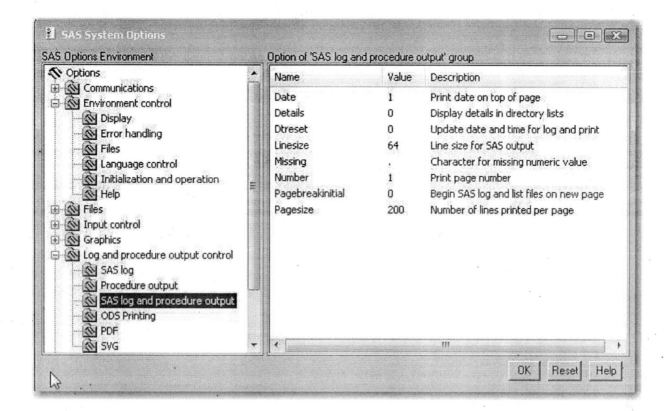

Changing Options

To change an option:

Expand the groups and subgroups under SAS Options Environment until you find the option that you want to change. (Options in subgroups are listed in the right pane of the window.)

Click the name of the option that you want to change, and display its pop-up menu. Then select one of the choices:

Modify Value opens a window in which you type or select a new value for the option.

Set to Default immediately resets the option to its default value.

For example, the SAS System Options window above shows options for the **SAS log and procedure output** subgroup under the group **Log and procedure output control**.

Finding Options Quickly

To locate an option in the SAS System Options window:

Place your cursor over the name of any option group or subgroup, and display its pop-up menu.

Click **Find Option**. The Find Option dialog box appears.

Type the name of the option that you want to locate, and click **OK**.

The SAS System Options window expands to the appropriate option subgroup. All subgroup options also appear, and the option that you located is highlighted.

Overview

Introduction

Raw data can be organized in several ways.

```
1---+----10---+----20---+----
BIRD FEEDER    LG088   3 $29.95
GLASS MUGS     SB082   6 $25.00
GLASS TRAY     BQ049  12 $39.95
PADDED HANGRS  MN256  15 $9.95
JEWELRY BOX    AJ498  23 $45.00
RED APRON      AQ072   9 $6.50
CRYSTAL VASE   AQ672  27 $29.95
PICNIC BASKET  LS930  21 $15.00
```

This external file contains data that is arranged in columns or fixed fields. You can specify a beginning and ending column for each field. However, this file contains nonstandard data, because one of the variable's values includes a special character, the dollar sign ($).

This external file contains no special characters, but its data is free-format, meaning that it is not arranged in columns. Notice that the values for a particular field do not begin and end in the same columns.

```
1---+----10---+----20---+--
BARNES NORTHWEST 36098.45
FARLSON SOUTHWEST 24394.09
LAWRENCE NORTHEAST 19504.26
NELSON SOUTHEAST 16930.84
STEWART MIDWEST 23845.13
TAYLOR MIDWEST 12354.42
TREADWAY SOUTHWEST 41092.84
WALSTON SOUTHEAST 28938.71
```

How your data is organized and what type of data you have determine which input style you should use to read the data. SAS provides three primary input styles: column input, formatted input, and list input. This chapter teaches you how to use column input and formatted input to read standard and nonstandard data that is arranged in fixed fields.

Objectives

In this chapter, you learn to

distinguish between standard and nonstandard numeric data

read standard fixed-field data

read nonstandard fixed-field data.

Overview

Introduction

As you have seen, one of the many features of PROC REPORT is the ability to summarize large amounts of data by producing descriptive statistics. However, there are SAS procedures that are designed specifically to produce various types of descriptive statistics and to display them in meaningful reports. The type of descriptive statistics that you need and the SAS procedure that you should use depend on whether you need to summarize continuous data values or discrete data values.

If the data values that you want to describe are continuous numeric values (for example, people's ages), then you can use the MEANS procedure or the SUMMARY procedure to calculate statistics such as the mean, sum, minimum, and maximum.

MEANS Procedure Output

Variable	N	Mean	Std Dev	Minimum	Maximum
Age	20	47	13	15	63
Height	20	67	4	61	75
Weight	20	175	36	102	240
Pulse	20	75	8	65	100
FastGluc	20	299	126	152	568
PostGluc	20	355	126	206	625

If the data values that you want to describe are discrete (for example, the color of people's eyes), then you can use the FREQ procedure to show the distribution of these values, such as percentages and counts.

FREQ Procedure Output

Eye Color	Frequency	Percent	Cumulative Frequency	Cumulative Percent
Brown	92	58.60	92	58.60
Blue	65	41.40	157	100.00

This chapter will show you how to use the MEANS, SUMMARY, and FREQ procedures to describe your data.

ATDATETIME audit trail variable

ATMESSAGE audit trail variable

ATOBSNO audit trail variable

Reading Hierarchical Files

Overview

Introduction

When planning modifications to SAS data sets, be sure to examine the many SAS functions that are available. SAS functions are pre-written routines that provide programming shortcuts for many calculations and manipulations of data.

This chapter teaches you how to use a variety of functions, such as those shown in the table below. You learn to convert data from one data type to another, to work with SAS date and time values, and to manipulate the values of character variables.

Selected SAS Functions and Their Descriptions

Function	Description	Form	Sample Value
YEAR	Extracts the year value from a SAS date value.	YEAR*(date)*	2002
QTR	Extracts the quarter value from a SAS date value.	QTR*(date)*	1
MONTH	Extracts the month value from a SAS date value.	MONTH*(date)*	12
DAY	Extracts the day value from a SAS date value.	DAY*(date)*	5

Objectives

In this chapter, you learn to

convert character data to numeric data
convert numeric data to character data
create SAS date values
extract the month, year, and interval from a SAS date value
perform calculations with date and datetime values and time intervals
extract, edit, and search the values of character variables
replace or remove all occurrences of a particular word within a character string.

Chapter Quiz

Select the best answer for each question. After completing the quiz, check your answers using the answer key in the appendix.

Which statement is *false* regarding an ARRAY statement?
It is an executable statement.
It can be used to create variables.
It must contain either all numeric or all character elements.
It must be used to define an array before the array name can be referenced.
What belongs within the braces of this ARRAY statement?

array contrib{?} qtr1-qtr4;

quarter

quarter*

1-4

4

For the program below, select an iterative DO statement to process all elements in the contrib array.

```
data work.contrib;
  array contrib{4} qtr1-qtr4;
    ...
    contrib{i}=contrib{i}*1.25;
  end;
run;
```


do i=4;

do i=1 to 4;

do until i=4;

do while i le 4;

What is the value of the index variable that references Jul in the statements below?

```
array quarter{4} Jan Apr Jul Oct;
do i=1 to 4;
   yeargoal=quarter{i}*1.2;
end;
```

1

2

3

4

Which DO statement would *not* process all the elements in the factors array shown below?

array factors{*} age height weight bloodpr;

do i=1 to dim(factors);

do i=1 to dim(*);

do i=1,2,3,4;

do i=1 to 4;

Which statement below is *false* regarding the use of arrays to create variables?
The variables are added to the program data vector during the compilation of the DATA step.
You do not need to specify the array elements in the ARRAY statement.
By default, all character variables are assigned a length of eight.
Only character variables can be created.
For the first observation, what is the value of diff{i} at the end of the second iteration of the DO loop?

Weight1	Weight2	Weight3
192	200	215
137	130	125
220	210	213

```
array wt{*} weight1-weight10;
array diff{9};
do i=1 to 9;
  diff{i}=wt{i+1}-wt{i};
end;
```

15

10

8

-7

Finish the ARRAY statement below to create temporary array elements that have initial values of **9000**, **9300**, **9600**, and **9900**.

```
array goal{4} ... ;
```

temporary (9000 9300 9600 9900)

temporary (9000 9300 9600 9900)

temporary 9000 9300 9600 9900

(temporary) 9000 9300 9600 9900

Based on the ARRAY statement below, select the array reference for the array element q50.

```
array ques{3,25} q1-q75;
```

ques{q50}

ques{1,50}

ques{2,25}

ques{3,0}

Select the ARRAY statement that defines the array in the following program.

```
data coat;
   input category high1-high3 / low1-low3;
   array compare{2,3} high1-high3 low1-low3;
   do i=1 to 2;
     do j=1 to 3;
       compare{i,j}=round(compare{i,j}*1.12);
     end;
   end;
datalines;
5555 9 8 7 6
4 3 2 1
8888 21 12 34 64
13 14 15 16
;
run;
```

array compare{1,6} high1-high3 low1-low3;

array compare{2,3} high1-high3 low1-low3;

array compare{3,2} high1-high3 low1-low3;

array compare{3,3} high1-high3 low1-low3;

Chapter Quiz

Select the best answer for each question. After completing the quiz, you can check your answers using the answer key in the appendix.

SAS date values are the number of days since which date?
January 1, 1900
January 1, 1950
January 1, 1960
January 1, 1970
A great advantage of storing dates and times as SAS numeric date and time values is that
they can easily be edited.
they can easily be read and understood.
they can be used in text strings like other character values.

they can be used in calculations like other numeric values.

SAS does not automatically make adjustments for daylight saving time, but it *does* make adjustments for:

leap seconds

leap years

Julian dates

time zones

An input data file has date expressions in the form 10222001. Which SAS informat should you use to read these dates?

DATE6.

DATE8.

MMDDYY6.

MMDDYY8.

The minimum width of the TIME*w*. informat is:

4

5

6

7

Shown below are date and time expressions and corresponding SAS datetime informats. Which date and time expression *cannot* be read by the informat that is shown beside it?

30May2000:10:03:17.2 **DATETIME20.**

30May00 10:03:17.2 **DATETIME18.**

30May2000/10:03 **DATETIME15.**

30May2000/1003 **DATETIME14.**

What is the default value of the YEARCUTOFF= system option?

1920

1910

1900

1930

Suppose your input data file contains the date expression 13APR2009. The YEARCUTOFF= system option is set to 1910. SAS will read the date as:

13APR1909

13APR1920

13APR2009

13APR2020

Suppose the YEARCUTOFF= system option is set to 1920. An input file contains the date expression 12/08/1925, which is being read with the MMDDYY8. informat. Which date will appear in your data?

08DEC1920

08DEC1925

08DEC2019

08DEC2025

Suppose your program creates two variables from an input file. Both variables are stored as SAS date values: FirstDay records the start of a billing cycle, and LastDay records the end of that cycle. The code for calculating the total number of days in the cycle would be:

TotDays=lastday-firstday;

TotDays=lastday-firstday+1;

TotDays=lastday/firstday;

You cannot use date values in calculations.

Defining a Unique Format

Overview

You can use the VALUE statement to define a format for displaying one or more values.

General form, VALUE statement:

VALUE *format-name*

range1='label1'
range2='label2'
...;

where *format-name*

> must begin with a dollar sign ($) if the format applies to character data
> must be a valid SAS name
> cannot be the name of an existing SAS format
> cannot end in a number
> does not end in a period when specified in a VALUE statement.

In SAS 8.2, the format name must be a SAS name up to eight characters in length, not ending in a number.

Beginning with SAS®9, a numeric format name can be up to 32 characters in length. A character format name can be up to 31 characters in length.

Notice that the statement begins with the keyword VALUE and ends with a semicolon after all the labels have been defined. The following VALUE statement creates the JOBFMT format to specify descriptive labels that will later be assigned to the variable JobTitle:

```
proc format lib=library;
    value jobfmt
        103='manager'
        105='text processor'
        111='assoc. technical writer'
        112='technical writer'
        113='senior technical writer';
run;
```

The VALUE range specifies

> a single value, such as **24** or 'S'.

a range of numeric values, such as **0-1500**.

a range of character values enclosed in quotation marks, such as **'A'-'M'**.

a list of unique values separated by commas, such as **90,180,270** or **'B'**, **'D'**, **'F'**. These values can be character values or numeric values, but not a combination of character and numeric values (because formats themselves are either character or numeric).

When the specified values are character values, they must be enclosed in quotation marks and must match the case of the variable's values. The format's name must also start with a dollar sign ($). For example, the VALUE statement below defines the $GRADE format, which displays the character values as text labels.

```
proc format lib=library;
   value $grade
      'A'='Good'
      'B'-'D'='Fair'
      'F'='Poor'
      'I','U'='See Instructor';
run;
```

When the specified values are numeric values, they are not enclosed in quotation marks, and the format's name should not begin with a dollar sign ($). The VALUE statement that defines the format JOBFMT assigns labels to numeric values.

Specifying Value Ranges

You can specify a non-inclusive range of numeric values by using the less than symbol (<) to avoid any overlapping. In this example, the range of values from **0** to less than **13** is labeled as child. The next range begins at **13**, so the label teenager would be assigned to the values **13** to **19**.

```
proc format lib=library;
   value agefmt
      0-<13='child'
      13-<20='teenager'
      20-<65='adult'
      65-100='senior citizen';
run;
```

You can also use the keywords LOW and HIGH to specify the lower and upper limits of a variable's value range. The keyword LOW does not include missing numeric values. The keyword OTHER can be used to label missing values as well as any values that are not specifically addressed in a range.

```
proc format lib=library;
   value agefmt
      low-<13='child'
      13-<20='teenager'
      20-<65='adult'
      65-high='senior citizen'
      other='unknown';
```

run;

🖰 If applied to a character format, the keyword LOW includes missing character values.

When specifying a label for displaying each range, remember to

enclose the label in quotation marks
limit the label to 256 characters
use two single quotation marks if you want an apostrophe to appear in the label, as in this example:

000='employee''s jobtitle unknown';

To define several formats, you can use multiple VALUE statements in a single PROC FORMAT step. In this example, each VALUE statement defines a different format.

```
proc format lib=library;
   value jobfmt
      103='manager'
      105='text processor'
      111='assoc. technical writer'
      112='technical writer'
      113='senior technical writer';
   value $respnse
      'Y'='Yes'
      'N'='No'
      'U'='Undecided'
      'NOP'='No opinion';
run;
```

The SAS log prints notes informing you that the formats have been created.

SAS Log

SAS Log (Partial Listing)

```
01   proc format lib=library;
02      value jobfmt
03            103='manager'   :
04            105='text processor'
05            111='assoc. technical writer'
06            112='technical writer'
07            113='senior technical writer';
     NOTE: Format JOBFMT has been written to LIBRARY.FORMATS.
```

Because you have defined the JOBFMT format for displaying the values of JobTitle, the format can be used with PROC PRINT for more legible output.

Data Set with Unformatted Values for JobTitle

	FirstName	LastName	JobTitle	Salary
1	Donny	Evans	112	29996.63
2	Lisa	Helms	105	18567.23
3	John	Higgins	111	25309.24
4	Amy	Larson	113	32696.78
5	Mary	Moore	112	28945.89
6	Jason	Powell	103	35099.55
7	Judy	Riley	111	25309.37
8	Neal	Ryan	112	28180.85

Data Set with Formatted Values for JobTitle

	FirstName	LastName	JobTitle	Salary
1	Donny	Evans	technical writer	29996.63
2	Lisa	Helms	text processor	18567.23
3	John	Higgins	assoc. technical writer	25309.24
4	Amy	Larson	senior technical writer	32696.78
5	Mary	Moore	technical writer	28945.89
6	Jason	Powell	manager	35099.55
7	Judy	Riley	assoc. technical writer	25309.37
8	Neal	Ryan	technical writer	28180.85

The next section will show how to apply your formats to variables.

Creating a Basic Report

To produce a simple list report, you first reference the library in which your SAS data set is stored. If you want, you can also set system options to control the appearance of your reports. Then you submit a basic PROC PRINT step.

General form, basic PROC PRINT step:

PROC PRINT DATA=_SAS-data-set_**;**

RUN;

where _SAS-data-set_ is the name of the SAS data set to be printed.

In the program below, the PROC PRINT statement invokes the PRINT procedure and specifies the data set Therapy in the SAS data library to which the libref Patients has been assigned.

```
libname patients 'c:\records\patients';
proc print data=patients.therapy;
```

run;

Notice the layout of the resulting report below. By default,

all observations and variables in the data set are printed
a column for observation numbers appears on the far left
variables and observations appear in the order in which they occur in the data set.

Patients.Therapy Data Set

The SAS System

Obs	Date	AerClass	WalkJogRun	Swim
1	JAN1999	56	78	14
2	FEB1999	32	109	19
3	MAR1999	35	106	22
4	APR1999	47	115	24
5	MAY1999	55	121	31
6	JUN1999	61	114	67
7	JUL1999	67	102	72
8	AUG1999	64	76	77
9	SEP1999	78	77	54
10	OCT1999	81	62	47
11	NOV1999	84	31	52
12	DEC1999	2	44	55
13	JAN2000	37	91	83
14	FEB2000	41	102	27
15	MAR2000	52	98	19
16	APR2000	61	118	22
17	MAY2000	49	88	29
18	JUN2000	24	101	54
19	JUL2000	45	91	69
20	AUG2000	63	65	53
21	SEP2000	60	49	68
22	OCT2000	78	70	41
23	NOV2000	82	44	58
24	DEC2000	93	57	47

Be sure to specify the equal sign in the DATA= option in SAS procedures. If you omit the equal sign, your program produces an error similar to the following in the SAS log:

Error Message

```
35    proc print data patients.therapy;
                       ----------------
                           73
ERROR 73-322: Expecting an =.
36    run;

NOTE: The SAS System stopped processing this step because of errors.
```

Raw Data Files

A raw data file is an external text file whose records contain data values that are organized in fields. Raw data files are non-proprietary and can be read by a variety of software programs. The sample raw data files in this chapter are shown with a ruler to help you identify where individual fields begin and end. The ruler is not part of the raw data file.

Raw Data File

The table below describes the record layout for a raw data file that contains readings from exercise stress tests that have been performed on patients at a health clinic. Exercise physiologists in the clinic use the test results to prescribe various exercise therapies. The file contains fixed fields. That is, values for each variable are in the same location in all records.

Record Layout for Raw Data

Field Name	Starting Column	Ending Column	Description of Field
ID	1	4	patient ID number
Name	6	25	patient name
RestHR	27	29	resting heart rate

- 1807 -

MaxHR	31	33	maximum heart rate during test
RecHR	35	37	recovery heart rate after test
TimeMin	39	40	time, complete minutes
TimeSec	42	43	time, seconds
Tolerance	45	45	comparison of stress test tolerance between this test and the last test (I=increased, D=decreased, S=same, N=no previous test)

Overview

Introduction

In SAS programming, a common task is to combine observations from two or more data sets into a new data set. Using the DATA step, you can combine data sets in several ways, including the following:

Method of Merging (Combining)	Illustration
One-to-one merging Creates observations that contain all of the variables from each contributing data set. Combines observations based on their relative position in each data set. Statement: SET	XisError: altImageDescription Element Should Not Be Blank. SAS Data Set C 	Num	VarA
-----	------
1	A1
3	A2
5	A3 | SAS Data Set D | Num	VarB
-----	------
2	B1
4	B2 | Merge Combined SAS Data Set | Num	VarA	VarB
-----	------	------
2	A1	B1
4	A2	B2	
Concatenating	XisError: altImageDescription Element Should Not Be Blank.

Appends the observations from one data set to another.

Statement: SET

Appending

Appending adds the observations in the second data set directly to the end of the original data set.

Procedure: APPEND

XisError: altImageDescription Element Should Not Be Blank.

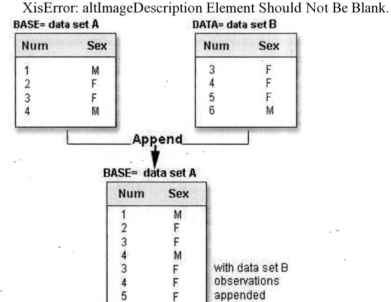

Interleaving

Intersperses observations from two or more data sets, based on one or more common variables.

Statements: SET, BY

XisError: altImageDescription Element Should Not Be Blank.

Match-merging

Matches observations from two or more data sets into a single observation in a new data set according to the values of a common variable.

Statements: MERGE, BY

XisError: altImageDescription Element Should Not Be Blank.

You can also use PROC SQL to join data sets according to common values. PROC SQL enables you to perform many other types of data set joins. See the *SQL Processing with SAS* e-learning course for additional training.

This chapter shows you how to combine SAS data sets using one-to-one combing or merging, concatenating, appending, interleaving, and match-merging. When you use the DATA step to combine data sets, you have a high degree of control in creating and manipulating data sets.

Objectives

In this chapter, you learn to

    perform one-to-one merging (combining) of data sets
    concatenate data sets
    append data sets
    interleave data sets

match-merge data sets
rename any like-named variables to avoid overwriting values
select only matched observations, if desired
predict the results of match-merging.

Execution Phase

Overview

After the DATA step is compiled, it is ready for execution. During the execution phase, the data portion of the data set is created. The data portion contains the data values.

During execution, each record in the input raw data file is read into the input buffer, copied to the program data vector, and then written to the new data set as an observation. The DATA step executes once for each record in the input file, unless otherwise directed by additional statements.

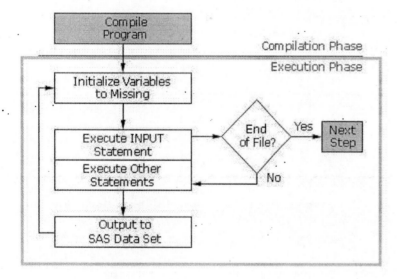

Example

The following DATA step reads values from the file Invent and executes nine times because there are nine records in the file.

```
data perm.update;
 infile invent;
 input Item $ 1-13 IDnum $ 15-19
   InStock 21-22 BackOrd 24-25;
```

```
  Total=instock+backord;
run;
```

Raw Data File Invent

```
1---+----10---+----20---+-
Bird Feeder    LG088  3 20
6 Glass Mugs   SB082  6 12
Glass Tray     BQ049 12  6
Padded Hangrs  MN256 15 20
Jewelry Box    AJ498 23  0
Red Apron      AQ072  9 12
Crystal Vase   AQ672 27  0
Picnic Basket  LS930 21  0
Brass Clock    AN910  2 10
```

Initializing Variables

At the beginning of the execution phase, the value of _N_ is **1**. Because there are no data errors, the value of _ERROR_ is **0**.

```
data perm.update;
  infile invent;
  input Item $ 1-13 IDnum $ 15-19
      InStock 21-22 BackOrd 24-25;
  Total=instock+backord;
run;
```

Program Data Vector

N	ERROR	Item	IDnum	InStock	BackOrd	Total
1	0			.	.	.

Initialized to Missing

The remaining variables are initialized to missing. Missing numeric values are represented by periods, and missing character values are represented by blanks.

INFILE Statement

Next, the INFILE statement identifies the location of the raw data.

```
data perm.update;
  infile invent;
  input Item $ 1-13 IDnum $ 15-19
      InStock 21-22 BackOrd 24-25;
  Total=instock+backord;
run;
```

Raw Data File Invent

```
1---+----10---+----20---+-
Bird Feeder    LG088  3 20
6 Glass Mugs   SB082  6 12
Glass Tray     BQ049 12  6
Padded Hangrs  MN256 15 20
Jewelry Box    AJ498 23  0
Red Apron      AQ072  9 12
Crystal Vase   AQ672 27  0
Picnic Basket  LS930 21  0
Brass Clock    AN910  2 10
```

Program Data Vector

N	ERROR	Item	IDnum	InStock	BackOrd	Total
1	0			•	•	•

INPUT Statement

Next, the INPUT statement reads a record into the input buffer. Then, the raw data in columns 1-13 is read and is assigned to Item in the program data vector.

```
data perm.update;
   infile invent;
   input Item $ 1-13 IDnum $ 15-19
        InStock 21-22 BackOrd 24-25;
   Total=instock+backord;
run;
```

Raw Data File Invent

```
1---+----10---+----20---+-
Bird Feeder    LG088   3 20
6 Glass Mugs   SB082   6 12
Glass Tray     BQ049  12  6
Padded Hangrs  MN256  15 20
Jewelry Box    AJ498  23  0
Red Apron      AQ072   9 12
Crystal Vase   AQ672  27  0
Picnic Basket  LS930  21  0
Brass Clock    AN910   2 10
```

Program Data Vector

N	ERROR	Item	IDnum	InStock	BackOrd	Total
1	0	Bird Feeder		•	•	•

```
data perm.update;
  infile invent;
  input Item $ 1-13 IDnum $ 15-19
      InStock 21-22 BackOrd 24-25;
  Total=instock+backord;
run;
```

Raw Data File Invent

```
1---+----10--v+----20---+-
Bird Feeder  •LG088   3 20
6 Glass Mugs   SB082   6 12
Glass Tray     BQ049  12  6
Padded Hangrs  MN256  15 20
Jewelry Box    AJ498  23  0
Red Apron      AQ072   9 12
Crystal Vase   AQ672  27  0
Picnic Basket  LS930  21  0
Brass Clock    AN910   2 10
```

Program Data Vector

N	ERROR	Item	IDnum	InStock	BackOrd	Total
1	0	Bird Feeder		•	•	•

Next, the data in columns 15-19 is read and is assigned to IDnum in the program data vector.

```
data perm.update;
  infile invent;
  input Item $ 1-13 IDnum $ 15-19
      InStock 21-22 BackOrd 24-25;
  Total=instock+backord;
run;
```

Raw Data File Invent

```
1---+----10---+----V0---+-
Bird Feeder   LG088  3 20
6 Glass Mugs  SB082  6 12
Glass Tray    BQ049 12  6
Padded Hangrs MN256 15 20
Jewelry Box   AJ498 23  0
Red Apron     AQ072  9 12
Crystal Vase  AQ672 27  0
Picnic Basket LS930 21  0
Brass Clock   AN910  2 10
```

Program Data Vector

N	ERROR	Item	IDnum	InStock	BackOrd	Total
1	0	Bird Feeder	LG088	.	.	.

Likewise, the INPUT statement reads the values for InStock from columns 21-22, and it reads the values for BackOrd from columns 24-25.

```
data perm.update;
  infile invent;
  input Item $ 1-13 IDnum $ 15-19
      InStock 21-22 BackOrd 24-25;
  Total=instock+backord;
run;
```

Raw Data File Invent

```
1---+----10---+----20---+V
Bird Feeder    LG088  3 20•
6 Glass Mugs   SB082  6 12
Glass Tray     BQ049 12  6
Padded Hangrs  MN256 15 20
Jewelry Box    AJ498 23  0
Red Apron      AQ072  9 12
Crystal Vase   AQ672 27  0
Picnic Basket  LS930 21  0
Brass Clock    AN910  2 10
```

Program Data Vector

N	ERROR	Item	IDnum	InStock	BackOrd	Total
1	0	Bird Feeder	LG088	3	20	•

Next, the assignment statement executes. The values for InStock and BackOrd are added to produce the values for Total.

```
data perm.update;
 infile invent;
 input Item $ 1-13 IDnum $ 15-19
     InStock 21-22 BackOrd 24-25;
 Total=instock+backord;
run;
```

Raw Data File Invent

```
1---+----10---+----20---+V
Bird Feeder    LG088  3 20•
6 Glass Mugs   SB082  6 12
Glass Tray     BQ049 12  6
Padded Hangrs  MN256 15 20
Jewelry Box    AJ498 23  0
Red Apron      AQ072  9 12
Crystal Vase   AQ672 27  0
Picnic Basket  LS930 21  0
Brass Clock    AN910  2 10
```

Program Data Vector

N	ERROR	Item	IDnum	InStock	BackOrd	Total
1	0	Bird Feeder	LG088	3	20	23

└──+──┘ = ↑

End of the DATA Step

At the end of the DATA step, several actions occur. First, the values in the program data vector are written to the output data set as the first observation.

```
data perm.update;
   infile invent;
   input Item $ 1-13 IDnum $ 15-19
        InStock 21-22 BackOrd 24-25;
   Total=instock+backord;
run;
```

Raw Data File Invent

```
1---+----10---+----20---+V
Bird Feeder    LG088  3 20·
6 Glass Mugs   SB082  6 12
Glass Tray     BQ049 12  6
Padded Hangrs  MN256 15 20
Jewelry Box    AJ498 23  0
Red Apron·     AQ072  9 12
Crystal Vase   AQ672 27  0
Picnic Basket  LS930 21  0
Brass Clock    AN910  2 10
```

Program Data Vector

N	ERROR	Item	IDnum	InStock	BackOrd	Total
1	0	Bird Feeder	LG088	3	20	23

SAS Data Set Perm.Update

Item	IDnum	InStock	BackOrd	Total
Bird Feeder	LG088	3	20	23

Next, control returns to the top of the DATA step and the value of _N_ increments from 1 to **2**. Finally, the variable values in the program data vector are re-set to missing. Notice that the automatic variable _ERROR_ is reset to zero if necessary.

```
data perm.update;
   infile invent;
   input Item $ 1-13 IDnum $ 15-19
        InStock 21-22 BackOrd 24-25;
```

```
   Total=instock+backord;
run;
```

Raw Data File Invent

```
V---+----10---+----20---+-
Bird Feeder     LG088  3 20
6 Glass Mugs    SB082  6 12
Glass Tray      BQ049 12  6
Padded Hangrs   MN256 15 20
Jewelry Box     AJ498 23  0
Red Apron       AQ072  9 12
Crystal Vase    AQ672 27  0
Picnic Basket   LS930 21  0
Brass Clock     AN910  2 10
```

Program Data Vector

N	ERROR	Item	IDnum	InStock	BackOrd	Total
2	0			•	•	•

Set to Missing

SAS Data Set Perm.Update

Item	IDnum	InStock	BackOrd	Total
Bird Feeder	LG088	3	20	23

Iterations of the DATA Step

You can see that the DATA step works like a loop, repetitively executing statements to read data values and create observations one by one. Each loop (or cycle of execution) is called an iteration. At the beginning of the second iteration, the value of _N_ is **2**, and _ERROR_ is still **0**. Notice that the input pointer points to the second record.

Raw Data File Invent

```
V---+----10---+----20---+-
Bird Feeder     LG088   3 20
6 Glass Mugs    SB082   6 12
Glass Tray      BQ049  12  6
Padded Hangrs   MN256  15 20
Jewelry Box     AJ498  23  0
Red Apron       AQ072   9 12
Crystal Vase    AQ672  27  0
Picnic Basket   LS930  21  0
Brass Clock     AN910   2 10
```

Program Data Vector

N	ERROR	Item	IDnum	InStock	BackOrd	Total
2	0	.		.	.	.

SAS Data Set Perm.Update

Item	IDnum	InStock	BackOrd	Total
Bird Feeder	LG088	3	20	23

As the INPUT statement executes for the second time, the values from the second record are read into the input buffer and then into the program data vector.

Raw Data File Invent

```
1---+----10---+----20---+V
Bird Feeder    LG088  3 20
6 Glass Mugs   SB082  6 12.
Glass Tray     BQ049 12  6
Padded Hangrs  MN256 15 20
Jewelry Box    AJ498 23  0
Red Apron      AQ072  9 12
Crystal Vase   AQ672 27  0
Picnic Basket  LS930 21  0
Brass Clock    AN910  2 10
```

Program Data Vector

N	ERROR	Item	IDnum	InStock	BackOrd	Total
2	0	6 Glass Mugs	SB082	6	12	

SAS Data Set Perm.Update

Item	IDnum	InStock	BackOrd	Total
Bird Feeder	LG088	3	20	23

Next, the value for Total is calculated based on the current values for InStock and BackOrd. The RUN statement indicates the end of the DATA step loop.

```
data perm.update;
   infile invent;
   input Item $ 1-13 IDnum $ 15-19
        InStock 21-22 BackOrd 24-25;
   Total=instock+backord;
run;
```

Raw Data File Invent

```
1---+----10---+----20---+V
Bird Feeder    LG088   3 20
6 Glass Mugs   SB082   6 12*
Glass Tray     BQ049  12  6
Padded Hangrs  MN256  15 20
Jewelry Box    AJ498  23  0
Red Apron      AQ072   9 12
Crystal Vase   AQ672  27  0
Picnic Basket  LS930  21  0
Brass Clock    AN910   2 10
```

Program Data Vector

N	ERROR	Item	IDnum	InStock	BackOrd	Total
2	0	6 Glass Mugs	SB082	6	12	18

```
           └─+─┴─=─┘↑
```

SAS Data Set Perm.Update

Item	IDnum	InStock	BackOrd	Total
Bird Feeder	LG088	3	20	23

At the bottom of the DATA step, the values in the program data vector are written to the data set as the second observation.

```
data perm.update;
   infile invent;
   input Item $ 1-13 IDnum $ 15-19
        InStock 21-22 BackOrd 24-25;
   Total=instock+backord;
run;
```

Next, the value of _N_ increments from 2 to **3**, control returns to the top of the DATA step, and the values for Item, IDnum, InStock, BackOrd, and Total are re-set to missing.

```
data perm.update;
   infile invent;
   input Item $ 1-13 IDnum $ 15-19
        InStock 21-22 BackOrd 24-25;
   Total=instock+backord;
run;
```

Raw Data File Invent

```
v---+-----10---+-----20---+-
Bird Feeder    LG088  3 20
6 Glass Mugs   SB082  6 12
Glass Tray     BQ049 12  6
Padded Hangrs  MN256 15 20
Jewelry Box    AJ498 23  0
Red Apron      AQ072  9 12
Crystal Vase   AQ672 27  0
Picnic Basket  LS930 21  0
Brass Clock    AN910  2 10
```

Program Data Vector

N	ERROR	Item	IDnum	InStock	BackOrd	Total
3	0			•	•	•

Reset to Missing

SAS Data Set Perm.Update

Item	IDnum	InStock	BackOrd	Total
Bird Feeder	LG088	3	20	23
6 Glass Mugs	SB082	6	12	18

End-of-File Marker

The execution phase continues in this manner until the end-of-file marker is reached in the raw data file. When there are no more records in the raw data file to be read, the data portion of the new data set is complete and the DATA step stops.

Raw Data File Invent

```
1---+-----10---+-----20---+-
Bird Feeder    LG088  3 20
6 Glass Mugs   SB082  6 12
Glass Tray     BQ049 12  6
Padded Hangrs  MN256 15 20
Jewelry Box    AJ498 23  0
Red Apron      AQ072  9 12
Crystal Vase   AQ672 27  0
Picnic Basket  LS930 21  0
Brass Clock    AN910  2 10
```

This is the output data set that SAS creates:

SAS Data Set Perm.Udpate

Item	IDnum	InStock	BackOrd	Total
Bird Feeder	LG088	3	20	23
6 Glass Mugs	SB082	6	12	18
Glass Tray	BQ049	12	6	18
Padded Hangrs	MN256	15	20	35
Jewelry Box	AJ498	23	0	23
Red Apron	AQ072	9	12	21
Crystal Vase	AQ672	27	0	27
Picnic Basket	LS930	21	0	21
Brass Clock	AN910	2	10	12

When reading variables from raw data, SAS sets the value of each variable in the DATA step to missing at the beginning of each cycle of execution, with these exceptions:

- variables that are named in a RETAIN statement
- variables that are created in a sum statement
- data elements in a _TEMPORARY_ array.
- any variables that are created with options in the FILE or INFILE statements
- automatic variables.

In contrast, when reading variables from a SAS data set, SAS sets the values to missing only before the first cycle of execution of the DATA step. Therefore, the variables retain their values until new values become available (for example, through an assignment statement or through the next execution of a SET or MERGE statement). Variables that are created with options in the SET or MERGE statements also retain their values from one cycle of execution to the next. (You learn about reading SAS data sets, working with arrays, and using the SET and MERGE statements in later chapters.)

Summary of the Execution Phase

You've seen how the DATA step iteratively reads records in the raw data file. Now take a minute to review execution-phase processing.

During the execution phase

- variables in the program data vector are initialized to missing before each execution of the DATA step
- each statement is executed sequentially
- the INPUT statement reads into the input buffer the next record from the external file identified by the INFILE statement, and then reads the data into the program data vector
- other statements can then further modify the current observation
- the values in the program data vector are written to the SAS data set at the end of the DATA step
- program flow returns to the top of the DATA step

the DATA step is executed until the end-of-file marker is reached in the external file.

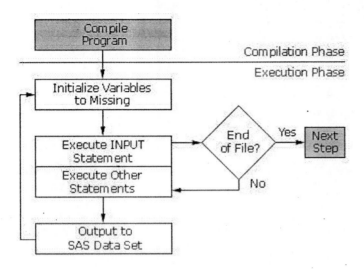

End of the Execution Phase

At the end of the execution phase, the SAS log confirms that the raw data file was read, and it displays the number of observations and variables in the data set.

SAS Log

```
NOTE: 9 records were read from the infile INVENT.
NOTE: The data set PERM.UPDATE has 9 observations
      and 5 variables.
```

You already know how to display the data set with the PRINT procedure.

proc print data=perm.update;
run;

Output from the PRINT Procedure

Obs	Item	IDnum	InStock	BackOrd	Total
1	Bird Feeder	LG088	3	20	23
2	6 Glass Mugs	SB082	6	12	18
3	Glass Tray	BQ049	12	6	18
4	Padded Hangrs	MN256	15	20	35
5	Jewelry Box	AJ498	23	0	23
6	Red Apron	AQ072	9	12	21
7	Crystal Vase	AQ672	27	0	27
8	Picnic Basket	LS930	21	0	21
9	Brass Clock	AN910	2	10	12

Creating Excel Worksheets

In addition to being able to read Excel data, SAS can also create Excel worksheets from SAS data sets.

To do this, you use the SAS/ACCESS LIBNAME statement. For example, to create a new worksheet named **high_stress** from the temporary SAS data set **work.high_stress** and save this worksheet in the new Excel file **newExcel.xlsx**, you would submit the following LIBNAME statement and DATA step:

```
libname clinic 'c:\Users\mylaptop\admitxl.xlsx' mixed=yes;
data clinic.admit;
   set work.admit;
run;
```

Chapter Quiz

Select the best answer for each question. After completing the quiz, check your answers using the answer key in the appendix.

  Which statement is *false* regarding the use of DO loops?
  They can contain conditional clauses.
  They can generate multiple observations.
  They can be used to combine DATA and PROC steps.
  They can be used to read data.
  During each execution of the following DO loop, the value of Earned is calculated and is added to its previous value. How many times does this DO loop execute?

```
data finance.earnings;
  Amount=1000;
```

```
    Rate=.075/12;
    do month=1 to 12;
      Earned+(amount+earned)*rate;
    end;
run;
```

      0
      1
     12
     13

On January 1 of each year, $5000 is invested in an account. Complete the DATA step below to determine the value of the account after 15 years if a constant interest rate of ten percent is expected.

```
data work.invest;
    ...
    Capital+5000;
    capital+(capital*.10);
  end;
run;
```

```
do count=1 to 15;
```

```
do count=1 to 15 by 10%;
```

```
do count=1 to capital;
```

```
do count=capital to (capital*.10);
```

In the data set Work.Invest, what would be the stored value for Year?

```
data work.invest;
  do year=1990 to 2004;
    Capital+5000;
    capital+(capital*.10);
  end;
run;
```

     missing
     1990
     2004
     2005

Which of the following statements is *false* regarding the program shown below?

```
data work.invest;
  do year=1990 to 2004;
    Capital+5000;
    capital+(capital*.10);
    output;
  end;
```

run;

The OUTPUT statement writes current values to the data set immediately.
The last value for Year in the new data set is **2005**.
The OUTPUT statement overrides the automatic output at the end of the DATA step.
The DO loop performs 15 iterations.
How many observations will the data set Work.Earn contain?

```
data work.earn;
   Value=2000;
   do year=1 to 20;
      Interest=value*.075;
      value+interest;
      output;
   end;
run;
```

    0
    1
    19
    20

Which of the following would you use to compare the result of investing $4,000 a year for five years in three different banks that compound interest monthly? Assume a fixed rate for the five-year period.
DO WHILE statement
nested DO loops
DO UNTIL statement
a DO group

Which statement is *false* regarding DO UNTIL statements?
The condition is evaluated at the top of the loop, before the enclosed statements are executed.
The enclosed statements are always executed at least once.
SAS statements in the DO loop are executed until the specified condition is true.
The DO loop must have a closing END statement.

Select the DO WHILE statement that would generate the same result as the program below.

```
data work.invest;
capital=100000;
   do until(Capital gt 500000);
      Year+1;
      capital+(capital*.10);
   end;
run;
```

do while(Capital ge 500000);

do while(Capital=500000);

do while(Capital le 500000);

```
do while(Capital>500000);
```

In the following program, complete the statement so that the program stops generating observations when Distance reaches 250 miles or when 10 gallons of fuel have been used.

```
data work.go250;
  set perm.cars;
  do gallons=1 to 10 ... ;
    Distance=gallons*mpg;
    output;
  end;
run;
```

```
while(Distance<250)
```

```
when(Distance>250)
```

```
over(Distance le 250)
```

```
until(Distance=250)
```

Debugging a DATA Step

Diagnosing Errors in the Compilation Phase

Now that you know how a DATA step is processed, you can use that knowledge to correct errors.Editing and Debugging SAS Programsprovided examples of errors that are detected during the compilation phase, including

misspelled keywords and data set names
unbalanced quotation marks
invalid options.

During the compilation phase, SAS can interpret some syntax errors (such as the keyword DATA misspelled as DAAT). If it cannot interpret the error, SAS

prints the word ERROR followed by an error message in the log
compiles but does not execute the step where the error occurred, and prints the following message to warn you:
NOTE: The SAS System stopped processing this step because of errors.

Some errors are explained fully by the message that SAS prints; other error messages are not as easy to interpret. For example, because SAS statements are free-format, when you fail to end a SAS statement with a semicolon, SAS cannot detect the error.

Diagnosing Errors in the Execution Phase

As you have seen, errors can occur in the compilation phase, resulting in a DATA step that is compiled but not executed. Errors can also occur during the execution phase. When SAS detects an error in the execution phase, the following can occur, depending on the type of error:

A note, warning, or error message is displayed in the log.
The values that are stored in the program data vector are displayed in the log.
The processing of the step either continues or stops.

Example

Suppose you misspelled the fileref in the INFILE statement below. This is not a syntax error, because SAS does not validate the file that you reference until the execution phase. During the compilation phase, the fileref Invnt is assumed to reference some external raw data file.

```
data perm.update;
   infile invnt;
   input Item $ 1-13 IDnum $ 15-19
      InStock 21-22 BackOrd 24-25;
   Total=instock+backord;
run;
```

This error is not detected until the execution phase begins. Because there is no external file that is referenced by the fileref Invnt, the DATA step stops processing.

```
3486   data perm.update;
3487      infile invnt;
3488      input Item $ 1-13 IDnum $ 15-19 InStock 21-22 BackOrd 24-25;
3489      Total=instock+backord;
3490
3491   run;

ERROR: No logical assign for filename INVNT.
NOTE: The SAS System stopped processing this step because of errors.
WARNING: The data set  PERM.UPDATE may be incomplete.  When this step was
         stopped there were 0 observations and 5 variables.
WARNING: Data set PERM.UPDATE was not replaced because this step was stopped.
         stopped.
NOTE: DATA statement used (Total process time):
      real time          0.01 seconds
      cpu time           0.01 seconds
```

Because Invent is misspelled, the statement in the DATA step that identifies the raw data is incorrect. Note, however, that the correct number of variables was defined in the descriptor portion of the data set.

Incorrectly identifying a variable's type is another common execution-time error. As you know, the values for IDnum are character values. Suppose you forget to place the dollar sign ($) after the variable's name in your INPUT statement. This is not a compile-time error, because SAS cannot verify IDnum's type until the data values for IDnum are read.

Raw Data File Invent

```
----+----10---+----20---+-
Bird Feeder    LG088  3 20
6 Glass Mugs   SB082  6 12
Glass Tray     BQ049 12  6
Padded Hangrs  MN256 15 20
Jewelry Box    AJ498 23  0
Red Apron      AQ072  9 12
Crystal Vase   AQ672 27  0
Picnic Basket  LS930 21  0
Brass Clock    AN910  2 10
```

```
data perm.update;
   infile invent;
   input Item $ 1-13 IDnum 15-19
        InStock 21-22 BackOrd 24-25;
   Total=instock+backord;
run;
```

In this case, the DATA step completes the execution phase, and the observations are written to the data set. However, several notes appear in the log.

SAS Log

```
NOTE: Invalid data for IDnum in line 7 15-19.
RULE:  ----+----1----+----2----+----3----+----4--
07     Crystal Vase  AQ672 27 0
Item=Crystal Vase IDnum=. InStock=27 BackOrd=0
Total=27 _ERROR_=1 _N_=7
NOTE: Invalid data for IDnum in line 8 15-19.
08     Picnic Basket LS930 21 0
Item=Picnic Basket IDnum=. InStock=21 BackOrd=0
Total=21 _ERROR_=1 _N_=8
NOTE: Invalid data for IDnum in line 9 15-19.
09     Brass Clock   AN910 2 10
Item=Brass Clock IDnum=. InStock=2 BackOrd=10
Total=12 _ERROR_=1 _N_=9

NOTE: 9 records were read from the infile INVENT.
NOTE: The data set PERM.UPDATE has 9 observations
      and 5 variables.
```

Each note identifies the location of the invalid data for each observation. In this example, the invalid data is located in columns 15-19 for all observations.

The second line in each note (excluding the RULE line) displays the raw data record. Notice that the second field displays the values for IDnum, which are obviously character values.

SAS Log

```
NOTE: Invalid data for IDnum in line 7 15-19.
RULE: ----+----1----+----2----+----3----+----4--
07      Crystal Vase   AQ672 27 0
Item=Crystal Vase IDnum=. InStock=27 BackOrd=0
Total=27 _ERROR_=1 _N_=7
NOTE: Invalid data for IDnum in line 8 15-19.
08      Picnic Basket LS930 21 0
Item=Picnic Basket IDnum=. InStock=21 BackOrd=0
Total=21 _ERROR_=1 _N_=8
NOTE: Invalid data for IDnum in line 9 15-19.
09      Brass Clock    AN910 2 10
Item=Brass Clock IDnum=. InStock=2 BackOrd=10
Total=12 _ERROR_=1 _N_=9


NOTE: 9 records were read from the infile INVENT.
NOTE: The data set PERM.UPDATE has 9 observations
      and 5 variables.
```

The third and fourth lines display the values that are stored in the program data vector. Here, the values for IDnum are missing, although the other values have been correctly assigned to their respective variables. Notice that _ERROR_ has a value of **1**, indicating that a data error has occurred.

SAS Log

```
NOTE: Invalid data for IDnum in line 7 15-19.
RULE: ----+----1----+----2----+----3----+----4--
07     Crystal Vase  AQ672 27 0
Item=Crystal Vase IDnum=. InStock=27 BackOrd=0
Total=27 _ERROR_=1 _N_=7
NOTE: Invalid data for IDnum in line 8 15-19.
08     Picnic Basket LS930 21 0
Item=Picnic Basket IDnum=. InStock=21 BackOrd=0
Total=21 _ERROR_=1 _N_=8
NOTE: Invalid data for IDnum in line 9 15-19.
09     Brass Clock  AN910 2 10
Item=Brass Clock IDnum=. InStock=2 BackOrd=10
Total=12 _ERROR_=1 _N_=9

NOTE: 9 records were read from the infile INVENT.
NOTE: The data set PERM.UPDATE has 9 observations
      and 5 variables.
```

The PRINT procedure displays the data set, showing that the values for IDnum are missing. In this example, the periods indicate that IDnum is a numeric variable, although it should have been defined as a character variable.

proc print data=perm.update;
run;

Output from the PRINT Procedure Showing Missing Values for IDnum

Obs	Item	IDnum	InStock	BackOrd	Total
1	Bird Feeder	.	3	20	23
2	6 Glass Mugs	.	6	12	18
3	Glass Tray	.	12	6	18
4	Padded Hangrs	.	15	20	35
5	Jewelry Box	.	23	0	23
6	Red Apron	.	9	12	21
7	Crystal Vase	.	27	0	27
8	Picnic Basket	.	21	0	21
9	Brass Clock	.	2	10	12

When you read raw data with the DATA step, it's important to check the SAS log to verify that your data was read correctly. Here is a typical message:

SAS Log

```
WARNING: The data set PERM.UPDATE may be incomplete.
         When this step was stopped there were
         0 observations and 5 variables.
```

When no observations are written to the data set, you should check to see whether your DATA step was completely executed. Most likely, a syntax error or another error was detected at the beginning of the execution phase.

Validating and Cleaning Data

Data errors occur when data values are not appropriate for the SAS statements that are specified in a program. SAS detects data errors during program execution. When a data error is detected, SAS continues to execute the program.

In general, SAS procedures analyze data, produce output, or manage SAS files. In addition, SAS procedures can be used to detect invalid data. The following procedures can be used to detect invalid data:

    PROC PRINT
    PROC FREQ
    PROC MEANS

The PRINT procedure displays the data set, showing that the values for IDnum are missing. Periods indicate that IDnum is a numeric variable, although it should have been defined as a character variable.

```
proc print data=perm.update;
run;
```

Output from the PRINT Procedure Showing Missing Values for IDnum

Obs	Item	IDnum	InStock	BackOrd	Total
1	Bird Feeder	.	3	20	23
2	6 Glass Mugs	.	6	12	18
3	Glass Tray	.	12	6	18
4	Padded Hangrs	.	15	20	35
5	Jewelry Box	.	23	0	23
6	Red Apron	.	9	12	21
7	Crystal Vase	.	27	0	27
8	Picnic Basket	.	21	0	21
9	Brass Clock	.	2	10	12

The FREQ procedure detects invalid character and numeric values by looking at distinct values. You can use PROC FREQ to identify any variables that were not given an expected value.

General form, FREQ procedure:

PROC FREQ DATA=*SAS-data-set* *<NLEVELS>*;

TABLES *variable(s);*

RUN;

where

  The TABLES statement specifies the frequency tables to produce.
  The NLEVELS option displays a table that provides the number of distinct values for each variable named in the TABLES statement.

In the following example, the data set contains invalid characters for the variables Gender and Age. PROC FREQ displays the distinct values of variables and is therefore useful for finding invalid values in data. You can use PROC FREQ with the TABLES statement to produce a frequency table for specific variables.

```
proc freq data=work.Patients;
    tables Gender Age;
```

run;

In the output you can see both the valid (**M** and **F**) and invalid (**G**) values for Gender, and the valid and invalid (242) values for age. In both the gender and age FREQ tables, one observation needs data cleaned as shown below:

The FREQ Procedure

Gender	Frequency	Percent	Cumulative Frequency	Cumulative Percent
F	2	50.00	2	50.00
G	1	25.00	3	75.00
M	1	25.00	4	100.00

Age	Frequency	Percent	Cumulative Frequency	Cumulative Percent
44	1	25.00	1	25.00
61	1	25.00	2	50.00
64	1	25.00	3	75.00
242	1	25.00	4	100.00

The MEANS procedure can also be used to validate data because it produces summary reports displaying descriptive statistics. For example, PROC MEANS can show whether the values for a particular variable are within their expected range.

General form, MEANS procedure:

PROC MEANS DATA=*SAS-data-set* *<statistics>*;

VAR *variable(s)*;

RUN;

> The VAR statement specifies the analysis variables and their order in the results.
> The statistics to display can be specified in the PROC MEANS statement.

Using the same data set as in the previous example, we can submit PROC MEANS to determine if the Age of all test subjects is within a reasonable range. Notice the VAR statement is specified with that particular variable to get the statistical information, or range, of the data values.

```
proc means data=work.Patients;
    var Age;
run;
```

The output for the MEANS procedure displays a range of 44 to 242, which clearly indicates that there is invalid data somewhere in the Age column.

The MEANS Procedure

		Analysis Variable : Age		
N	Mean	Std Dev	Minimum	Maximum
4	102.7500000	93.2501117	44.0000000	242.0000000

Cleaning the Data

You can use an assignment statement or a conditional clause to programmatically clean invalid data once it is identified. For example, if your input data contains a field called Gender, and that field has an invalid value (a value other than M or F), then you can clean your data by changing the invalid value to a valid value for Gender. To avoid overwriting your original data set, you can use the DATA statement to create a new data set. The new data set will contain all of the data from your original data set, along with the correct values for invalid data.

The following example assumes that in your input data, Gender has an invalid value of G. This error might be the result of a data entry error. After examining your data, you determine that G should actually be F. You can fix the invalid data for Gender by using an assignment statement along with an IF-THEN statement:

```
data work.clean_data;
   set work.patients;
   gender=upcase(Gender);
   if Gender='G' then Gender='F';
run;

proc print data=work.clean_data;
run;
```

When you examine your input data further, you find that two observations contain invalid values for Age. These values exceed a maximum value of 110. You can uniquely identify each of the observations by the variable Empid. By checking the date of birth in each of the observations, you determine the correct value for Age. To change the data, you can use an IF-THEN-ELSE statement:

```
data work.clean_data;
   set work.patients;
   if empid=3294 then age=65;
   else if empid=7391 then age=75;
run;

proc print data=work.clean_data;
run;
```

Another way of ensuring that your output data set contains valid data is to programmatically identify invalid data and delete the associated observations from your output data set:

```
data work.clean_data;
   set work.patients;
   if Age>110 then delete;
run;

proc print data=work.clean_data;
run;
```

Selecting Statistics

The default statistics that the MEANS procedure produces (*n*-count, mean, standard deviation, minimum, and maximum) are not always the ones that you need. You might prefer to limit output to the mean of the values. Or you might need to compute a different statistic, such as the median or range of the values.

To specify statistics, include statistic keywords as options in the PROC MEANS statement. When you specify a statistic in the PROC MEANS statement, default statistics are not produced. For example, to see the median and range of Perm.Survey numeric values, add the MEDIAN and RANGE keywords as options.

```
proc means data=perm.survey median range;
run;
```

MEANS Procedure Output Displaying Median and Range

MEANS Procedure Output Displaying Median and Range

The MEANS Procedure

Variable	Median	Range
Item1	4.0000000	3.0000000
Item2	3.0000000	4.0000000
Item3	4.0000000	1.0000000
Item4	3.5000000	3.0000000
Item5	3.0000000	4.0000000
Item6	4.0000000	3.0000000
Item7	3.0000000	4.0000000
Item8	3.0000000	3.0000000
Item9	2.5000000	3.0000000
Item10	3.0000000	3.0000000
Item11	3.0000000	4.0000000
Item12	3.0000000	1.0000000
Item13	3.0000000	3.0000000
Item14	2.5000000	3.0000000
Item15	3.0000000	4.0000000
Item16	2.0000000	4.0000000
Item17	3.0000000	2.0000000
Item18	3.0000000	3.0000000

The following keywords can be used with PROC MEANS to compute statistics:

Descriptive Statistics

Keyword	Description
CLM	Two-sided confidence limit for the mean
CSS	Corrected sum of squares
CV	Coefficient of variation
KURTOSIS	Kurtosis

LCLM	One-sided confidence limit below the mean
MAX	Maximum value
MEAN	Average
MODE	Value that occurs most frequently (new in SAS 9.2)
MIN	Minimum value
N	Number of observations with nonmissing values
NMISS	Number of observations with missing values
RANGE	Range
SKEWNESS	Skewness
STDDEV / STD	Standard deviation
STDERR	Standard error of the mean
SUM	Sum
SUMWGT	Sum of the Weight variable values
UCLM	One-sided confidence limit above the mean
USS	Uncorrected sum of squares
VAR	Variance

Quantile Statistics

Keyword	Description
MEDIAN / P50	Median or 50th percentile
P1	1st percentile
P5	5th percentile
P10	10th percentile
Q1 / P25	Lower quartile or 25th percentile
Q3 / P75	Upper quartile or 75th percentile
P90	90th percentile
P95	95th percentile
P99	99th percentile
QRANGE	Difference between upper and lower quartiles: Q3-Q1

Hypothesis Testing

Keyword	Description
PROBT	Probability of a greater absolute value for the t value
T	Student's t for testing the hypothesis that the population mean is 0

Overview

Introduction

SAS provides many informats for reading raw data values in various forms. <u>Reading Raw Data in Fixed Fields</u>explained how informats can be used to read standard and nonstandard data. In this chapter, you learn how to use a special category of SAS informats called date and time informats. These informats enable you to read a variety of common date and time expressions. After you read date and time values, you can also perform calculations with them.

```
options yearcutoff=1920;
data perm.aprbills;
   infile aprdata;
   input LastName $8. @10 DateIn mmddyy8. +1 DateOut
      mmddyy8. +1 RoomRate 6. @35 EquipCost 6.;
   Days=dateout-datein+1;
   RoomCharge=days*roomrate;
   Total=roomcharge+equipcost;
run;
```

Program Data Vector

Program Data Vector

LastName	DateIn	DateOut	RoomRate	EquipCost	Days	RoomCharge	Total
Akron	14339	14343	175.00	298.45	5	875.00	1173.45

+1

Objectives

In this chapter, you learn how

> SAS stores date and time values
> to use SAS informats to read common date and time expressions
> to handle two-digit year values
> to calculate time intervals by subtracting two dates
> to multiply a time interval by a rate
> to display various date and time values.

Reading Repeating Blocks of Data

Overview

Each record in the file Tempdata contains three blocks of data. Each block contains a date followed by the day's high temperature in a small city located in the southern United States.

Raw Data File Tempdata

```
       Raw Data File Tempdata
1---+----10---+----20---+----30--
01APR90 68 02APR90 67 03APR90 70
04APR90 74 05APR90 72 06APR90 73
07APR90 71 08APR90 75 09APR90 76
10APR90 78 11APR90 70 12APR90 69
13APR90 71 14APR90 72 15APR90 74
16APR90 73 17APR90 71 18APR90 75
19APR90 75 20APR90 73 21APR90 75
22APR90 77 23APR90 78 24APR90 80
25APR90 78 26APR90 77 27APR90 79
28APR90 81 29APR90 81 30APR90 84
```

You could write a DATA step that reads each record and creates three different Date and Temp variables.

Three Date and Temp Variables

SAS Data Set

Date1	Temp1	Date2	Temp2	Date3	Temp3
11048	68	11049	67	11050	70

Alternatively, you could create a separate observation for each block of data in a record. This data set is better structured for analysis and reporting with SAS procedures.

Separate Observations for Each Block of Data in a Record

SAS Data Set

Date	HighTemp
11048	68
11049	67
11050	70

Holding the Current Record with a Line-Hold Specifier

You need to hold the current record so the input statement can read, and SAS can output, repeated blocks of data on the same record. This is easily accomplished by using a line-hold specifier in the INPUT statement.

SAS provides two line-hold specifiers.

The trailing at sign (@) holds the input record for the execution of the next INPUT statement.
The double trailing at sign (@@) holds the input record for the execution of the next INPUT statement, even across iterations of the DATA step.

The term *trailing* indicates that the @ or @@ must be the *last* item specified in the INPUT statement. For example, input Name $20. @; or input Name $20. @@;

This chapter teaches you how the trailing @@ can be used to hold a record across multiple iterations of the DATA step.

Using the Double Trailing At Sign (@@) to Hold the Current Record

Normally, each time a DATA step executes, the INPUT statement reads the next record. But when you use the trailing @@, the INPUT statement continues reading from the same record.

Example with the Double Trailing At Sign

Input Score;

Input Score @@;

Raw Data File and Program Data Vector

Raw Data File and Program Data Vector

The double trailing at sign (@@)

> works like the trailing @ except it holds the data line in the input buffer across multiple executions of the DATA step
>> typically is used to read multiple SAS observations from a single data line
>> should not be used with the @ pointer control, with column input, nor with the MISSOVER option.

A record that is held by the double trailing at sign (@@) is not released until either of the following events occurs:

> the input pointer moves past the end of the record. Then the input pointer moves down to the next record.

Raw Data File

```
1---+----10--▼+-
102 92 78 103
84 23 36 75
```

an INPUT statement that has no trailing at sign executes.

input ID $ @@;

.

.

input Department 5.;

The following example requires only one INPUT statement to read the values for Date and HighTemp, but the INPUT statement must execute three times for each record.

The INPUT statement reads a block of values for Date and HighTemp, and holds the current record by using the trailing @@. The values in the program data vector are written to the data set as an observation, and control returns to the top of the DATA step.

```
data perm.april90;
   infile tempdata;
   input Date : date. HighTemp @@;
```

Control Returned to the Top of the DATA Step

```
          Raw Data File Tempdata
1---+----1▼---+----20---+----30--
01APR90 68 02APR90 67 03APR90 70
04APR90 74 05APR90 72 06APR90 73
07APR90 71 08APR90 75 09APR90 76
```

In the next iteration, the INPUT statement reads the next block of values for Date and HighTemp from the same record.

Date and High Temp

```
          Raw Data File Tempdata
1---+----10---+----2▼---+----30--
01APR90 68 02APR90 67 03APR90 70
04APR90 74 05APR90 72 06APR90 73
07APR90 71 08APR90 75 09APR90 76
```

Completing the DATA Step

You can add a FORMAT statement to the DATA step to display the date or time values with a specified format. The FORMAT statement below uses the DATE*w.* format to display the values for Date in the form *ddmmmyyyy*.

```
data perm.april90;
   infile tempdata;
   input Date : date. HighTemp @@;
   format date date9.;
run;
```

Displaying Dates in a Specified Format

```
         Raw Data File Tempdata
1---+----10---+----20---+----30--
01APR90  68  02APR90  67  03APR90  70
04APR90  74  05APR90  72  06APR90  73
07APR90  71  08APR90  75  09APR90  76
```

DATA Step Processing of Repeating Blocks of Data

Complete DATA Step

```
data perm.april90;
   infile tempdata;
   input Date : date. HighTemp @@;
   format date date9.;
run;
```

Example

As the execution phase begins, the input pointer rests on column 1 of record 1.

Input Pointer on Column 1 of Record 1

```
         Raw Data File Tempdata
>V---+----10---+----20---+----30--
01APR90  68  02APR90  67  03APR90  70
04APR90  74  05APR90  72  06APR90  73
07APR90  71  08APR90  75  09APR90  76
10APR90  78  11APR90  70  12APR90  69
13APR90  71  14APR90  72  15APR90  74
```

Program Data Vector

N	Date	HighTemp
1	.	.

During the first iteration of the DATA step, the first block of values for Date and High Temp are read into the program data vector.

Reading the First Block of Values

Raw Data File Tempdata

The first observation is written to the data set.

Control Returns to the Top of the DATA Step

Raw Data File Tempdata

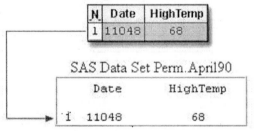

Control returns to the top of the DATA step, and the values are reset to missing.

Reset Values

Program Data Vector

During the second iteration, the @@ prevents the input pointer from moving down to the next record. Instead, the INPUT statement reads the second block of values for Date and HighTemp from the first record.

Reading the Second Block of Values from the First Record

Raw Data File Tempdata

```
>----+----10---+----20V--+----30--
01APR90 68 02APR90 67 03APR90 70
04APR90 74 05APR90 72 06APR90 73
07APR90 71 08APR90 75 09APR90 76
10APR90 78 11APR90 70 12APR90 69
13APR90 71 14APR90 72 15APR90 74
```

Program Data Vector

N	Date	HighTemp
2	11049	67

The second observation is written to the data set, and control returns to the top of the DATA step.

Writing the Second Observation to the Data Set

Raw Data File Tempdata

```
>----+----10---+----20V--+----30--
01APR90 68 02APR90 67 03APR90 70
04APR90 74 05APR90 72 06APR90 73
07APR90 71 08APR90 75 09APR90 76
10APR90 78 11APR90 70 12APR90 69
13APR90 71 14APR90 72 15APR90 74
```

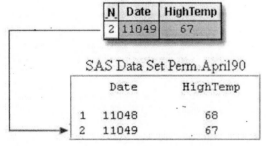

Program Data Vector

N	Date	HighTemp
2	11049	67

SAS Data Set Perm.April90

	Date	HighTemp
1	11048	68
2	11049	67

During the third iteration, the last block of values is read and written to the data set as the third observation.

Writing the Third Observation to the Data Set

Raw Data File Tempdata

Program Data Vector

N	Date	HighTemp
3	11050	70

SAS Data Set Perm.April90

	Date	HighTemp
1	11048	68
2	11049	67
3	11050	70

During the fourth iteration, the first block of values in the second record is read and written as the fourth observation.

Writing the Fourth Observation to the Data Set

Raw Data File Tempdata

Program Data Vector

N	Date	HighTemp
4	11051	74

SAS Data Set Perm.April90

	Date	HighTemp
1	11048	68
2	11049	67
3	11050	70
4	11051	74

The execution phase continues until the last block of data is read.

Writing the Last Observation to the Data Set

Raw Data File Tempdata

```
>----+----10---+----20---+----30-V
01APR90 68 02APR90 67 03APR90 70
04APR90 74 05APR90 72 06APR90 73
07APR90 71 08APR90 75 09APR90 76
10APR90 78 11APR90 70 12APR90 69
13APR90 71 14APR90 72 15APR90 74
```

SAS Data Set Perm.April90

	Date	HighTemp
1	11048	68
	.	
	.	
	.	
13	11060	71
14	11061	72
15	11062	74

You can display the data set with the PRINT procedure.

```
proc print data=perm.april90;
run;
```

PROC PRINT Output of the Data Set.

Obs	Date	HighTemp
1	01APR1990	68
2	02APR1990	67
3	03APR1990	70
4	04APR1990	74
5	05APR1990	72
6	06APR1990	73
7	07APR1990	71
8	08APR1990	75
9	09APR1990	76
10	10APR1990	78
11	11APR1990	70
12	12APR1990	69
13	13APR1990	71
14	14APR1990	71
15	15APR1990	74

Overview

Introduction

When you begin a SAS session, it's often convenient to set up your environment first. For example, you may want to

define libraries that contain the SAS data sets that you intend to use

specify whether your procedure output is created as HTML (Hyper Text Markup Language) output, LISTING output, or another type of output.

set features of your LISTING output, if you are creating any, such as whether the date and time appear

specify how two-digit year values should be interpreted.

This chapter shows you how to define libraries, reference SAS files, and specify options for your SAS session. You also learn how to specify the form(s) of output to produce.

SAS System Options Window

Objectives

In this chapter, you learn to

define new libraries by using programming statements

reference SAS files to be used during your SAS session

set results options to determine the type or types of output produced (HTML, LISTING output, or other) in desktop operating environments

set system options to determine how date values are read and to control the appearance of any LISTING output that is created during your SAS session.

Defining Libraries

Often the first step in setting up your SAS session is to define the libraries. You can also use programming statements to assign library names.

Remember that to reference a permanent SAS file, you

assign a name (*libref*) to the SAS library in which the file is stored

use the libref as the first part of the file's two-level name (*libref.filename*) to reference the file within the library.

Defining Libraries

This example shows the two-level name for a SAS data set, **Admit**, which is stored in a SAS library to which the libref **Clinic** has been assigned.

Assigning Librefs

To define libraries, you can use a LIBNAME statement. You can store the LIBNAME statement with any SAS program so that the SAS data library is assigned each time the program is submitted.

General form, basic LIBNAME statement:

LIBNAME *libref 'SAS-data-library'*;

where

    libref is 1 to 8 characters long, begins with a letter or underscore, and contains only letters, numbers, or underscores.
    SAS-data-library is the name of a SAS data library in which SAS data files are stored. The specification of the physical name of the library differs by operating environment.

The LIBNAME statement below assigns the libref Clinic to the SAS data library **D:\Users\Qtr\Reports** in the Windows environment.

libname clinic 'd:\users\qtr\reports';

Many of the examples in this book use the libref **sasuser**. The following LIBNAME statement assigns the libref sasuser to the c:\Users\name\sasuser folder in a Windows operating environment:

libname sasuser 'c:\Users\name\sasuser';

The table below gives some examples of physical names for SAS data libraries in various operating environments.

Physical Names for SAS Data Libraries

Environment	Sample Physical Name
Windows	c:\fitness\data
UNIX	/users/april/fitness/sasdata
z/OS (OS/390)	april.fitness.sasdata

 The code examples in this chapter are shown in the Windows operating environment. If you are running SAS within another operating environment, then the platform-specific names and locations will look different. Otherwise, SAS programming code will be the same across operating environments.

You can use multiple LIBNAME statements to assign as many librefs as needed.

Verifying Librefs

After assigning a libref, it is a good idea to check the Log window to verify that the libref has been assigned successfully.

Log Output for Clinic libref

```
Log - (Untitled)                                        _ □ ×
17      libname clinic 'd:\users\qtr\reports';
NOTE: Libref CLINIC was successfully assigned as follows:
      Engine:       V9
      Physical Name: d:\users\qtr\reports
```

How Long Librefs Remain in Effect

The LIBNAME statement is global, which means that the librefs remain in effect until you modify them, cancel them, or end your SAS session.

Therefore, the LIBNAME statement assigns the libref for the current SAS session only. Each time you begin a SAS session, you must assign a libref to each permanent SAS data library that contains files that you want to access in that session. (Remember that Work is the default libref for a temporary SAS data library.)

How Long Librefs Remain in Effect

When you end your SAS session or delete a libref, SAS no longer has access to the files in the library. However, the contents of the library still exist on your operating system.

Remember that you can also assign a library from the SAS Explorer using the New Library window. Libraries that are created with the New Library window can be automatically assigned at startup by selecting **Enable at Startup**.

Specifying Two-Level Names

After you assign a libref, you specify it as the first element in the two-level name for a SAS file.

Specifying Two-Level Names

This example shows the two-level name for a SAS data set, **Admit**, which is stored in a SAS data library to which the libref **Clinic** has been assigned.

For example, in order for the PRINT procedure to read Clinic.Admit, you specify the two-level name of the file as follows:

```
proc print data=clinic.admit;
run;
```

Referencing Files in Other Formats

You can use the LIBNAME statement to reference not only SAS files but also files that were created with other software products, such as database management systems.

SAS can read or write these files by using the appropriate engine for that file type. For some file types, you need to tell SAS which engine to use. For others, SAS automatically chooses the appropriate engine.

A SAS engine is a set of internal instructions that SAS uses for writing to and reading from files in a SAS library.

Referencing Files in Other Formats

Specifying Engines

To indicate which engine to use, you specify the engine name in the LIBNAME statement, as shown below.

General form, LIBNAME statement for files in other formats:

LIBNAME *libref engine 'SAS-data-library'*;

where

> *libref* is 1 to 8 characters long, begins with a letter or underscore, and contains only letters, numbers, or underscores.

> *engine* is the name of a library engine that is supported in your operating environment.

> *SAS-data-library* is the name of a SAS library in which SAS data files are stored. The specification of the physical name of the library differs by operating environment.

Interface Library Engines

Interface library engines support read-only access to BMDP, OSIRIS, and SPSS files. With these engines, the physical filename that is associated with a libref is an actual filename, not a SAS library. This is an exception to the rules for librefs.

Engines and Their Descriptions

Engine	Description
BMDP	allows read-only access to BMDP files
OSIRIS	allows read-only access to OSIRIS files

SPSS   allows read-only access to SPSS files

For example, the LIBNAME statement below specifies the libref Rptdata and the engine SPSS for the file **G:\Myspss.dat** in the Windows operating environment.

libname rptdata spss 'g:\myspss.spss';

For more information about interface library engines, see the SAS documentation for your operating environment.

SAS/ACCESS Engines

If your site licenses SAS/ACCESS software, you can use the LIBNAME statement to access data that is stored in a DBMS file. The types of data you can access depend on your operating environment and on which SAS/ACCESS products you have licensed.

Relational Databases and Their Associated Files

Relational Databases	Nonrelational Files	PC Files
ORACLE	ADABAS	Excel (.xls)
SYBASE	IMS/DL-I	Lotus (.wkn)
Informix	CA-IDMS	dBase
DB2 for z/OS	SYSTEM 2000	DIF
DB2 for UNIX and PC		
Oracle Rdb	Teradata	Access
ODBC	MySQL	SPSS
CA-OpenIngres	Netezza	Stata

Ole DB   Paradox

SAS® Certification Prep Guide
Advanced Programming for SAS®9
Third Edition

Clearing SAS Programming Windows

When you run SAS programs, text accumulates in the Output window and in the Log window.

You might find it helpful to clear the contents of your SAS programming windows. To clear the Output window, Editor window, Program Editor window, or Log window, activate each window individually and select **Edit** ⇒ **Clear All**.

Cleared Log Window

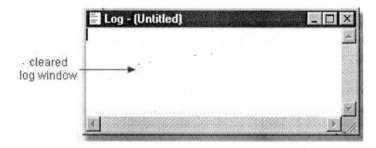

cleared log window

👆 You can also clear the contents of a window by activating the window and then issuing the CLEAR command.

⚠️ Text that has been cleared from windows cannot be recalled. However, in the Editor and Program Editor windows, you can select **Edit** ⇒ **Undo** to redisplay the text.

Creating and Managing Variables

Overview

Creating and Modifying Variables

Assigning Values Conditionally

Specifying Lengths for Variables

Subsetting Data

Chapter 21: Reading Hierarchical Files

When you write a DATA step to create one observation per detail record you need to

distinguish between header and detail records.

keep header data as a part of each observation until the next header record is encountered.

hold the current record so other values in the record can be read.

all of the above

Correct answer: d

In order to create one observation per detail record, it is necessary to distinguish between header and detail records. Use a RETAIN statement to keep header data as part of each observation until the next header record is encountered. You also need to use the @ line-hold specifier to hold the current record so other values in the record can be read.

Which SAS statement reads the value for code (the first field), and holds the record until an INPUT statement reads the remaining value from the same record in the same iteration of the DATA step?

XisError: altImageDescription Element Should Not Be Blank.

```
1---+----10---+----20---+----30
01 Office Supplies
02 Paper Clips
02 Tape
01 Art Supplies
02 Crayons
02 Finger Paint
02 Construction Paper
```

input code $2. @;

input code $2. @@;

retain code;

none of the above

Correct answer: a

An INPUT statement is used to read the value for code. The single @ sign at the end of the INPUT statement holds the current record for a later INPUT statement in the same iteration of the DATA step.

Which SAS statement checks for the condition that Record equals C and executes a single statement to read the values for Amount?

if record=c then input @3 Amount comma7.;

if record='C' then input @3 Amount comma7.;

if record='C' then do input @3 Amount comma7.;

if record=C then do input @3 Amount comma7.;

Correct answer: b

The IF-THEN statement defines the condition that Record equals C and executes an INPUT statement to read the value for Amount when the condition is true. C must be enclosed in quotation marks and must be specified exactly as shown because it is a character value.

After the value for code is read in the sixth iteration, which illustration of the program data vector is correct?

XisError: altImageDescription Element Should Not Be Blank.

```
1---+----10---+----20---+----30
H Lettuce
P Green Leaf    Quality Growers
P Iceberg       Pleasant Farm
P Romaine       Quality Growers
H Squash
P Yellow        Tasty Acres
P Zucchini      Pleasant Farm
```

```
data perm.produce (drop=code);
  infile orders;
  retain Vegetable;
  input code $1. @;
  if code='H' then input @3 vegetable $6.;
  if code='P';
  input @3 Variety : $10. @15 Supplier : $15.;
run;
proc print data=perm.produce;
run;
```

XisError: altImageDescription Element Should Not Be Blank.

_N_	Vegetable	code	Variety	Supplier
6		P		

XisError: altImageDescription Element Should Not Be Blank.

_N_	Vegetable	code	Variety	Supplier
6	Squash	P		

XisError: altImageDescription Element Should Not Be Blank.

_N_	Vegetable	code	Variety	Supplier
6	Squash	H		

XisError: altImageDescription Element Should Not Be Blank.

_N_	Vegetable	code	Variety	Supplier
6	Squash	H	Yellow	

Correct answer: b

The value of Vegetable is retained across iterations of the DATA step. As the sixth iteration begins, the INPUT statement reads the value for code and holds the record, so that the values for Variety and Supplier can be read with an additional INPUT statement.

What happens when the fourth iteration of the DATA step is complete?

XisError: altImageDescription Element Should Not Be Blank.

```
1---+----10---+----20---+----30
F Apples
V Gala              $2.50
V Golden Delicious $1.99
V Rome              $2.35
F Oranges
V Navel             $2.79
V Temple            $2.99
```

```
data perm.orders (drop=type);
   infile produce;
   retain Fruit;
   input type $1. @;
   if type='F' then input @3 fruit $7.;
   if type='V';
   input @3 Variety : $16. @20 Price comma5.;
run;
```

All of the values in the program data vector are written to the data set as the third observation.

All of the values in the program data vector are written to the data set as the fourth observation.

The values for Fruit, Variety, and Price are written to the data set as the third observation.

The values for Fruit, Variety, and Price are written to the data set as the fourth observation.

Correct answer: c

This program creates one observation for each detail record. The RETAIN statement retains the value for Fruit as part of each observation until the values for Variety and Price can be read. The DROP= option in the DATA statement prevents the variable for type from being written to the data set.

Which SAS statement indicates that several other statements should be executed when Record has a value of **A**?

XisError: altImageDescription Element Should Not Be Blank.

```
1---+----10---+----20---+----30
A 124153-01
C $153.02
D $20.00
D $20.00
```

if record='A' then do;

if record=A then do;

if record='A' then;

if record=A then;

Correct answer: a

The IF-THEN statement defines the condition that Record equals A and specifies a simple DO group. The keyword DO indicates that several executable statements follow until the DO group is closed by an END statement. The value A must be enclosed in quotation marks and specified exactly as shown because it is a character value.

Which is true for the following statements (X indicates a header record)?


```
if code='X' then do;
  if _n_ > 1 then output;
  Total=0;
  input Name $ 3-20;
end;
```


_N_ equals the number of times the DATA step has begun to execute.

When code='X' and _n_ > 1 are true, an OUTPUT statement is executed.

Each header record causes an observation to be written to the data set.

a and b

Correct answer: d

_N_ is an automatic variable whose value is the number of times the DATA step has begun to execute. The expression _n_ > 1 defines a condition where the DATA step has executed more than once. When the conditions code='X' and _n_ > 1 are true, an OUTPUT statement is executed, and

Total is initialized to zero. Thus, each header record except the first one causes an observation to be written to the data set.

What happens when the condition type='P' is false?

```
if type='P' then input @3 ID $5. @9 Address $20.;
else if type='V' then input @3 Charge 6.;
```

The values for ID and Address are read.

The values for Charge are read.

type is assigned the value of **V**.

The ELSE statement is executed.

Correct answer: d

The condition is false, so the values for ID and Address are not read. Instead, the ELSE statement is executed and defines another condition which may or may not be true.

What happens when last has a value other than zero?

```
data perm.househld (drop=code);
    infile citydata end=last;
    retain Address;
    input type $1. @;
    if code='A' then do;
        if _n_ > 1 then output;
        Total=0;
        input address $ 3-17;
    end;
    else if code='N' then total+1;
    if last then output;
run;
```

last has a value of **1**.

The OUTPUT statement writes the last observation to the data set.

The current value of last is written to the DATA set.

a and b

Correct answer: d

You can determine when the current record is the last record in an external file by specifying the END= option in the INFILE statement. last is a temporary numeric variable whose value is zero

- 1864 -

until the last line is read. last has a value of **1** after the last line is read. Like automatic variables, the END= variable is not written to the data set.

Based on the values in the program data vector, what happens next?

XisError: altImageDescription Element Should Not Be Blank.

_N_	last	Department	Extension	type	Total	Amount
5	0	Accounting	x3808	D	16.50	.

```
1---+----10---+----20---+----30
D Accounting    x3808
S Paper Clips   $2.50
S Paper         $4.95
S Binders       $9.05
D Personnel     x3810
S Markers       $8.98
S Pencils       $3.35
```

```
data work.supplies (drop=type amount);
   infile orders end=last;
   retain Department Extension;
   input type $1. @;
   if type='D' then do;
      if _n_ > 1 then output;
      Total=0;
      input @3 department $10. @16 extension $5.;
   end;
   else if type='S' then do;
      input @16 Amount comma5.;
      total+amount;
      if last then output;
         end;
run;
```

All the values in the program data vector are written to the data set as the first observation.

The values for Department, Total, and Extension are written to the data set as the first observation.

The values for Department, Total, and Extension are written to the data set as the fourth observation.

The value of last changes to **1**.

Correct answer: b

This program creates one observation for each header record and combines information from each detail record into the summary variable, Total. When the value of type is **D** and the value of _N_ is greater than **1**, the OUTPUT statement executes, and the values for Department, Total and Extension are written to the data set as the first observation. The variables _N_ , last, type and Amount are not written to the data set.

Specifying Titles and Footnotes

Overview

Now you've learned how to structure your PRINT procedure output. However, you might also want to make your reports easy to interpret by

adding titles and footnotes

replacing variable names with descriptive labels

formatting variable values.

Although this chapter focuses on PROC PRINT, you can apply these enhancements to most SAS procedure output.

TITLE and FOOTNOTE Statements

To make your report more meaningful and self-explanatory, you can associate up to 10 titles with procedure output by using TITLE statements before the PROC step. Likewise, you can specify up to 10 footnotes by using FOOTNOTE statements before the PROC step.

Because TITLE and FOOTNOTE statements are global statements, place them anywhere within or before the PRINT procedure. Titles and footnotes are assigned as soon as TITLE or FOOTNOTE statements are read; they apply to all subsequent output.

General form, TITLE and FOOTNOTE statements:

TITLE<*n*> *'text'*;

FOOTNOTE<*n*> *'text'*;

where *n* is a number from 1 to 10 that specifies the title or footnote line, and *'text'* is the actual title or footnote to be displayed. The maximum title or footnote length depends on your operating environment and on the value of the LINESIZE= option.

The keyword **title** is equivalent to title1. Likewise, **footnote** is equivalent to footnote1. If you don't specify a title, the default title is The SAS System. No footnote is printed unless you specify one.

Be sure to match quotation marks that enclose the title or footnote text.

Using the TITLES and FOOTNOTES Windows

You can also specify titles in the TITLES window and footnotes in the FOOTNOTES window. Titles and footnotes that you specify in these windows are not stored with your program, and they remain in effect only during your SAS session.

To open the TITLES window, issue the TITLES command. To open the FOOTNOTES window, issue the FOOTNOTES command.

To specify a title or footnote, type in the text you want next to the number of the line where the text should appear. To cancel a title or footnote, erase the existing text. Notice that you do not enclose text in quotation marks in these windows.

Titles Window

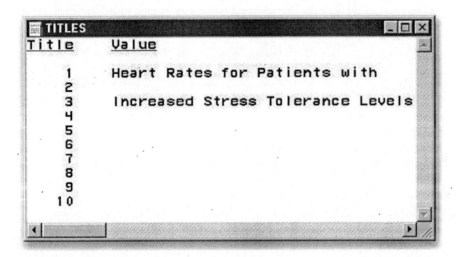

Example: Titles

The two TITLE statements below, specified for lines 1 and 3, define titles for the PROC PRINT output.

```
title1 'Heart Rates for Patients with';
title3 'Increased Stress Tolerance Levels';
proc print data=clinic.stress;
   var resthr maxhr rechr;
   where tolerance='I';
run;
```

Title lines for HTML output appear differently depending on the version of SAS that you use. In SAS Version 8, title lines simply appear consecutively, without extra spacing to indicate skipped title numbers. In SAS®9 HTML output, title line 2 is blank.

HTML Output with Titles: SAS®8

SAS Version 8 HTML Output:

Heart Rates for Patients with Increased Stress Tolerance Levels

Obs	RestHR	MaxHR	RecHR
2	68	171	133
3	78	177	139
8	70	167	122
11	65	181	141
14	74	152	113
15	75	158	108
20	78	189	138

HTML Output with Titles: SAS®9

SAS®9 HTML Output:

Heart Rates for Patients with

Increased Stress Tolerance Levels

Obs	RestHR	MaxHR	RecHR
2	68	171	133
3	78	177	139
8	70	167	122
11	65	181	141
14	74	152	113
15	75	158	108
20	78	189	138

In SAS LISTING output for all versions of SAS, title line 2 is blank, as shown below. Titles are centered by default.

LISTING Output with Titles: All Versions

```
        Heart Rates for Patients with

      Increased Stress Tolerance Levels

       OBS       RestHR       MaxHR       RecHR

          2         68          171         133
          3         78          177         139
          8         70          167         122
         11         65          181         141
         14         74          152         113
         15         75          158         108
         20         78          189         138
```

Example: Footnotes

The two FOOTNOTE statements below, specified for lines 1 and 3, define footnotes for the PROC PRINT output. Since there is no footnote2, a blank line is inserted between footnotes 1 and 2 in the output.

```
footnote1 'Data from Treadmill Tests';
footnote3 '1st Quarter Admissions';
proc print data=clinic.stress;
   var resthr maxhr rechr;
   where tolerance='I';
run;
```

Footnotes appear at the bottom of each page of procedure output. Notice that footnote lines are *pushed up* from the bottom. The FOOTNOTE statement that has the largest number appears on the bottom line.

HTML Output with Footnotes

Obs	RestHR	MaxHR	RecHR
2	68	171	133
3	78	177	139
8	70	167	122
11	65	181	141
14	74	152	113
15	75	158	108
20	78	189	138

Data from Treadmill Tests
1st Quarter Admissions

In SAS LISTING output, footnote line 2 is blank, as shown below. Footnotes are centered by default.

LISTING Output with Footnotes

```
   OBS        RestHR        MaxHR        RecHR


    2           68           171          133
    3           78           177          139
    8           70           167          122
   11           65           181          141
   14           74           152          113
   15           75           158          108
   20           78           189          138


        Data from Treadmill Tests

          1st Quarter Admissions
```

Modifying and Canceling Titles and Footnotes

TITLE and FOOTNOTE statements are global statements. That is, after you define a title or footnote, it remains in effect until you modify it, cancel it, or end your SAS session.

For example, the footnotes that are assigned in the PROC PRINT step below also appear in the output from the PROC TABULATE step.

```
footnote1 'Data from Treadmill Tests';
footnote3 '1st Quarter Admissions';
proc print data=clinic.stress;
   var resthr maxhr rechr;
   where tolerance='I';
run;
proc tabulate data=clinic.stress;
   where tolerance='I';
   var resthr maxhr;
   table mean*(resthr maxhr);
run;
```

Redefining a title or footnote line cancels any higher-numbered title or footnote lines, respectively. In the example below, defining a title for line 2 in the second report automatically cancels title line 3.

```
title3 'Participation in Exercise Therapy';
proc print data=clinic.therapy;
   var swim walkjogrun aerclass;
run;
title2 'Report for March';
proc print data=clinic.therapy;
run;
```

To cancel all previous titles or footnotes, specify a null TITLE or FOOTNOTE statement (a TITLE or FOOTNOTE statement with no number or text) or a TITLE1 or FOOTNOTE1 statement with no text. This will also cancel the default title The SAS System.

For example, in the program below, the null TITLE1 statement cancels all titles that are in effect before either PROC step executes. The null FOOTNOTE statement cancels all footnotes that are in effect after the PROC PRINT step executes. The PROC TABULATE output appears without a title or a footnote.

```
title1;
footnote1 'Data from Treadmill Tests';
footnote3 '1st Quarter Admissions';
proc print data=clinic.stress;
   var resthr maxhr rechr;
   where tolerance='I';
run;
footnote;
proc tabulate data=clinic.stress;
   var timemin timesec;
   table max*(timemin timesec);
run;
```

Chapter Summary

Text Summary

How SAS Stores Date and Time Values

SAS stores dates as numeric SAS date values, which represent the number of days from January 1, 1960. SAS time values are the number of seconds since midnight.

Reading Dates and Times with Informats

Use SAS informats to read date and time expressions and convert them to SAS date and time values.

MMDDYY*w.* reads dates such as 053090, 05/30/90, or 05 30 1990.

DATE*w.* reads dates such as 30May1990, 30May90, or 30-May-1990.

TIME*w.* reads times such as 17:00, 17:00:01.34, or 2:34.

DATETIME*w.* reads dates and times such as 30May1990:10:03:17.2, 30May90 10:03:17.2, or 30May1990/10:03.

Two-digit year values require special consideration. When a two-digit year value is read, SAS defaults to a year within a 100-year span that is determined by the YEARCUTOFF= system option. The default value of YEARCUTOFF= is **1920**. You can check or reset the value of this option in your SAS session to use a different 100-year span for date informats.

Using Dates and Times in Calculations

Date and time values can be used in calculations like other numeric values. In addition to tracking time intervals, SAS date and time values can be used with SAS functions and with complex calculations.

Using Date and Time Formats

SAS provides many specialized date and time formats that enable you to specify how date and time values are displayed. You can use the WEEKDATE*w.* format to write date values in the form *day-of-week, month-name dd, yy* (or *yyyy*). You can use the WORDDATE*w.* format to write date values in the form *month-name dd, yyyy*.

Syntax

OPTIONS YEARCUTOFF=*yyyy*;

DATA *SAS-data-set*;

INFILE *file-specification*;
INPUT *<pointer-control> variable informat.*;

RUN;

PROC PRINT DATA=*SAS-data-set*;

FORMAT *variable format.*;

RUN;

Sample Program

```
options yearcutoff=1920;
data perm.aprbills;
   infile aprdata;
   input LastName $8. @10 DateIn mmddyy8.
      +1 DateOut mmddyy8. +1 RoomRate 6.
      @35 EquipCost 6.;
   Days=dateout-datein+1;
   RoomCharge=days*roomrate;
   Total=roomcharge+equipcost;
run;
proc print data=perm.aprbills;
   format datein dateout worddate12.;
run;
```

Points to Remember

SAS makes adjustments for leap years, but not for leap seconds or daylight saving time.

The minimum acceptable field width for the TIME*w*. informat is 5. If you specify a *w* value less than **5**, you'll receive an error message in the SAS log.

The default value of the YEARCUTOFF= option is **1920**. When you work with two-digit year data, remember to check the default value of the YEARCUTOFF= option, and change it if necessary.

The value of the YEARCUTOFF= system option does not affect four-digit year values. Four-digit values are always read correctly.

Be sure to specify the proper informat for reading a date value, and specify the correct field width so that the entire value is read.

If SAS date values appear in your program output, use a date format to display them in legible form.

Writing Basic DATA Steps

Creating SAS Data Sets from External Files explained how to write a DATA step to create a permanent SAS data set from raw data that is stored in an external file.

```
data clinic.stress;
   infile tests;
   input ID 1-4 Name $ 6-25 RestHR 27-29
      MaxHR 31-33 RecHR 35-37
      TimeMin 39-40 TimeSec 42-43
      Tolerance $ 45;
run;
```

Partial Raw Data File Tests

```
1---+----10---+----20---+----30---+----40---+-
2458 Murray,  W          72   185 128 12 38 D
2462 Almers,  C          68   171 133 10  5 I
2501 Bonaventure, T      78   177 139 11 13 I
2523 Johnson, R          69   162 114  9 42 S
2539 LaMance, K          75   168 141 11 46 D
2544 Jones, M            79   187 136 12 26 N
2552 Reberson, P         69   158 139 15 41 D
2555 King, E             70   167 122 13 13 I
```

You learned how to submit the DATA step and how to check the log to see whether the step ran successfully.

```
NOTE: The infile TESTS is:
      Filename=c:\rawdata\tests,
      RECFM=V,LRECL=256,File Size (bytes)=376,
      Last Modified=16May2011:11:23:09,
      Create Time=17May2011:07:42:32

NOTE: 8 records were read from the infile TESTS.
      The minimum record length was 45.
      The maximum record length was 45.
NOTE: The data set CLINIC.STRESS has 8 observations and 8 variables.
NOTE: DATA statement used (Total process time):
      real time           0.01 seconds
      cpu time            0.00 seconds
```

You also learned how to display the contents of the data set with the PRINT procedure.

```
proc print data=clinic.stress;
run;
```

Output from the PRINT Procedure

Obs	ID	Name	RestHr	MaxHR	RecHR	TimeMin	TimeSec	Tolerance
1	2458	Murray, W	72	185	128	12	38	D
2	2462	Almers, C	68	171	133	10	5	I
3	2501	Bonaventure, T	78	177	139	11	13	I
4	2523	Johnson, R	69	162	114	9	42	S
5	2539	LaMance, K	75	168	141	11	46	D
6	2544	Jones, M	79	187	136	12	26	N
7	2552	Reberson, P	69	158	139	15	41	D
8	2555	King, E	70	167	122	13	13	I

The IMPORT Wizard

Importing Data

As an alternative to using programming statements, you can use the Import Wizard to guide you through the process of creating a SAS data set from both raw data and from Excel worksheets. The Import Wizard enables you to create a SAS data set from different types of external files, such as

dBase files (*.dbf)

Excel 2007 (or earlier version) workbooks (*.xls, *.xlsx, *.xlsb, or *.xlsm)

Microsoft Access tables (*.mdb, *.accdb)

Delimited files (*.*)

Comma-separated values (*.csv).

The data sources that are available to you depend on which SAS/ACCESS products you have licensed. If you do not have any SAS/ACCESS products licensed, the only type of data source files available to you are CSV files, TXT files, and delimited files.

To access the Import Wizard, select **File** ➤ **Import Data** from the menu bar. The Import Wizard opens with the **Select import type** screen.

Import Wizard

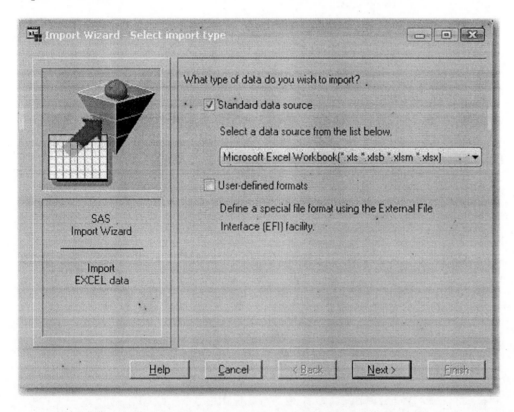

Follow the instructions on each screen of the Import Wizard to read in your data. If you need additional information, select the **Help** button at the bottom of each screen in the wizard.

Just as you can create a SAS data set from raw data by using the Import Wizard, you can use the Export Wizard to read data from a SAS data set and to write the data to an external data source. To access the Export Wizard, select **File ➤ Export Data** from the menu bar.

Editing and Debugging SAS Programs

Overview

Opening a Stored SAS Program

Editing SAS Programs

Clearing SAS Programming Windows

Interpreting Error Messages

Correcting Errors

Resolving Common Problems

Additional Features

Chapter Summary

Chapter Quiz

Reading a Varying Number of Repeating Fields

Overview

So far, each record in the file Data97 has contained the same number of repeating fields.

Raw Data File Data97

```
                    Raw Data File Data97
1---+----10---+----20---+----30---+----40
0734 1,323.34 2,472.85 3,276.65 5,345.52
0943 1,908.34 2,560.38 3,472.09 5,290.86
1009 2,934.12 3,308.41 4,176.18 7,581.81
1043 1,295.38 5,980.28 8,876.84 6,345.94
1190 2,189.84 5,023.57 2,794.67 4,243.35
1382 3,456.34 2,065.83 3,139.08 6,503.49
1734 2,345.83 3,423.32 1,034.43 1,942.28
```

But suppose that some of the employees quit at various times. Their records might not contain sales totals for the second, third, or fourth quarter. These records contain a variable number of repeating fields.

Raw Data File Data97 Showing Empty Records

```
                 Raw Data File Data97
1---+----10---+----20---+----30---+----40
1824 1,323.34 2,472.85
1943 1,908.34
2046 1,423.52 1,673.46 3,276.65
2063 2,345.34 2,452.45 3,523.52 2,983.01
```

The DATA step that you just wrote won't work with a variable number of repeating fields because now the value of Quarter is not constant for every record.


```
data perm.sales97;
   infile data97;
   input ID $ @;
   do Quarter=1 to 4;
      input Sales : comma. @;
      output;
   end;
run;
```

Using the MISSOVER Option

You can adapt the DATA step to accommodate a varying number of Sales values.

Like the previous example with the same number of repeating fields, your DATA step must read the same record repeatedly. However, you need to prevent the input pointer from moving to the next record when there are missing Sales values.

You can use the MISSOVER option in an INFILE statement to prevent SAS from reading the next record when missing values are encountered at the end of a record. Essentially, records that have a varying number of repeating fields are records that contain missing values, so you need to specify the MISSOVER option here as well.

Because there is at least one value for the repeating field, Sales, in each record, the first INPUT statement reads *both* the value for ID and the first Sales value for each record. The trailing @ holds the record so that any subsequent repeating fields can be read.


```
data perm.sales97;
   infile data97 missover;
   input ID $ Sales : comma. @;
```


Holding a Record

```
               Raw Data File Data97
1---+----10--V+----20---+----30---+----40
1824 1,323.34 2,472.85
1943 1,908.34
2046 1,423.52 1,673.46 3,276.65
2063 2,345.34 2,452.45 3,523.52 2,983.01
```

SAS provides several options to control reading past the end of a line. You've seen the MISSOVER option for setting remaining INPUT statement variables to missing values if the pointer reaches the end of a record. You can also use other options such as the TRUNCOVER option, which reads column or formatted input when the last variable that is read by the INPUT statement contains varying-length data. The TRUNCOVER option assigns the contents of the input buffer to a variable when the field is shorter than expected.

Other related options include FLOWOVER (the default), STOPOVER, and SCANOVER. For more information about TRUNCOVER and related options, see the SAS documentation.

Executing SAS Statements While a Condition Is True

Now consider how many times to read each record. Earlier, you created an index variable named Quarter whose value ranged from 1 to 4 because there were four repeating fields.

Now you want to read the record only while a value for Sales exists. Use a DO WHILE statement instead of the iterative DO statement, enclosing the expression in parentheses. In the example below, the DO WHILE statement executes while the value of Sales is not equal to a missing value (which is represented by a period).

```
data perm.sales97;
   infile data97 missover;
   input ID $ Sales : comma. @;
   do while (sales ne .);
```

Creating a Counter Variable

Because the DO WHILE statement does not create an index variable, you can create your own "counter" variable. You can use a sum statement to increment the value of the counter variable each time the DO WHILE loop executes.

In the example below, the assignment statement that precedes the loop creates the counter variable Quarter and assigns it an initial value of zero. Each time the DO WHILE loop executes, the sum statement increments the value of Quarter by one.

```
data perm.sales97;
   infile data97 missover;
   input ID $ Sales : comma. @;
   Quarter=0;
   do while (sales ne .);
      quarter+1;
```

Completing the DO WHILE Loop

Now look at the other statements that should be executed in the DO WHILE loop. First, you need an OUTPUT statement to write the current observation to the data set. Then, another INPUT statement reads the next value for Sales and holds the record. You complete the DO WHILE loop with an END statement.

```
data perm.sales97;
   infile data97 missover;
   input ID $ Sales : comma. @;
   Quarter=0;
   do while (sales ne .);
     quarter+1;
     output;
     input sales : comma. @;
   end;
run;
```

Processing a DATA Step That Has a Varying Number of Repeating Fields

This example uses the following DATA step:

```
data perm.sales97;
   infile data97 missover;
   input ID $ Sales : comma. @;
   Quarter=0;
   do while (sales ne .);
     quarter+1;
     output;
     input sales : comma. @;
   end;
run;
```

During the first iteration of the DATA step, values for ID and Sales are read. Quarter is initialized to *0*.

Initializing the Value of Quarter to 0

The DO WHILE statement checks to see if Sales has a value, which it does, so the other statements in the DO loop execute. The Value of Quarter is incremented by 1 and the current observation is written to the data set.

Executing the DO Loop

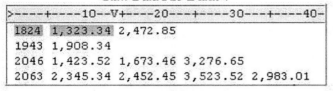

Raw Data File Data97

```
>----+----10--V+----20---+----30---+----40-
1824 1,323.34 2,472.85
1943 1,908.34
2046 1,423.52 1,673.46 3,276.65
2063 2,345.34 2,452.45 3,523.52 2,983.01
```

Program Data Vector

N	ID	Sales	Quarter
1	1824	1323.34	1

SAS Data Set Perm.Sales97

	ID	Sales	Quarter
1	1824	1323.34	1

The INPUT statement reads the next value for Sales, the end of the loop is reached, and control returns to the DO WHILE statement.

Returning Control to the DO WHILE Statement

Raw Data File Data97

```
>----+----10---+----20-V-+----30---+----40-
1824 1,323.34 2,472.85
1943 1,908.34
2046 1,423.52 1,673.46 3,276.65
2063 2,345.34 2,452.45 3,523.52 2,983.01
```

Program Data Vector

N	ID	Sales	Quarter
1	1824	2472.85	1

SAS Data Set Perm.Sales97

	ID	Sales	Quarter
1	1824	1323.34	1

The condition is checked and Sales still has a value, so the loop executes again.

Executing the Loop Again

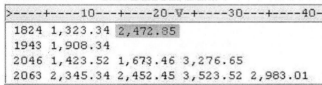

Raw Data File Data97

```
>----+----10---+----20-V-+----30---+----40-
1824 1,323.34 2,472.85
1943 1,908.34
2046 1,423.52 1,673.46 3,276.65
2063 2,345.34 2,452.45 3,523.52 2,983.01
```

Program Data Vector

N	ID	Sales	Quarter
1	1824	2472.85	1

SAS Data Set Perm.Sales97

	ID	Sales	Quarter
1	1824	1323.34	1

Quarter is incremented to 2, and the values in the program data vector are written as the second observation.

Raw Data File Data97

```
>----+----10---+----20-V-+----30---+----40-
1824 1,323.34 2,472.85
1943 1,908.34
2046 1,423.52 1,673.46 3,276.65
2063 2,345.34 2,452.45 3,523.52 2,983.01
```

Program Data Vector

N	ID	Sales	Quarter
1	1824	2472.85	2

SAS Data Set Perm.Sales97

	ID	Sales	Quarter
1	1824	1323.34	1
2	1824	2472.85	2

The INPUT statement executes again. The MISSOVER option prevents the input pointer from moving to the next record in search of another value for Sales. Therefore, SALEs receives a missing value.

Raw Data File Data97

```
>----+----10---+----20-V-+----30---+----40-
1824 1,323.34 2,472.85
1943 1,908.34
2046 1,423.52 1,673.46 3,276.65
2063 2,345.34 2,452.45 3,523.52 2,983.01
```

Program Data Vector

N	ID	Sales	Quarter
1	1824	•	2

SAS Data Set Perm.Sales97

	ID	Sales	Quarter
1	1824	1323.34	1
2	1824	2472.85	2

The end of the loop is reached, and control returns to the DO WHILE statement. Because the condition is now false, the statements in the loop are not executed and the values in the PDV are not output.

Returning Control the DO WHILE Statement

Raw Data File Data97

```
>----+----10---+----20-V-+----30---+----40-
 1824 1,323.34 2,472.85
 1943 1,908.34
 2046 1,423.52 1,673.46 3,276.65
 2063 2,345.34 2,452.45 3,523.52 2,983.01
```

Program Data Vector

N	ID	Sales	Quarter
1	1824	.	2

SAS Data Set Perm.Sales97

	ID	Sales	Quarter
1	1824	1323.34	1
2	1824	2472.85	2

Instead, control returns to the top of the DATA step, the values in the program data vector are reset to missing, and the input statement reads the next record. The DATA step continues executing until the end of the file.

Returning Control to the Top of the DATA Step

Raw Data File Data97

```
>V---+----10---+----20---+----30---+----40-
 1824 1,323.34 2,472.85
 1943 1,908.34
 2046 1,423.52 1,673.46 3,276.65
 2063 2,345.34 2,452.45 3,523.52 2,983.01
```

Program Data Vector

N	ID	Sales	Quarter
2	.	.	.

SAS Data Set Perm.Sales97

	ID	Sales	Quarter
1	1824	1323.34	1
2	1824	2472.85	2

PROC PRINT output for the data set shows a varying number of observations for each employee.

```
proc print data=perm.sales97;
run;
```

Output of PROC PRINT

Obs	ID	Sales	Quarter
1	1824	1323.34	1
2	1824	2472.85	2
3	1943	2199.23	1
4	2046	3598.48	1
5	2046	4697.98	2
6	2046	4598.45	3
7	2063	4963.87	1
8	2063	3434.42	2
9	2063	2241.64	3
10	2063	2759.11	4

Review of Column Input

Overview

In Creating SAS Data Sets from External Files, you learned how to use column input to read raw data that is stored in an external file.

You can use column input to read the values for Item, IDnum, InStock, and BackOrd from the raw data file that is referenced by the fileref Invent.

```
input Item $ 1-13 IDnum $ 15-19 InStock 21-22
    BackOrd 24-25;
```

```
            Raw Data File Invent
1---+----10---+----20---+--
BIRD FEEDER    LG088   3 20
GLASS MUGS     SB082   6 12
GLASS TRAY     BQ049  12  6
PADDED HANGRS  MN256  15 20
JEWELRY BOX    AJ498  23  0
RED APRON      AQ072   9 12
CRYSTAL VASE   AQ672  27  0
PICNIC BASKET  LS930  21  0
```

Notice that the INPUT statement lists the variables with their corresponding column locations in order from left to right. However, one of the features of column input is the ability to read fields in any order.

For example, you could have read the values for InStock and BackOrd before the values for Item and IDnum.

input InStock 21-22 BackOrd 24-25 Item $ 1-13
    IDnum $ 15-19;

When you print a report that is based on this data set, the variables will be listed in the order in which they were created by default.

InStock	BackOrd	Item	IDnum
3	20	BIRD FEEDER	LG088
6	12	GLASS MUGS	SB082
12	6	GLASS TRAY	BQ049
15	20	PADDED HANGRS	MN256
23	0	JEWELRY BOX	AJ498
9	12	RED APRON	AQ072
27	0	CRYSTAL VASE	AQ672
21	0	PICNIC BASKET	LS930

Column Input Features

Column input has several features that make it useful for reading raw data.

It can be used to read character variable values that contain embedded blanks.

input Name $ 1-25;

```
1---+----10---+----20---+-
JOSEPH PAUL THACKERY JR. .
```

No placeholder is required for missing data. A blank field is read as missing and does not cause other fields to be read incorrectly.

input Item $ 1-13 IDnum $ 15-19
   InStock 21-22 BackOrd 24-25;

```
1---+----10---+----20---+--
PADDED HANGRS MN256 15 20
JEWELRY BOX   AJ498      0
RED APRON     AQ072  9 12
```

Fields or parts of fields can be re-read.

input Item $ 1-13 IDnum $ 15-19 Supplier $ 15-16
   InStock 21-22 BackOrd 24-25;

```
1---+----10---+----20---+--
PADDED HANGRS MN256 15 20
JEWELRY BOX   AJ498 23  0
RED APRON     AQ072  9 12
```

Fields do not have to be separated by blanks or other delimiters.

input Item $ 1-13 IDnum $ 14-18 InStock 19-20
     BackOrd 21-22;

```
1---+----10---+----20---+--
PADDED HANGRSMN2561520
JEWELRY BOX   AJ49823 0
RED APRON     AQ072 912
```

Chapter 12: Combining SAS Data Sets

Which program will combine Brothers.One and Brothers.Two to produce Brothers.Three?

XisError: altImageDescription Element Should Not Be Blank.

```
data brothers.three;
   set brothers.one;
   set brothers.two;
run;



data brothers.three;
   set brothers.one brothers.two;
run;



data brothers.three;
   set brothers.one brothers.two;
   by varx;
```

```
                run;
```

```
                data brothers.three;
                    merge brothers.one brothers.two;
                    by varx;
                run;
```

Correct answer: a

This example is a case of one-to-one matching, which requires multiple SET statements. Where same-named variables occur, values that are read from the second data set replace those read from the first data set. Also, the number of observations in the new data set is the number of observations in the smallest original data set.

Which program will combine Actors.Props1 and Actors.Props2 to produce Actors.Props3?

XisError: altImageDescription Element Should Not Be Blank.

Actors.Props1		+	Actors.Props2		=	Actors.Props3	
Actor	**Prop**		**Actor**	**Prop**		**Actor**	**Prop**
Curly	Anvil		Curly	Ladder		Curly	Anvil
Larry	Ladder		Moe	Pliers		Curly	Ladder
Moe	Poker					Larry	Ladder
						Moe	Poker
						Moe	Pliers

```
                data actors.props3;
                    set actors.props1;
                    set actors.props2;
                run;
```

```
                data actors.props3;
                    set actors.props1 actors.props2;
                run;
```

```
                data actors.props3;
                    set actors.props1 actors.props2;
                    by actor;
                run;
```

```
data actors.props3;
    merge actors.props1 actors.props2;
    by actor;
run;
```

Correct answer: c

This is a case of interleaving, which requires a list of data set names in the SET statement and one or more BY variables in the BY statement. Notice that observations in each BY group are read sequentially, in the order in which the data sets and BY variables are listed. The new data set contains all the variables from all the input data sets, as well as the total number of records from all input data sets.

If you submit the following program, which new data set is created?

XisError: altImageDescription Element Should Not Be Blank.

Work.Dataone

Career	Supervis	Finance
72	26	9
63	76	7
96	31	7
96	98	6
84	94	6

Work.Datatwo

Variety	Feedback	Autonomy
10	11	70
85	22	93
83	63	73
82	75	97
36	77	97

```
data work.jobsatis;
    set work.dataone work.datatwo;
run;
```

XisError: altImageDescription Element Should Not Be Blank.

Career	Supervis	Finance	Variety	Feedback	Autonomy
72	26	9	.	.	.
63	76	7	.	.	.
96	31	7	.	.	.
96	98	6	.	.	.
84	94	6	.	.	.
.	.	.	10	11	70
.	.	.	85	22	93
.	.	.	83	63	73
.	.	.	82	75	97
.	.	.	36	77	97

XisError: altImageDescription Element Should Not Be Blank.

Career	Supervis	Finance	Variety	Feedback	Autonomy
72	26	9	10	11	70
63	76	7	85	22	93
96	31	7	83	63	73
96	98	6	82	75	97
84	94	6	36	77	97

XisError: altImageDescription Element Should Not Be Blank.

Career	Supervis	Finance
72	26	9
63	76	7
96	31	7
96	98	6
84	94	6
10	11	70
85	22	93
83	63	73
82	75	97
36	77	97

none of the above

Correct answer: a

Concatenating appends the observations from one data set to another data set. The new data set contains the total number of records from all input data sets, so b is incorrect. All the variables from all the input data sets appear in the new data set, so c is incorrect.

If you concatenate the data sets below in the order shown, what is the value of Sale in observation 2 of the new data set?

XisError: altImageDescription Element Should Not Be Blank.

Sales.Reps	
ID	Name
1	Nay Rong
2	Kelly Windsor
3	Julio Meraz
4	Richard Krabill

Sales.Close	
ID	Sale
1	$28,000
2	$30,000
2	$40,000
3	$15,000
3	$20,000
3	$25,000
4	$35,000

Sales.Bonus	
ID	Bonus
1	$2,000
2	$4,000
3	$3,000
4	$2,500

missing

$30,000

$40,000

you cannot concatenate these data sets

Correct answer: a

The concatenated data sets are read sequentially, in the order in which they are listed in the SET statement. The second observation in Sales.Reps does not contain a value for Sale, so a missing value appears for this variable. (Note that if you merge the data sets, the value of Sale for the second observation is **$30,000**.)

What happens if you merge the following data sets by the variable SSN?

XisError: altImageDescription Element Should Not Be Blank.

SSN	Age
029-46-9261	39
074-53-9892	34
228-88-9649	32
442-21-8075	12
446-93-2122	36
776-84-5391	28
929-75-0218	27

SSN	Age	Date
029-46-9261	37	02/15/95
074-53-9892	32	05/22/97
228-88-9649	30	03/04/96
442-21-8075	10	11/22/95
446-93-2122	34	07/08/96
776-84-5391	26	12/15/96
929-75-0218	25	04/30/97

The values of Age in the 1st data set overwrite the values of Age in the 2nd data set.

The values of Age in the 2nd data set overwrite the values of Age in the 1st data set.

The DATA step fails because the two data sets contain same-named variables that have different values.

The values of Age in the 2nd data set are set to missing.

Correct answer: b

If you have variables with the same name in more than one input data set, values of the same-named variable in the first data set in which it appears are overwritten by values of the same-named variable in subsequent data sets.

Suppose you merge data sets Health.Set1 and Health.Set2 below:

XisError: altImageDescription Element Should Not Be Blank.

Health.Set1

ID	Sex	Age
1129	F	48
1274	F	50
1387	F	57
2304	F	16
2486	F	63
4425	F	48
4759	F	60
5438	F	42
6488	F	59
9012	F	39
9125	F	56

Health.Set2

ID	Height	Weight
1129	61	137
1387	64	142
2304	61	102
5438	62	168
6488	64	154
9012	63	157
9125	64	159

Which output does the following program create?

```
data work.merged;
  merge health.set1(in=in1) health.set2(in=in2);
  by id;
  if in1 and in2;
run;
proc print data=work.merged;
run;
```

XisError: altImageDescription Element Should Not Be Blank.

Obs	ID	Sex	Age	Height	Weight
1	1129	F	48	61	137
2	1274	F	50	.	.
3	1387	F	57	64	142
4	2304	F	16	61	102
5	2486	F	63	.	.
6	4425	F	48	.	.
7	4759	F	60	.	.
8	5438	F	42	62	168
9	6488	F	59	64	154
10	9012	F	39	63	157
11	9125	F	56	64	159

XisError: altImageDescription Element Should Not Be Blank.

Obs	ID	Sex	Age	Height	Weight
1	1129	F	48	61	137
2	1387	F	50	64	142
3	2304	F	57	61	102
4	5438	F	16	62	168
5	6488	F	63	64	154
6	9012	F	48	63	157
7	9125	F	60	64	159
8	5438	F	42		
9	6488	F	59		
10	9012	F	39		
11	9125	F	56		

XisError: altImageDescription Element Should Not Be Blank.

Obs	ID	Sex	Age	Height	Weight
1	1129	F	48	61	137
2	1387	F	57	64	142
3	2304	F	16	61	102
4	5438	F	42	62	168
5	6488	F	59	64	154
6	9012	F	39	63	157
7	9125	F	56	64	159

none of the above

Correct answer: c

The DATA step uses the IN= data set option and the subsetting IF statement to exclude unmatched observations from the output data set. So a and b, which contain unmatched observations, are incorrect.

The data sets Ensemble.Spring and Ensemble.Summer both contain a variable named Blue. How do you prevent the values of the variable Blue from being overwritten when you merge the two data sets?

```
data ensemble.merged;
   merge ensemble.spring(in=blue)
         ensemble.summer;
```

```
            by fabric;
          run;
```

```
        data ensemble.merged;
          merge ensemble.spring(out=blue)
               ensemble.summer;
            by fabric;
          run;
```

```
        data ensemble.merged;
          merge ensemble.spring(blue=navy)
               ensemble.summer;
            by fabric;
          run;
```

```
        data ensemble.merged;
          merge ensemble.spring(rename=(blue=navy))
               ensemble.summer;
            by fabric;
          run;
```

Correct answer: d

Match-merging overwrites same-named variables in the first data set with same-named variables in subsequent data sets. To prevent overwriting, rename variables by using the RENAME= data set option in the MERGE statement.

What happens if you submit the following program to merge Blood.Donors1 and Blood.Donors2, shown below?

```
data work.merged;
  merge blood.donors1 blood.donors2;
  by id;
run
```

XisError: altImageDescription Element Should Not Be Blank.

Blood.Donors1		
ID	Type	Units
2304	O	16
1129	A	48
1129	A	50
1129	A	57
2486	B	63

Blood.Donors2		
ID	Code	Units
6488	65	27
1129	63	32
5438	62	39
2304	61	45
1387	64	67

The Merged data set contains some missing values because not all observations have matching observations in the other data set.

The Merged data set contains eight observations.

The DATA step produces errors.

Values for Units in Blood.Donors2 overwrite values of Units in Blood.Donors1.

Correct answer: c

The two input data sets are not sorted by values of the BY variable, so the DATA step produces errors and stops processing.

If you merge Company.Staff1 and Company.Staff2 below by ID, how many observations does the new data set contain?

XisError: altImageDescription Element Should Not Be Blank.

Company.Staff1			
ID	Name	Dept	Project
000	Miguel	A12	Document
111	Fred	B45	Survey
222	Diana	B45	Document
888	Monique	A12	Document
999	Vien	D03	Survey

Company.Staff2		
ID	Name	Hours
111	Fred	35
222	Diana	40
777	Steve	0
888	Monique	37

4

5

6

9

Correct answer: c

In this example, the new data set contains one observation for each unique value of ID. The merged data set is shown below.

XisError: altImageDescription Element Should Not Be Blank.

ID	Name	Dept	Project	Hours
000	Miguel	A12	Document	.
111	Fred	B45	Survey	35
222	Diana	B45	Document	40
777	Steve			0
888	Monique	A12	Document	37
999	Vien	D03	Survey	.

If you merge data sets Sales.Reps, Sales.Close, and Sales.Bonus by ID, what is the value of Bonus in the third observation in the new data set?

XisError: altImageDescription Element Should Not Be Blank.

Sales.Reps

ID	Name
1	Nay Rong
2	Kelly Windsor
3	Julio Meraz
4	Richard Krabill

Sales.Close

ID	Sale
1	$28,000
2	$30,000
2	$40,000
3	$15,000
3	$20,000
3	$25,000
4	$35,000

Sales.Bonus

ID	Bonus
1	$2,000
2	$4,000
3	$3,000
4	$2,500

$4,000

$3,000

missing

can't tell from the information given

Correct answer: a

In the new data set, the third observation is the second observation for ID number 2 (Kelly Windsor). The value for Bonus is retained from the previous observation because the BY variable value didn't change. The new data set is shown below.

XisError: altImageDescription Element Should Not Be Blank.

ID	Name	Sale	Bonus
1	Nay Rong	$28,000	$2,000
2	Kelly Windsor	$30,000	$4,000
2	Kelly Windsor	$40,000	$4,000
3	Julio Meraz	$15,000	$3,000
3	Julio Meraz	$20,000	$3,000
3	Julio Meraz	$25,000	$3,000
4	Richard Krabill	$35,000	$2,500

Using Options to Specify Links and Paths

Overview

When ODS generates HTML files for the body, contents, and frame, it also generates links between the files using the HTML filenames that you specify in the ODS HTML statement. If you specify complete pathnames, ODS uses those pathnames in the links that it generates.

The ODS statement below creates a frame file that has links to **c:\records\toc.html** and **c:\records\data.html**, and a contents file that has links to **c:\records\data.html**.

```
ods html body='c:\records\data.html'
    contents='c:\records\toc.html'
    frame='c:\records\frame.html';
```

A portion of the source code for the HTML file frame.html is shown below. Notice that the links have the complete pathnames specified in the file specifications for the contents and body files.

Source Code for the HTML File Frame.html

```
<FRAME MARGINWIDTH="4" MARGINHEIGHT="0" SRC="c:\records\toc.html"
    NAME="contents" SCROLLING=auto>
<FRAME MARGINWIDTH="9" MARGINHEIGHT="0" SRC="c:\records\data.html"
    NAME="body" SCROLLING=auto>
```

These links work when you are viewing the HTML files locally. If you want to place these files on a Web server so that other people could access them, then the link needs to include either the complete URL for an absolute link or the HTML filename for a relative link.

The URL= Suboption

By specifying the URL= suboption in the BODY= or CONTENTS= file specification, you can provide a URL that ODS uses in all the links that it creates to the file. You can use the URL= suboption in any ODS file specification except FRAME= (because no ODS file references the frame file).

General form, URL= suboption in a file specification:

(**URL**=*'Uniform-Resource-Locator'*)

where *Uniform-Resource-Locator* is the name of an HTML file or the full URL of an HTML file. ODS uses this URL instead of the file specification in all the links and references that it creates that point to the file.

The URL= suboption is useful for building HTML files that might be moved from one location to another. If the links from the contents and page files are constructed with a simple URL (one name), they work as long as the contents, page, and body files are all in the same location.

Example: Relative URLs

In this ODS HTML statement, the URL= suboption specifies only the HTML filename. This is the most common style of linking between files because maintenance is easier. The files can be moved as long as they all remain in the same directory or storage location.

```
ods html body='c:\records\data.html' (url='data.html')
     contents='c:\records\toc.html' (url='toc.html')
     frame='c:\records\frame.html';
```

The source code for frame.html has only the HTML filename as specified on the URL= suboptions for the body and contents files.

Source Code Frame.html

```
<FRAME MARGINWIDTH="4" MARGINHEIGHT="0" SRC="toc.htm"
       NAME="contents" SCROLLING=auto>
<FRAME MARGINWIDTH="9" MARGINHEIGHT="0" SRC="data.htm"
       NAME="body" SCROLLING=auto>
```

Example: Absolute URLs

Alternatively, in this ODS HTML statement, the URL= suboptions specify complete URLs using Hypertext Transfer Protocol (HTTP). These files can be stored in the same or different locations.

```
ods html body='c:\records\data.html'
     (url='http://mysite.com/myreports/data.html')
```

```
contents='c:\records\toc.html'
(url='http://mysite.com/mycontents/toc.html')
frame='c:\records\frame.html';
```

As you would expect, the source code for Frame.html has the entire HTTP addresses that you specified in the URL= suboptions for the body and contents files.

Source Code Frame.html

```
<FRAME MARGINWIDTH="4" MARGINHEIGHT="0" SRC="http://mysite.com/myreports/data.html"
     NAME="contents" SCROLLING=auto>
<FRAME MARGINWIDTH="9" MARGINHEIGHT="0" SRC="http://mysite.com/myreports/toc.html"
     NAME="body" SCROLLING=auto>
```

When you use the URL= suboption to specify a complete URL, you might need to move your files to that location before you can view them.

The PATH= Option

So far, you've learned to specify the complete pathname for HTML files in the BODY=, CONTENTS=, and FRAME= specifications when you want to save HTML files to specific locations. You can use the following options to streamline your ODS HTML statement:

PATH= option

specifies the location where you want to store your HTML output

URL=NONE suboption

prevents ODS from using the pathname in any links that it creates in your files

General form, PATH= option with the URL= suboption:

PATH=file-location-specification <(URL= NONE |'Uniform-Resource-Locator')>

where

file-location-specification identifies the location where you want HTML files to be saved. It can be one of the following:

the complete pathname to an aggregate storage location, such as a directory or partitioned data set

a fileref (file shortcut) that has been assigned to a storage location

a SAS catalog (libname.catalog).

Uniform-Resource-Locator provides a URL for links in the HTML files that ODS generates. If you specify the keyword **NONE**, no information from the PATH= option appears in the links or references.

If you do not use the URL= suboption, information from the PATH= option is added to links and references in the files that are created.

⚠ In the z/OS operating environment, if you store your HTML files as members in a partitioned data set, the PATH= value must be a PDSE, not a PDS. You can allocate a PDSE within SAS as shown in this example:

```
filename pdsehtml '.example.htm'

  dsntype=library dsorg=po

  disp=(new, catlg, delete);
```

Also, you should specify valid member names for the HTML files (without extensions).

Example: PATH= Option with URL=NONE

In the program below, the PATH= option directs the files data.html, toc.html, and frame.html to the **C:\Records** directory in the Windows operating environment. The links from the frame file to the body and contents files contain only the HTML filenames data.html and toc.html.

```
ods html path='c:\records' (url=none)
     body='data.html'
     contents='toc.html'
     frame='frame.html';
proc print data=clinic.admit;
run;
proc print data=clinic.stress2;
run;
ods html close;
ods html;
```

This program generates the same files and links as the previous example in which you learned to use the URL= suboption with the BODY= and CONTENTS= file specifications. However, it is a bit simpler to specify the path only once in the PATH= option and to specify URL=NONE.

🕮 If you plan to move your HTML files, you should specify URL=NONE with the PATH= option to prevent information from the PATH= option from creating URLs that are invalid or incorrect.

Example: PATH= Option without the URL= Suboption

In the program below, the PATH= option directs the files data.html, toc.html, and frame.html to the **C:\Records** directory in the Windows operating environment. The links from the frame file to the body and contents files contain the complete pathname, **c:\records\data.html** and **c:\records\toc.html**:

```
ods html path='c:\records'
     body='data.html'
     contents='toc.html'
     frame='frame.html';
proc print data=clinic.admit;
run;
proc print data=clinic.stress2;
run;
ods html close;
ods html;
```

Example: PATH= Option with a Specified URL

In the program below, the PATH= option directs the files data.html, toc.html, and frame.html to the **C:\Records** directory in the Windows operating environment. The links from the frame file to the body and contents files contain the specified URL, **http://mysite.com/myreports/data.html** and **http://mysite.com/myreports/toc.html**:

```
ods html path='c:\records'(url='http://mysite.com/myreports/')
     body='data.html'
     contents='toc.html'
     frame='frame.html';
proc print data=clinic.admit;
run;
proc print data=clinic.stress2;
run;
ods html close;
ods html;
```

Reading Instream Data

Overview

Throughout this chapter, our program has contained an INFILE statement that identifies an external file to read.

```
data sasuser.stress;
   infile tests;
   input ID $ 1-4 Name $ 6-25 RestHR 27-29 MaxHR 31-33
       RecHR 35-37 TimeMin 39-40 TimeSec 42-43
       Tolerance $ 45;
   if tolerance='D';
   TotalTime=(timemin*60)+timesec;
 run;
```

However, you can also read instream data lines that you enter directly in your SAS program, rather than data that is stored in an external file. Reading instream data is extremely helpful if you want to create data and test your programming statements on a few observations that you can specify according to your needs.

To read instream data, you use

> a DATALINES statement as the last statement in the DATA step and immediately preceding the data lines

> a null statement (a single semicolon) to indicate the end of the input data.

```
data sasuser.stress;
   input ID $ 1-4 Name $ 6-25 RestHR 27-29 MaxHR 31-33
      RecHR 35-37 TimeMin 39-40 TimeSec 42-43
      Tolerance $ 45;
   datalines;
   .
   .
   .
```

data lines go here

```
   .
   .
   .
;
```

General form, DATALINES statement:

DATALINES;

> You can use only one DATALINES statement in a DATA step. Use separate DATA steps to enter multiple sets of data.

> You can also use LINES; or CARDS; as the last statement in a DATA step and immediately preceding the data lines. Both LINES and CARDS are aliases for the DATALINES statement.

> If your data contains semicolons, use the DATALINES4 statement plus a null statement that consists of four semicolons (;;;;).

Example

To read the data for the treadmill stress tests as instream data, you can submit the following program:

```
data sasuser.stress;
   input ID $ 1-4 Name $ 6-25 RestHR 27-29 MaxHR 31-33
      RecHR 35-37 TimeMin 39-40 TimeSec 42-43
      Tolerance $ 45;
   if tolerance='D';
   TotalTime=(timemin*60)+timesec;
```

```
    datalines;
2458 Murray, W         72 185 128 12 38 D
2462 Almers, C         68 171 133 10 5 I
2501 Bonaventure, T    78 177 139 11 13 I
2523 Johnson, R        69 162 114 9 42 S
2539 LaMance, K        75 168 141 11 46 D
2544 Jones, M          79 187 136 12 26 N
2552 Reberson, P       69 158 139 15 41 D
2555 King, E           70 167 122 13 13 I
2563 Pitts, D          71 159 116 10 22 S
2568 Eberhardt, S      72 182 122 16 49 N
2571 Nunnelly, A       65 181 141 15 2 I
2572 Oberon, M         74 177 138 12 11 D
2574 Peterson, V       80 164 137 14 9 D
2575 Quigley, M        74 152 113 11 26 I
2578 Cameron, L        75 158 108 14 27 I
2579 Underwood, K      72 165 127 13 19 S
2584 Takahashi, Y      76 163 135 16 7 D
2586 Derber, B         68 176 119 17 35 N
2588 Ivan, H           70 182 126 15 41 N
2589 Wilcox, E         78 189 138 14 57 I
2595 Warren, C         77 170 136 12 10 S
;
```

⚠ Notice that you do not need a RUN statement following the null statement (the semicolon after the data lines). The DATALINES statement functions as a step boundary, so the DATA step is executed as soon as SAS encounters it.

Nesting SAS Functions

Throughout this chapter, you've seen examples of individual functions. For example, in this assignment statement the SCAN function selects the middle name (third word) from the variable Name:

```
MiddleName=scan(name,3);
```

Then this assignment statement uses the SUBSTR function to select the first letter from the variable MiddleName:

```
MiddleInitial=substr(MiddleName,1,1);
```

To write more efficient programs, however, you can nest functions as appropriate. For example, you can nest the SCAN function within the SUBSTR function in an assignment statement to compute the value for MiddleInitial:

MiddleInitial=substr(scan(name,3),1,1);

This example of nested numeric functions determines the number of years between June 15, 1999, and today:

Years=intck('year','15jun1999'd,today());

⟐ You can nest any functions as long as the function that is used as the argument meets the requirements for the argument.

Creating and Modifying Variables

Overview

So far in this chapter, you've read existing data. But sometimes existing data doesn't provide the information you need. To modify existing values or to create new variables, you can use an assignment statement in any DATA step.

General form, assignment statement:

variable=expression;

where

   variable names a new or existing variable

   expression is any valid SAS expression

⟐ The assignment statement is one of the few SAS statements that doesn't begin with a keyword.

For example, here is an assignment statement that assigns the character value **Toby Witherspoon** to the variable Name:

Name='Toby Witherspoon';

SAS Expressions

You use SAS expressions in assignment statements and many other SAS programming statements to

   transform variables

   create new variables

conditionally process variables

calculate new values

assign new values.

An expression is a sequence of operands and operators that form a set of instructions. The instructions are performed to produce a new value:

Operands are variable names or constants. They can be numeric, character, or both.

Operators are special-character operators, grouping parentheses, or functions. You can learn about functions in <u>Transforming Data with SAS Functions</u>.

Using Operators in SAS Expressions

To perform a calculation, you use arithmetic operators. The table below lists arithmetic operators.

Using Operators in SAS Expressions

Operator	Action	Example	Priority
-	negative prefix	**negative=-x;**	I
**	exponentiation	**raise=x**y;**	I
*	multiplication	**mult=x*y;**	II
/	division	**divide=x/y;**	II
+	addition	**sum=x+y;**	III
-	subtraction	**diff=x-y;**	III

When you use more than one arithmetic operator in an expression,

operations of priority I are performed before operations of priority II, and so on

consecutive operations that have the same priority are performed

from right to left within priority I

from left to right within priority II and III

you can use parentheses to control the order of operations.

⚠ When a value that is used with an arithmetic operator is missing, the result of the expression is missing. The assignment statement assigns a missing value to a variable if the result of the expression is missing.

You use the following comparison operators to express a condition.

Comparison Operators

Operator	Meaning	Example
= or eq	equal to	**name='Jones, C.'**
^= or ne	not equal to	**temp ne 212**
> or gt	greater than	**income>20000**
< or lt	less than	**partno lt "BG05"**
>= or ge	greater than or equal to	**id>='1543'**
<= or le	less than or equal to	**pulse le 85**

To link a sequence of expressions into compound expressions, you use logical operators, including the following:

Logical Operators

Operator	Meaning
AND or #38	and, both. If both expressions are true, then the compound expression is true.

OR or | or, either. If either expression is true, then the compound expression is true.

More Examples of Assignment Statements

The assignment statement in the DATA step below creates a new variable, TotalTime, by multiplying the values of TimeMin by 60 and then adding the values of TimeSec.

```
data sasuser.stress;
   infile tests;
   input ID $ 1-4 Name $ 6-25 RestHR 27-29 MaxHR 31-33
      RecHR 35-37 TimeMin 39-40 TimeSec 42-43
      Tolerance $ 45;
   TotalTime=(timemin*60)+timesec;
run;
```

Assignment Statement Output

SAS Data Set Sasuser.Stress (Partial Listing)

ID	Name	RestHR	MaxHR	RecHR	TimeMin	TimeSec	Tolerance	TotalTime
2458	Murray, W	72	185	128	12	38	D	758
2462	Almers, C	68	171	133	10	5	I	605
2501	Bonaventure, T	78	177	139	11	13	I	673
2523	Johnson, R	69	162	114	9	42	S	582
2539	LaMance, K	75	168	141	11	46	D	706

The expression can also contain the variable name that is on the left side of the equal sign, as the following assignment statement shows. This statement re-defines the values of the variable RestHR as 10 percent higher.

```
data sasuser.stress;
   infile tests;
   input ID $ 1-4 Name $ 6-25 RestHR 27-29 MaxHR 31-33
      RecHR 35-37 TimeMin 39-40 TimeSec 42-43
      Tolerance $ 45;
   resthr=resthr+(resthr*.10);
run;
```

When a variable name appears on both sides of the equal sign, the original value on the right side is used to evaluate the expression. The result is assigned to the variable on the left side of the equal sign.

```
data sasuser.stress;
   infile tests;
   input ID $ 1-4 Name $ 6-25 RestHR 27-29 MaxHR 31-33
      RecHR 35-37 TimeMin 39-40 TimeSec 42-43
      Tolerance $ 45;
   resthr=resthr+(resthr*.10);
run;  ^     ^
```

result   original value

Date Constants

You can assign date values to variables in assignment statements by using date constants. To represent a constant in SAS date form, specify the date as *'ddmmmyy'* or *'ddmmmyyyy'*, immediately followed by a D.

General form, date constant:

'ddmmmyy'd

or

"ddmmmyy"d

where

dd is a one- or two-digit value for the day

mmm is a three-letter abbreviation for the month (JAN, FEB, and so on)

yy or yyyy is a two- or four-digit value for the year, respectively.

🖰   Be sure to enclose the date in quotation marks.

Example

In the following program, the second assignment statement assigns a date value to the variable TestDate.

```
data sasuser.stress;
   infile tests;
   input ID $ 1-4 Name $ 6-25 RestHR 27-29 MaxHR 31-33
      RecHR 35-37 TimeMin 39-40 TimeSec 42-43
      Tolerance $ 45;
   TotalTime=(timemin*60)+timesec;
   TestDate='01jan2000'd;
run;
```

🖰   You can also use SAS time constants and SAS datetime constants in assignment statements.

Time='9:25't;

DateTime='18jan2005:9:27:05'dt;

Chapter Summary

Text Summary

The Output Delivery System

The Output Delivery System (ODS) makes new report formatting options available in SAS. ODS separates your output into component parts so that the output can be sent to any ODS destination that you specify.

Opening and Closing ODS Destinations

Each ODS destination creates a different type of formatted output. By default, the HTML destination is open and SAS creates simple HTML output. Because an open destination uses system resources, it is a good idea to close the HTML destination if you don't need to create HTML output. Using ODS statements, you can create multiple output objects at the same time. When you have several ODS destinations open, you can close them all using the ODS _ALL_ CLOSE statement.

Creating HTML Output with Option

The HTML destination is open by default. However, you can use the ODS HTML statement to specify options. Use the BODY= or FILE= specification to create a custom named HTML body file containing procedure results. You can also use the ODS HTML statement to direct the HTML output from multiple procedures to the same HTML file.

Creating HTML Output with a Table of Contents

In order to manage multiple pieces of procedure output, you can use the CONTENTS= and FRAME = options with the ODS HTML statement to create a table of contents that links to your HTML output. The table of contents contains a heading for each procedure that creates output.

Specifying a Path for Output

You can also use the PATH= option to specify the directory where you want to store your HTML output. When you use the PATH= option, you don't need to specify the complete pathname for the body, contents, or frame files. By specifying the URL= suboption in the file specification, you can provide a URL that ODS uses in all the links that it creates to the file.

Changing the Appearance of HTML Output

You can change the appearance of your output using the STYLE= option in the ODS HTML statement. Several predefined styles are shipped with SAS.

Additional Features

ODS provides ways for you to customize HTML output using style definitions. Definitions are created using PROC TEMPLATE and describe how to render the HTML output or part of the HTML output.

Syntax

LIBNAME *libref 'SAS-data-library'*;

ODS LISTING CLOSE;

ODS HTML PATH=*file-specification*

```
<(URL='Uniform-Resource-Locator' | NONE)>
BODY=file-specification
CONTENTS=<file-specification>
FRAME=<file-specification>
STYLE=<style-name>;

PROC PRINT DATA=SAS-data-set;

RUN;

ODS HTML CLOSE;

ODS LISTING;
```

Sample Program

```
libname clinic 'c:\data98\patients';
ods html path='c:\records'(url=none)
     body='data.html'
     contents='toc.html'
     frame='frame.html'
     style=brick;
proc print data=clinic.admit label;
   var id sex age height weight actlevel;
   label actlevel='Activity Level';
run;
proc print data=clinic.stress2;
   var id resthr maxhr rechr;
run;
ods html close;
ods html;
```

Points to Remember

An open destination uses system resources. Therefore, it is a good idea to close the HTML destination before you create other types of output and reopen the HTML destination after you close all destinations destination.

You do not need the ODS HTML CLOSE statement to create simple HTML output. However, if you want to create HTML with options, then use the ODS HTML CLOSE statement to close the HTML destination. The ODS HTML CLOSE statement is added *after* the RUN statement for the procedure.

If you use the CONTENTS= and FRAME= options, open the frame file from within your Web browser to view the procedure output *and* the table of contents.

Referencing a SAS Library

Using a LIBNAME Statement

As you begin to write the program, remember that you might need to use a LIBNAME statement to reference the permanent SAS library in which the data set will be stored.

To do this...	Use this SAS statement...	Example
Reference a SAS library	LIBNAME statement	**libname taxes 'c:\users\name\sasuser';**

For example, the LIBNAME statement below assigns the libref Taxes to the SAS library in the folder **C:\Acct\Qtr1\Report** in the Windows environment.

libname taxes 'c:\acct\qtr1\report';

You do not need to use a LIBNAME statement in all situations. For example, if you are storing the data set in a temporary SAS data set or if SAS has automatically assigned the libref for the permanent library that you are using.

Many of the examples in this chapter use the libref Sasuser, which SAS automatically assigns.

Understanding SAS Functions

Overview

SAS functions are built-in routines that enable you to complete many types of data manipulations quickly and easily. Generally speaking, functions provide programming shortcuts. There are many types of SAS functions: arithmetic functions, financial functions, character functions, probability functions, and many more.

SAS Function Catagories

Categories of SAS Functions

Array	Probability
Bitwise Logical Operations	Quantile
Character	Random Number

Character String Matching	Sample Statistics
Date and Time	SAS File I/O
Dynamic Link Library	Special
External Files	State and ZIP Code
Financial	Trigonometric
Hyperbolic	Truncation
Macro	Variable Control
Mathematical	Variable Information

MultiByte Character Set

SAS Functions That Compute Sample Statistics

Function	Syntax	Calculates...
SUM	sum(argument, argument,...)	sum of values
MEAN	mean(argument, argument,...)	average of nonmissing values
MIN	min(argument, argument,...)	minimum value
MAX	max(argument, argument,...)	maximum value
VAR	var(argument, argument,...)	variance of the values
STD	std(argument, argument,...)	standard deviation of the values

Uses of SAS Functions

Using SAS functions, you can

calculate sample statistics

create SAS date values

convert U.S. ZIP codes to state postal codes

round values

generate random numbers

extract a portion of a character value

convert data from one data type to another.

This chapter concentrates on functions that

convert data

manipulate SAS date values

modify values of character variables.

However, be sure to explore the many other SAS functions, which are described in the SAS documentation.

Example of a SAS Function

SAS functions can be used in DATA step programming statements. A SAS function can be specified anywhere that you would use a SAS expression, as long as the function is part of a SAS statement.

Let's look at a simple example of a SAS function. The assignment statement below uses the MEAN function to calculate the average of three exam scores that are stored in the variables Exam1, Exam2, and Exam3.

```
AvgScore=mean(exam1,exam2,exam3);
```

When you reference a SAS function, the function returns a value that is based on the function arguments. The MEAN function above contains three arguments: the variables Exam1, Exam2, and Exam3. The function calculates the mean of the three variables that are listed as arguments.

Some functions require a specific number of arguments, whereas other functions can contain any number of arguments. Some functions require no arguments.

Understanding DATA Step Processing

Overview

Writing Basic DATA Steps

How SAS Processes Programs

Compilation Phase

Execution Phase

Debugging a DATA Step

Testing Your Programs

Chapter Summary

Chapter Quiz

Specifying the Length of Character Variables

Overview

Remember that when you use list input to read raw data, character variables are assigned a default length of 8. Let's see what happens when list input is used to read character variables whose values are longer than 8.

The raw data file referenced by the fileref Citydata contains 1970 and 1980 population figures for several large U.S. cities. Notice that some city names are rather long.

Raw Data File with Character Values That Are Longer than 8

```
1---+----10---+----20---+----
ANCHORAGE 48081 174431
ATLANTA 495039 425022
BOSTON 641071 562994
CHARLOTTE 241420 314447
CHICAGO 3369357 3005072
DALLAS 844401 904078
DENVER 514678 492365
DETROIT 1514063 1203339
MIAMI 334859 346865
PHILADELPHIA 1949996 1688210
SACRAMENTO 257105 275741
```

The longer character values are truncated when they are read into the program data vector.

Program Data Vector

Program Data Vector

N	Rank	City	Pop70	Pop80
1	1	ANCHORAG	48081	174431

PROC PRINT output shows the truncated values for City.

```
data sasuser.growth;
   infile citydata.dat;
   input City $ Pop70 Pop80;
run;
proc print data=sasuser.growth;
```

run;

Output with Truncated Values

Obs	City	Pop70	Pop80
1	ANCHORAG	48081	174431
2	ATLANTA	495039	425022
3	BOSTON	641071	562994
4	CHARLOTT	241420	314447
5	CHICAGO	3369357	3005072
6	DALLAS	844401	904078
7	DENVER	514678	492365
8	DETROIT	1514063	1203339
9	MIAMI	334859	346865
10	PHILADEL	1949996	1688210
11	SACRAMEN	257105	275741

The LENGTH Statement

Remember, variable attributes are defined when the variable is first encountered in the DATA step. In the program below, the LENGTH statement precedes the INPUT statement and defines both the length and type of the variable City. A length of 12 has been assigned to accommodate **PHILADELPHIA**, which is the longest value for City.

```
data sasuser.growth;
   infile citydata.dat;
   length City $ 12;
   input city $ Pop70 Pop80;
run;
proc print data=sasuser.growth;
run;
```

Raw Data File with Character Values That Are Longer than 8

```
1---+----10---+----20---+----
ANCHORAGE 48081 174431
ATLANTA 495039 425022
BOSTON 641071 562994
CHARLOTTE 241420 314447
CHICAGO 3369357 3005072
DALLAS 844401 904078
DENVER 514678 492365
DETROIT 1514063 1203339
MIAMI 334859 346865
PHILADELPHIA 1949996 1688210
SACRAMENTO 257105 275741
```

Using this method, you do not need to specify City's type in the INPUT statement. However, leaving the $ in the INPUT statement will not produce an error. Your output should now display the complete values for City.

Output Using Length Statement

Obs	City	Pop70	Pop80
1	ANCHORAGE	48081	174431
2	ATLANTA	495039	425022
3	BOSTON	641071	562994
4	CHARLOTTE	241420	314447
5	CHICAGO	3369357	3005072
6	DALLAS	844401	904078
7	DENVER	514678	492365
8	DETROIT	1514063	1203339
9	MIAMI	334859	346865
10	PHILADELPHIA	1949996	1688210
11	SACRAMENTO	257105	275741

Because variable attributes are defined when the variable is first encountered in the DATA step, a variable that is defined in a LENGTH statement (if it precedes an INPUT statement) will appear first in the data set, regardless of the order of the variables in the INPUT statement.

Chapter 6: Understanding DATA Step Processing

Which of the following is *not* created during the compilation phase?

the data set descriptor

the first observation

the program data vector

the _N_ and _ERROR_ automatic variables

Correct answer: b

During the compilation phase, the program data vector is created. The program data vector includes the two automatic variables _N_ and _ERROR_. The descriptor portion of the new SAS data set is created at the end of the compilation phase. The descriptor portion includes the name of the data set, the number of observations and variables, and the names and attributes of the variables. Observations are not written until the execution phase.

During the compilation phase, SAS scans each statement in the DATA step, looking for syntax errors. Which of the following is *not* considered a syntax error?

incorrect values and formats

invalid options or variable names

missing or invalid punctuation

missing or misspelled keywords

Correct answer: a

Syntax checking can detect many common errors, but it cannot verify the values of variables or the correctness of formats.

Unless otherwise directed, the DATA step executes...

once for each compilation phase.

once for each DATA step statement.

once for each record in the input file.

once for each variable in the input file.

Correct answer: c

The DATA step executes once for each record in the input file, unless otherwise directed.

At the beginning of the execution phase, the value of _N_ is **1**, the value of _ERROR_ is **0**, and the values of the remaining variables are set to:

0

1

undefined

missing

Correct answer: d

The remaining variables are initialized to missing. Missing numeric values are represented by periods, and missing character values are represented by blanks.

Suppose you run a program that causes three DATA errors. What is the value of the automatic variable _ERROR_ when the observation that contains the third error is processed?

0

1

2

3

Correct answer: b

The default value of _ERROR_ is **0**, which means there is no data error. When an error occurs, whether one error or multiple errors, the value is set to **1**.

Which of the following actions occurs at the beginning of an iteration of the DATA step?

The automatic variables _N_ and _ERROR_ are incremented by one.

The DATA step stops execution.

The descriptor portion of the data set is written.

The values of variables created in programming statements are re-set to missing in the program data vector.

Correct answer: d

By default, at the end of the DATA step, the values in the program data vector are written to the data set as an observation, control returns to the top of the DATA step, the value of the automatic variable _N_ is incremented by one, and the values of variables created in programming statements are reset to missing. The automatic variable _ERROR_ is reset to 0 if necessary.

Based on the DATA step shown below, in what order will the variables be stored in the new data set?

```
data perm.update;
  infile invent;
  input IDnum $ Item $ 1-13 Instock 21-22
     BackOrd 24-25;
  Total=instock+backord;
run;
```

IDnum Item InStock BackOrd Total

Item IDnum InStock BackOrd Total

Total IDnum Item InStock BackOrd

Total Item IDnum InStock BackOrd

Correct answer: a

The order in which variables are defined in the DATA step determines the order in which the variables are stored in the data set.

If SAS detects syntax errors, then...

data set variables will contain missing values.

the DATA step does not compile.

the DATA step still compiles, but it does not execute.

the DATA step still compiles and executes.

Correct answer: c

When SAS cannot detect syntax errors, the DATA step compiles, but it does not execute.

What is wrong with this program?

```
data perm.update;
   infile invent
   input Item $ 1-13 IDnum $ 15-19 Instock 21-22
       BackOrd 24-25;
   total=instock+backord;
run;
```

missing semicolon on second line

missing semicolon on third line

incorrect order of variables

incorrect variable type

- 1918 -

Correct answer: a

A semicolon is missing from the second line. It will cause an error because the INPUT statement will be interpreted as invalid INFILE statement options.

Look carefully at this section of a SAS session log. Based on the note, what was the most likely problem with the DATA step?

XisError: altImageDescription Element Should Not Be Blank.

```
NOTE: Invalid data for IDnum in line 7 15-19.
RULE: ----+----1----+----2----+----3----+----4
7        Bird Feeder LG088 3 20
Item=Bird Feeder IDnum=. InStock=3 BackOrd=20
Total=23 _ERROR_=1 _N_=1
```

A keyword was misspelled in the DATA step.

A semicolon was missing from the INFILE statement.

A variable was misspelled in the INPUT statement.

A dollar sign was missing in the INPUT statement.

Correct answer: d

The third line of the log displays the value for IDnum, which is clearly a character value. The fourth line displays the values in the program data vector and shows a period, the symbol for a missing numeric value, for IDnum, the other values are correctly assigned. Thus, it appears that numeric values were expected for IDnum. A dollar sign, to indicate character values, is missing from the INPUT statement.

Chapter 13: Transforming Data with SAS Functions

Which function calculates the average of the variables Var1, Var2, Var3, and Var4?

mean(var1,var4)

mean(var1-var4)

mean(of var1,var4)

mean(of var1-var4)

Correct answer: d

Use a variable list to specify a range of variables as the function argument. When specifying a variable list, be sure to precede the list with the word OF. If you omit the word OF, the function argument might not be interpreted as expected.

Within the data set Hrd.Temp, PayRate is a character variable and Hours is a numeric variable. What happens when the following program is run?

```
data work.temp;
  set hrd.temp;
  Salary=payrate*hours;
run;
```

      SAS converts the values of PayRate to numeric values. No message is written to the log.

      SAS converts the values of PayRate to numeric values. A message is written to the log.

      SAS converts the values of Hours to character values. No message is written to the log.

      SAS converts the values of Hours to character values. A message is written to the log.

Correct answer: b

When this DATA step is executed, SAS automatically converts the character values of PayRate to numeric values so that the calculation can occur. Whenever data is automatically converted, a message is written to the SAS log stating that the conversion has occurred.

A typical value for the character variable Target is **123,456**. Which statement correctly converts the values of Target to numeric values when creating the variable TargetNo?

      TargetNo=input(target,comma6.);

      TargetNo=input(target,comma7.);

      TargetNo=put(target,comma6.);

      TargetNo=put(target,comma7.)

Correct answer: b

You explicitly convert character values to numeric values by using the INPUT function. Be sure to select an informat that can read the form of the values.

A typical value for the numeric variable SiteNum is **12.3**. Which statement correctly converts the values of SiteNum to character values when creating the variable Location?

Location=dept||'/'||input(sitenum,3.1);

Location=dept||'/'||input(sitenum,4.1);

Location=dept||'/'||put(sitenum,3.1);

Location=dept||'/'||put(sitenum,4.1);

Correct answer: d

You explicitly convert numeric values to character values by using the PUT function. Be sure to select a format that can read the form of the values.

Suppose the YEARCUTOFF= system option is set to 1920. Which MDY function creates the date value for January 3, 2020?

MDY(1,3,20)

MDY(3,1,20)

MDY(1,3,2020)

MDY(3,1,2020)

Correct answer: c.

Because the YEARCUTOFF= system option is set to 1920, SAS sees the two-digit year value **20** as **1920**. Four-digit year values are always read correctly.

The variable Address2 contains values such as **Piscataway, NJ**. How do you assign the two-letter state abbreviations to a new variable named State?

State=scan(address2,2);

State=scan(address2,13,2);

State=substr(address2,2);

State=substr(address2,13,2);

Correct answer: a

The SCAN function is used to extract words from a character value when you know the order of the words, when their position varies, and when the words are marked by some delimiter. In this case, you don't need to specify delimiters, because the blank and the comma are default delimiters.

The variable IDCode contains values such as **123FA** and **321MB**. The fourth character identifies sex. How do you assign these character codes to a new variable named Sex?

Sex=scan(idcode,4);

Sex=scan(idcode,4,1);

Sex=substr(idcode,4);

Sex=substr(idcode,4,1);

Correct answer: d

The SUBSTR function is best used when you know the exact position of the substring to extract from the character value. You specify the position to start from and the number of characters to extract.

Due to growth within the 919 area code, the telephone exchange 555 is being reassigned to the 920 area code. The data set Clients.Piedmont includes the variable Phone, which contains telephone numbers in the form 919-555-1234. Which of the following programs will correctly change the values of Phone?

```
data work.piedmont(drop=areacode exchange);
  set clients.piedmont;
  Areacode=substr(phone,1,3);
  Exchange=substr(phone,5,3);
  if areacode='919' and exchange='555'
    then scan(phone,1,3)='920';
run;
```

```
data work.piedmont(drop=areacode exchange);
  set clients.piedmont;
  Areacode=substr(phone,1,3);
  Exchange=substr(phone,5,3);
  if areacode='919' and exchange='555'
    then phone=scan('920',1,3);
run;
```

```
data work.piedmont(drop=areacode exchange);
  set clients.piedmont;
  Areacode=substr(phone,1,3);
  Exchange=substr(phone,5,3);
  if areacode='919' and exchange='555'
    then substr(phone,5,3)='920';
run;
```

```
data work.piedmont(drop=areacode exchange);
  set clients.piedmont;
  Areacode=substr(phone,1,3);
  Exchange=substr(phone,5,3);
  if areacode='919' and exchange='555'
    then phone=substr('920',1,3);
run;
```

Correct answer: c

The SUBSTR function replaces variable values if it is placed on the left side of an assignment statement. When placed on the right side (as in Question 7), the function extracts a substring.

Suppose you need to create the variable FullName by concatenating the values of FirstName, which contains first names, and LastName, which contains last names. What's the best way to remove extra blanks between first names and last names?

```
        data work.maillist;
          set retail.maillist;
          length FullName $ 40;
          fullname=trim firstname||' '||lastname;
        run;



        data work.maillist;
          set retail.maillist;
          length FullName $ 40;
          fullname=trim(firstname)||' '||lastname;
        run;



        data work.maillist;
          set retail.maillist;
          length FullName $ 40;
          fullname=trim(firstname)||' '||trim(lastname);
        run;



        data work.maillist;
          set retail.maillist;
          length FullName $ 40;
          fullname=trim(firstname||' '||lastname);
        run;
```

Correct answer: b

The TRIM function removes trailing blanks from character values. In this case, extra blanks must be removed from the values of FirstName. Although answer c also works, the extra TRIM function for the variable LastName is unnecessary. Because of the LENGTH statement, all values of FullName are padded to 40 characters.

Within the data set Furnitur.Bookcase, the variable Finish contains values such as **ash/cherry/teak/matte-black**. Which of the following creates a subset of the data in which the values of Finish contain the string **walnut**? Make the search for the string case-insensitive.

```
        data work.bookcase;
          set furnitur.bookcase;
          if index(finish,walnut) = 0;
        run;



        data work.bookcase;
          set furnitur.bookcase;
```

```
        if index(finish,'walnut') > 0;
   run;



   data work.bookcase;
     set furnitur.bookcase;
     if index(lowcase(finish),walnut) = 0;
   run;



   data work.bookcase;
     set furnitur.bookcase;
     if index(lowcase(finish),'walnut') > 0;
   run;
```

Correct answer: d

Use the INDEX function in a subsetting IF statement, enclosing the character string in quotation marks. Only those observations in which the function locates the string and returns a value greater than 0 are written to the data set.

Correcting Errors

Overview

To modify programs that contain errors, you can edit them in the code editing window. You can correct simple errors, such as the spelling error in the following program, by typing over the incorrect text, deleting text, or inserting text.

```
data clinic.admitfee;
   set clinic.admit;
run;
proc prin data=clinic.admitfee;
   var id name actlevel fee;
run;
```

🖑 If you use the Program Editor window, you usually need to recall the submitted statements from the recall buffer to the Program Editor window, where you can correct the problems. Remember that you can recall submitted statements by issuing the RECALL command or by selecting **Run ➪ Recall Last Submit**.

In the program below, the missing t has been inserted into the PRINT keyword that is specified in the PROC PRINT statement.

Corrected Program

```
program.sas *                    _ □ ✕
  data clinic.admitfee;
       set clinic.admit;
  run;
  proc print data=clinic.admitfee;
       var id name actlevel fee;
  run;
```

Some problems are relatively easy to diagnose and correct. But sometimes you might not know right away how to correct errors. The online Help provides information about individual procedures as well as help that is specific to your operating environment. From the **Help** menu, you can also select **SAS on the Web** for links to Technical Support and Frequently Asked Questions, if you have Internet access.

Resubmitting a Revised Program

After correcting your program, you can submit it again. However, before doing so, it is a good idea to clear the messages from the Log window so that you don't confuse the old error messages with the new messages. Then you can resubmit the program and view any resulting output.

Correct PROC PRINT Output

The SAS System

Obs	ID	Name	ActLevel	Fee
1	2458	Murray, W	HIGH	85.20
2	2462	Almers, C	HIGH	124.80
3	2501	Bonaventure, T	LOW	149.75
4	2523	Johnson, R	MOD	149.75
5	2539	LaMance, K	LOW	124.80
6	2544	Jones, M	HIGH	124.80
7	2552	Reberson, P	MOD	149.75
8	2555	King, E	MOD	149.75
9	2563	Pitts, D	LOW	124.80
10	2568	Eberhardt, S	LOW	124.80
11	2571	Nunnelly, A	HIGH	149.75
12	2572	Oberon, M	LOW	85.20
13	2574	Peterson, V	MOD	149.75
14	2575	Quigley, M	HIGH	124.80
15	2578	Cameron, L	MOD	124.80
16	2579	Underwood, K	LOW	149.75
17	2584	Takahashi, Y	MOD	124.80
18	2586	Derber, B	HIGH	85.20
19	2588	Ivan, H	LOW	85.20
20	2589	Wilcox, E	HIGH	149.75
21	2595	Warren, C	MOD	149.75

Remember to check the Log window again to verify that your program ran correctly.

Log Message with No Errors

```
Log - (Untitled)                                    [_][□][X]

54        data clinic.admitfee;                          ▲
55          set clinic.admit;
56        run;

NOTE: The data set CLINIC.ADMITFEE has
      21 observations and 9 variables.
NOTE: DATA statement used:
      real time              0.09 seconds
      cpu time               0.03 seconds


57        proc print data=clinic.admitfee;
58          var id name actlevel fee;
59        run;

NOTE: PROCEDURE PRINT used:
      real time              1.78 seconds
      cpu time               0.03 seconds         ▼
◄ │                                              │ ► │
```

Because submitted steps remain in the recall buffer, resubmitting error-free steps wastes system resources. You can place SAS comment symbols before and after your error-free code until you debug the rest of your program. SAS ignores text between comment symbols during processing. When your entire program is error-free, remove the comment symbols and your entire SAS program is intact. See Additional Features for instructions about creating a SAS comment statement.

To resubmit a section of code in the Windows operating environment, highlight the selected code in the code editing window. Then select **Run** ➧ **Submit**.

This and other chapters show you the Enhanced Editor window only. If you are not using the Enhanced Editor as a code editing window, be sure to adapt the directions for the Program Editor window. For example, you might need to recall programs.

Creating a Summarized Data Set Using PROC SUMMARY

You can also create a summarized output data set with PROC SUMMARY. When you use PROC SUMMARY, you use the same code to produce the output data set that you would use with PROC MEANS. The difference between the two procedures is that PROC MEANS produces a report by default (remember that you can use the NOPRINT option to suppress the default report). By contrast, to produce a report in PROC SUMMARY, you must include a PRINT option in the PROC SUMMARY statement.

Example

The following example creates an output data set but does not create a report:

```
proc summary data=clinic.diabetes;
   var age height weight;
   class sex;
   output out=work.sum_gender
      mean=AvgAge AvgHeight AvgWeight;
run;
```

If you placed a PRINT option in the PROC SUMMARY statement above, this program would produce the same report as if you replaced the word SUMMARY with MEANS.


```
proc summary data=clinic.diabetes print;
   var age height weight;
   class sex;
   output out=work.sum_gender
     mean=AvgAge AvgHeight AvgWeight;
run;
```

Output Created by the SUMMARY Procedure with the PRINT Option Specified

The SUMMARY Procedure

Sex	N Obs	Variable	N	Mean	Std Dev	Minimum	Maximum
F	11	Age	11	48.9090909	13.3075508	16.0000000	63.0000000
		Height	11	63.9090909	2.1191765	61.0000000	68.0000000
		Weight	11	150.4545455	18.4464828	102.0000000	168.0000000
M	9	Age	9	44.0000000	12.3895117	15.0000000	54.0000000
		Height	9	70.6666667	2.6457513	66.0000000	75.0000000
		Weight	9	204.2222222	30.2893454	140.0000000	240.0000000

Subsetting Data

As you read your data, you can subset it by processing only those observations that meet a specified condition. To do this, you can use a subsetting IF statement in any DATA step.

Using a Subsetting IF Statement

The subsetting IF statement causes the DATA step to continue processing only those observations that meet the condition of the expression specified in the IF statement. The resulting SAS data set or data sets contain a subset of the original external file or SAS data set.

   General form, subsetting IF statement:

IF *expression*;

where *expression* is any valid SAS expression.

   If the expression is *true*, the DATA step continues to process that observation.

   If the expression is *false*, no further statements are processed for that observation, and control returns to the top of the DATA step.

Example

The subsetting IF statement below selects only observations whose values for Tolerance are **D**. It is positioned in the DATA step so that other statements do not need to process unwanted observations.

```
data sasuser.stress;
   infile tests;
   input ID $ 1-4 Name $ 6-25 RestHR 27-29 MaxHR 31-33
       RecHR 35-37 TimeMin 39-40 TimeSec 42-43
       Tolerance $ 45;
   if tolerance='D';
   TotalTime=(timemin*60)+timesec;
run;
```

Because Tolerance is a character variable, the value **D** must be enclosed in quotation marks, and it must be the same case as in the data set.

See the SAS documentation for a comparison of the WHERE and subsetting IF statements when they are used in the DATA step.

Chapter Quiz

Select the best answer for each question. After completing the quiz, you can check your answers using the answer key in the appendix.

Which SAS statement associates the fileref Crime with the raw data file **C:\States\Data\crime.dat**?

filename crime 'c:\states\data\crime.dat';

filename crime c:\states\data\crime.dat;

fileref crime 'c:\states\data\crime.dat';

filename 'c:\states\data\crime' crime.dat;

Filerefs remain in effect until . . .

you change them.

you cancel them.

you end your SAS session.

all of the above

Which statement identifies the name of a raw data file to be read with the fileref Products and specifies that the DATA step read-only records 1-15?

infile products obs 15;

infile products obs=15;

input products obs=15;

input products 1-15;

Which of the following programs correctly writes the observations from the data set below to a raw data file?

Data Set work.patients

SAS data set Work.Patients

ID	Sex	Age	Height	Weight	Pulse
2304	F	16	61	102	100
1128	M	43	71	218	76
4425	F	48	66	162	80
1387	F	57	64	142	70
9012	F	39	63	157	68
6312	M	52	72	240	77
5438	F	42	62	168	83
3788	M	38	73	234	71
9125	F	56	64	159	70
3438	M	15	66	140	67

data _null_;
    set work.patients;

```
      infile 'c:\clinic\patients\referals.dat';
      input id $ 1-4 sex 6 $ age 8-9 height 11-12
            weight 14-16 pulse 18-20;
   run;




   data referals.dat;
      set work.patients;
      input id $ 1-4 sex $ 6 age 8-9 height 11-12
            weight 14-16 pulse 18-20;
   run;




   data _null_;
      set work.patients;
      file c:\clinic\patients\referals.dat;
      put id $ 1-4 sex 6 $ age 8-9 height 11-12
            weight 14-16 pulse 18-20;
   run;




   data _null_;
      set work.patients;
      file 'c:\clinic\patients\referals.dat';
      put id $ 1-4 sex 6 $ age 8-9 height 11-12
            weight 14-16 pulse 18-20;
   run;
```

Which raw data file can be read using column input?

Raw Data File A

```
1---+----10---+----20---+
Henderson CA 26 ADM
Josephs SC 33 SALES
Williams MN 40 HRD
Rogan NY RECRTN
```

Raw Data File B

```
1---+----10---+----20---+----30
2803 Deborah Campos   173.97
2912 Bill    Marin    205.14
3015 Helen   Stinson  194.08
3122 Nicole  Terry    187.65
```

Raw Data File C

```
1---+----10---+----20---+
Avery John       $601.23
Davison Sherrill $723.15
Holbrook Grace   $489.76
Jansen Mike      $638.42
```

all of the above.

Which program creates the output shown below?

Raw Data and SAS Output Data Set

```
1---+----10---+----20---+----30
3427 Chen     Steve Raleigh
1436 Davis    Lee   Atlanta
2812 King     Vicky Memphis
1653 Sanchez Jack  Atlanta
```

Obs	ID	LastName	FirstName	City
1	3427	Chen	Steve	Raleigh
2	1436	Davis	Lee	Atlanta
3	2812	King	Vicky	Memphis
4	1653	Sanchez	Jack	Atlanta

```
data work.salesrep;
  infile empdata;
  input ID $ 1-4 LastName $ 6-12
      FirstName $ 14-18 City $ 20-29;
run;
proc print data=work.salesrep;
run;
```

```
data work.salesrep;
  infile empdata;
  input ID $ 1-4 Name $ 6-12
      FirstName $ 14-18 City $ 20-29;
run;
proc print data=work.salesrep;
run;
```

```
data work.salesrep;
  infile empdata;
  input ID $ 1-4 name1 $ 6-12
      name2 $ 14-18 City $ 20-29;
run;
proc print data=work.salesrep;
run;
```

all of the above.

Which statement correctly reads the fields in the following order: StockNumber, Price, Item, Finish, Style?

Field Name	Start Column	End Column	Data Type
StockNumber	1	3	character
Finish	5	9	character
Style	11	18	character
Item	20	24	character
Price	27	32	numeric

Raw Data

```
1---+----10---+----20---+----30---+
310 oak     pedestal table  329.99
311 maple pedestal table  369.99
312 brass floor     lamp   79.99
313 glass table     lamp   59.99
313 oak     rocking   chair  153.99
```

input StockNumber $ 1-3 Finish $ 5-9 Style $ 11-18
    Item $ 20-24 Price 27-32;

input StockNumber $ 1-3 Price 27-32
    Item $ 20-24 Finish $ 5-9 Style $ 11-18;

input $ StockNumber 1-3 Price 27-32 $

Item 20-24 $ Finish 5-9 $ Style 11-18;

input StockNumber $ 1-3 Price $ 27-32
    Item $ 20-24 Finish $ 5-9 Style $ 11-18;

Which statement correctly re-defines the values of the variable Income as 100 percent higher?

income=income*1.00;

income=income+(income*2.00);

income=income*2;

income=*2;

Which program correctly reads instream data?


```
data finance.newloan;
   input datalines;
   if country='JAPAN';
   MonthAvg=amount/12;
1998 US    CARS  194324.12
1998 US    TRUCKS 142290.30
1998 CANADA CARS    10483.44
1998 CANADA TRUCKS  93543.64
1998 MEXICO CARS    22500.57
1998 MEXICO TRUCKS  10098.88
1998 JAPAN  CARS    15066.43
1998 JAPAN  TRUCKS  40700.34
;
```


```
data finance.newloan;
   input Year 1-4 Country $ 6-11
       Vehicle $ 13-18 Amount 20-28;
   if country='JAPAN';
   MonthAvg=amount/12;
   datalines;
run;
```

```
data finance.newloan;
   input Year 1-4 Country 6-11
      Vehicle 13-18 Amount 20-28;
   if country='JAPAN';
   MonthAvg=amount/12;
   datalines;
1998 US     CARS  194324.12
1998 US     TRUCKS 142290.30
1998 CANADA CARS   10483.44
1998 CANADA TRUCKS  93543.64
1998 MEXICO CARS   22500.57
1998 MEXICO TRUCKS 10098.88
1998 JAPAN  CARS   15066.43
1998 JAPAN  TRUCKS 40700.34
;
```

```
data finance.newloan;
   input Year 1-4 Country $ 6-11
      Vehicle $ 13-18 Amount 20-28;
   if country='JAPAN';
   MonthAvg=amount/12;
   datalines;
1998 US     CARS  194324.12
1998 US     TRUCKS 142290.30
1998 CANADA CARS   10483.44
1998 CANADA TRUCKS  93543.64
1998 MEXICO CARS   22500.57
1998 MEXICO TRUCKS 10098.88
1998 JAPAN  CARS   15066.43
1998 JAPAN  TRUCKS 40700.34
;
```

Which SAS statement subsets the raw data shown below so that only the observations in which Sex (in the second field) has a value of **F** are processed?

Raw Data

```
----+----10---+----20---+--
Alfred   M 14 69.0 112.5
Becka    F 13 65.3 98.0
Gail     F 14 64.3 90.0
Jeffrey  M 13 62.5 84.0
John     M 12 59.0 99.5
Karen    F 12 56.3 77.0
Mary     F 15 66.5 112.0
Philip   M 16 72.0 150.0
Sandy    F 11 51.3 50.5
Tammy    F 14 62.8 102.5
William  M 15 66.5 112.0
```

if sex=f;

if sex=F;

if sex='F';

a or b

Identifying Nonstandard Numeric Data

Standard Numeric Data

Standard numeric data values can contain only

numbers

decimal points

numbers in scientific, or E, notation (23E4)

minus signs and plus signs.

Some examples of standard numeric data are 15, -15, 15.4, +.05, 1.54E3, and -1.54E-3.

Nonstandard Numeric Data

Nonstandard numeric data includes

values that contain special characters, such as percent signs (%), dollar signs ($), and commas (,) date and time values

data in fraction, integer binary, real binary, and hexadecimal forms.

The external file referenced by the fileref Empdata contains the personnel information for the technical writing department of a small computer manufacturer. The fields contain values for each employee's last name, first name, job title, and annual salary.

```
         Raw Data File Empdata
1---+----10---+----20---+---
EVANS    DONNY  112 29,996.63
HELMS    LISA   105 18,567.23
HIGGINS  JOHN   111 25,309.00
LARSON   AMY    113 32,696.78
MOORE    MARY   112 28,945.89
POWELL   JASON  103 35,099.50
RILEY    JUDY   111 25,309.00
RYAN     NEAL   112 28,180.00
WILSON   HENRY  113 31,875.46
WOODS    CHIP   105 17,098.71
```

Notice that the values for Salary contain commas. So, the values for Salary are considered to be nonstandard numeric values.

Expanding Your Use of Arrays

Creating Variables in an ARRAY Statement

So far, you have learned several ways to reference existing variables in an ARRAY statement. You can also create variables in an ARRAY statement by omitting the array elements from the statement. If you do not reference existing variables, SAS automatically creates new variables for you and assigns default names to them. The default name is the array-name followed by consecutive numbers 1 to the dimension of the array.

General form, ARRAY statement to create new variables:

ARRAY *array-name{dimension}*;

where

   array-name specifies the name of the array.

   dimension describes the number and arrangement of array elements.

For example, suppose you need to calculate the weight gain or loss from week to week for each member of a fitness class, shown below.

SAS Data Set Hrd.Convert

Name	Weight1	Weight2	Weight3	Weight4	Weight5	Weight6
Alicia	153.4	151.9	151.7	148.6	145.5	145.9
Betsy	116.0	116.0	114.0	111.1	109.8	108.2
Brenda	151.2	149.0	147.7	146.4	145.1	143.7
Carl	149.0	146.8	145.5	144.2	142.9	141.5
Carmela	140.2	137.8	136.5	135.4	134.0	128.3

You'd like to create variables that contain this weekly difference. To perform the calculation, you first group the variables Weight1 through Weight6 into an array.

```
data hrd.diff;
   set hrd.convert;
   array wt{6} weight1-weight6;
```

Next, you want to create the new variables to store the differences between the six recorded weights. You can use an additional ARRAY statement without elements to create the new variables, WgtDiff1 to WgtDiff5.

```
data hrd.diff;
   set hrd.convert;
   array wt{6} weight1-weight6;
   array WgtDiff{5};
```

SAS Data Set Hrd.Convert

Name	Weight1	Weight2	Weight3	Weight4	Weight5	Weight6
Alicia	153.4	<-1->151.9	<-2->151.7	<-3->148.6	<-4->145.5	<-5->145.9
Betsy	116.0	116.0	114.0	111.1	109.8	108.2
Brenda	151.2	149.0	147.7	146.4	145.1	143.7
Carl	149.0	146.8	145.5	144.2	142.9	141.5
Carmela	140.2	137.8	136.5	135.4	134.0	128.3

Remember, when creating variables in an ARRAY statement, you do not need to specify array elements as long as you specify how many elements will be in the array.

```
array WgtDiff{5};
```

Default Variable Names

The default variable names are created by concatenating the array name and the numbers 1, 2, 3, and so on, up to the array dimension.

array WgtDiff{5};

    . . . . .

    . . . . .

    . . . . .

    . . . . .

    . . . . .

WgtDiff1 WgtDiff2 WgtDiff3 WgtDiff4 WgtDiff5

🖱   If you prefer, you can specify individual variable names. To specify variable names, you list each name as an element of the array. The following ARRAY statement creates the numeric variables Oct12, Oct19, Oct26, Nov02, and Nov09.

array WgtDiff{5} Oct12 Oct19 Oct26 Nov02 Nov09;
       array WgtDiff{5};

    . . . . .

    . . . . .

    . . . . .

    . . . . .

    . . . . .

Oct12 Oct19 Oct26 Nov02 Nov09

Arrays of Character Variables

To create an array of character variables, add a dollar sign ($) after the array dimension.

array firstname{5} $;

By default, all character variables that are created in an ARRAY statement are assigned a length of 8. You can assign your own length by specifying the length after the dollar sign.

array firstname{5} $ 24;

The length that you specify is automatically assigned to all variables that are created by the ARRAY statement.

During the compilation of the DATA step, the variables that this ARRAY statement creates are added to the program data vector and are stored in the resulting data set.


```
data hrd.diff;
  set hrd.convert;
  array wt{6}  Weight1-Weight6;
```

```
array WgtDiff{5};
```

Program Data Vector

N	Name	Weight1	Weight2	Weight3	Weight4	Weight5	Weight6

WgtDiff1	WgtDiff2	WgtDiff3	WgtDiff4	WgtDiff5

⚠ When referencing the array elements, be careful not to confuse the array references WgtDiff{1} through WgtDiff{5} (note the braces) with the variable names WgtDiff1 through WgtDiff5. The program data vector below shows the relationship between the array references and the corresponding variable names.

Program Data Vector

N	Name	Weight1	Weight2	Weight3	Weight4	Weight5	Weight6

WgtDiff{1}	WgtDiff{2}	WgtDiff{3}	WgtDiff{4}	WgtDiff{5}
WgtDiff1	WgtDiff2	WgtDiff3	WgtDiff4	WgtDiff5

Now you can use a DO loop to calculate the differences between each of the recorded weights. Notice that each value of WgtDiff{i} is calculated by subtracting wt{i} from wt{$i+1$}. By manipulating the index variable, you can easily reference any array element.

```
data hrd.diff;
   set hrd.convert;
   array wt{6} weight1-weight6;
   array WgtDiff{5};
   do i=1 to 5;
      wgtdiff{i}=wt{i+1}-wt{i};
   end;
run;
```

A portion of the resulting data set is shown below.

SAS Data Set Hrd.Diff

Name	WgtDiff1	WgtDiff2	WgtDiff3	WgtDiff4	WgtDiff5
Alicia	-1.54322	-0.22046	-3.08644	-3.08644	0.44092
Betsy	0.00000	-1.98414	-2.86598	-1.32276	-1.54322
Brenda	-2.20460	-1.32276	-1.32276	-1.32276	-1.32276

Assigning Initial Values to Arrays

Sometimes it is useful to assign initial values to elements of an array when you define the array.

array goal{4} g1 g2 g3 g4 (initial values);

To assign initial values in an ARRAY statement:

Place the values after the array elements.

     array goal{4} g1 g2 g3 g4 (9000 9300 9600 9900);

Specify one initial value for each corresponding array element.

     ↓ ↓ ↓ ↓
     array goal{4} g1 g2 g3 g4 (9000 9300 9600 9900);
          ↑ ↑ ↑ ↑

Separate each value with a comma or blank.

     ↓ ↓ ↓
     array goal{4} g1 g2 g3 g4 (9000 9300 9600 9900);

Enclose the initial values in parentheses.

     ↓   ↓
     array goal{4} g1 g2 g3 g4 (9000 9300 9600 9900);

Enclose each character value in quotation marks.

     ↓ ↓↓ ↓↓ ↓
     array col{3} $ color1-color3 ('red','green','blue');

It's also possible to assign initial values to an array without specifying each array element. The following statement creates the variables Var1, Var2, Var3, and Var4, and assigns them initial values of **1**, **2**, **3**, and **4**:

array Var{4} (1 2 3 4);

For this example, assume that you have the task of comparing the actual sales figures in the Finance.Qsales data set to the sales goals for each sales representative at the beginning of the year. The sales goals are not recorded in Finance.Qsales.

Description of Finance.Qsales

Variable	Type	Length
SalesRep	char	8
Sales1	num	8
Sales2	num	8
Sales3	num	8
Sales4	num	8

The DATA step below reads the Finance.Qsales data set to create the Finance.Report data set. The ARRAY statement creates an array to process sales data for each quarter.

```
data finance.report;
  set finance.qsales;
  array sale{4} sales1-sales4;
```

To compare the actual sales to the sales goals, you must create the variables for the sales goals and assign values to them.

```
data finance.report;
  set finance.qsales;
  array sale{4} sales1-sales4;
  array Goal{4} (9000 9300 9600 9900);
```

A third ARRAY statement creates the variables Achieved1 through Achieved4 to store the comparison of actual sales versus sales goals.

```
data finance.report;
  set finance.qsales;
  array sale{4} sales1-sales4;
  array Goal{4} (9000 9300 9600 9900);
  array Achieved{4};
  do i=1 to 4;
    achieved{i}=100*sale{i}/goal{i};
  end;
run;
```

A DO loop executes four times to calculate the value of each element of the achieved array (expressed as a percentage).

```
data finance.report;
   set finance.qsales;
   array sale{4} sales1-sales4;
   array Goal{4} (9000 9300 9600 9900);
   array Achieved{4};
   do i=1 to 4;
      achieved{i}=100*sale{i}/goal{i};
   end;
run;
```

Before submitting this DATA step, you can drop the index variable from the new data set by adding a DROP= option to the DATA statement.

```
data finance.report(drop=i);
   set finance.qsales;
   array sale{4} sales1-sales4;
   array Goal{4} (9000 9300 9600 9900);
   array Achieved{4};
   do i=1 to 4;
      achieved{i}=100*sale{i}/goal{i};
   end;
run;
```

This is an example of a simple table-lookup program. The resulting data set contains the variables that were read from Finance.Qsales, plus the eight variables that were created with ARRAY statements.

SAS Data Set Finance.Report

SalesRep	Sales1	Sales2	Sales3	Sales4	Goal1	Goal2
Britt	8400	8800	9300	9800	9000	9300
Fruchten	9500	9300	9800	8900	9000	9300
Goodyear	9150	9200	9650	11000	9000	9300

Goal3	Goal4	Achieved1	Achieved2	Achieved3	Achieved4
9600	9900	93.333	94.624	96.875	98.990
9600	9900	105.556	100.000	102.083	89.899
9600	9900	101.667	98.925	100.521	111.111

Variables to which initial values are assigned in an ARRAY statement are automatically retained.

The variables Goal1 through Goal4 should not be stored in the data set, because they are needed only to calculate the values of Achieved1 through Achieved4. The next example shows you how to create temporary array elements.

Creating Temporary Array Elements

To create temporary array elements for DATA step processing without creating new variables, specify _TEMPORARY_ after the array name and dimension.

```
data finance.report(drop=i);
  set finance.qsales;
  array sale{4} sales1-sales4;
  array goal{4} _temporary_ (9000 9300 9600 9900);
  array Achieved{4};
  do i=1 to 4;
    achieved{i}=100*sale{i}/goal{i};
  end;
run;
```

Temporary array elements do not appear in the resulting data set.

SAS Data Set Finance.Report

SalesRep	Sales1	Sales2	Sales3	Sales4
Britt	8400	8800	9300	9800
Fruchten	9500	9300	9800	8900
Goodyear	9150	9200	9650	11000

Achieved1	Achieved2	Achieved3	Achieved4
93.333	94.624	96.875	98.990
105.556	100.000	102.083	89.899
101.667	98.925	100.521	111.111

Temporary array elements are useful when the array is needed only to perform a calculation. You can improve performance time by using temporary array elements.

Understanding Multidimensional Arrays

So far, you have learned how to group variables into one-dimensional arrays. You can also group variables into table-like structures called multidimensional arrays. This section teaches you how to define and use two-dimensional arrays, which are a common type of multidimensional array.

Suppose you want to write a DATA step to compare responses on a quiz to the correct answers. As long as there is only one correct answer per question, this is a simple one-to-one comparison.

```
Resp1  →  Answer1
Resp2  →  Answer2
Resp3  →  Answer3
Resp4  →  Answer4
```

However, if there is more than one correct answer per question, you must compare each response to each possible correct answer in order to determine whether there is a match.

Resp1 → Answer1 Answer2 Answer3
Resp2 → Answer4 Answer5 Answer6
Resp3 → Answer7 Answer8 Answer9
Resp4 → Answer10 Answer11 Answer12 ·

You can process the above data more easily by grouping the Answer variables into a two-dimensional array. Just as you can think of a one-dimensional array as a single row of variables, as in this example ...

Answer1 Answer2 Answer3 Answer4 ... Answer9 Answer10 Answer11 Answer12

... you can think of a two-dimensional array as multiple rows of variables.

Answer1   Answer2   Answer3
Answer4   Answer5   Answer6
Answer7   Answer8   Answer9
Answer10 Answer11 Answer12

Defining a Multidimensional Array

To define a multidimensional array, you specify the number of elements in each dimension, separated by a comma. This ARRAY statement defines a two-dimensional array:

array new{3,4} x1-x12;

In a two-dimensional array, the two dimensions can be thought of as a table of rows and columns.

array new{r,c} x1-x12;

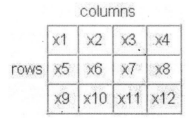

The first dimension in the ARRAY statement specifies the number of rows.

↓

array new{3,4} x1-x12;

x1	x2	x3	x4
x5	x6	x7	x8
x9	x10	x11	x12

rows

The second dimension specifies the number of columns.

↓

array new{3,4} x1-x12;

columns

x1	x2	x3	x4
x5	x6	x7	x8
x9	x10	x11	x12

You can reference any element of the array by specifying the two dimensions. In the example below, you can perform an action on the variable x7 by specifying the array reference new(2,3). You can easily locate the array element in the table by finding the row (2), then the column (3).

array new{3,4} x1-x12;
new(2,3)=0;

x1	x2	x3	x4
x5	x6	x7	x8
x9	x10	x11	x12

When you define a two-dimensional array, the array elements are grouped in the order in which they are listed in the ARRAY statement. For example, the array elements x1 through x4 can be thought of as the first row of the table.

↓ ↓ ↓ ↓
array new{3,4} x1 x2 x3 x4 x5 x6 x7 x8 x9 x10 x11 x12;

x1	x2	x3	x4
x5	x6	x7	x8
x9	x10	x11	x12

The elements x5 through x8 become the second row of the table, and so on.

↓ ↓ ↓ ↓

array new{3,4} x1 x2 x3 x4 x5 x6 x7 x8 x9 x10 x11 x12;

x1	x2	x3	x4
x5	x6	x7	x8
x9	x10	x11	x12

Referencing Elements of a Two-Dimensional Array

Multidimensional arrays are typically used with nested DO loops. The next example uses a one-dimensional array, a two-dimensional array, and a nested DO loop to re-structure a set of variables.

Your company's sales figures are stored by month in the SAS data set Finance.Monthly. Your task is to generate a new data set of quarterly sales rather than monthly sales.

Description of Finance.Monthly

Variable	Type	Length
Year	num	8
Month1	num	8
Month2	num	8
Month3	num	8
Month4	num	8
Month5	num	8
Month6	num	8
Month7	num	8
Month8	num	8
Month9	num	8
Month10	num	8
Month11	num	8
Month12	num	8

Defining the array m{4,3} puts the variables Month1 through Month12 into four groups of three months (calendar quarters).

Table Representation of m Array

Month1	Month2	Month3
Month4	Month5	Month6
Month7	Month8	Month9
Month10	Month11	Month12

```
data finance.quarters;
  set finance.monthly;
  array m{4,3} month1-month12;
```

Defining the array Qtr{4} creates the numeric variables Qtr1, Qtr2, Qtr3, Qtr4, which will be used to sum the sales for each quarter.

```
data finance.quarters;
  set finance.monthly;
  array m{4,3} month1-month12;
  array Qtr{4};
```

A nested DO loop is used to reference the values of the variables Month1 through Month12 and to calculate the values of Qtr1 through Qtr4. Because the variables i and j are used only for loop processing, the DROP= option is used to exclude them from the Finance.Quarters data set.

```
data finance.quarters(drop=i j);
  set finance.monthly;
  array m{4,3} month1-month12;
  array Qtr{4};
  do i=1 to 4;
    qtr{i}=0;
    do j=1 to 3;
      qtr{i}+m{i,j};
    end;
  end;
run;
```

Each element in the Qtr array represents the sum of one row in the m array. The number of elements in the Qtr array should match the first dimension of the m array (that is, the number of rows in the m array). The first DO loop executes once for each of the four elements of the Qtr array.

The assignment statement, qtr{i}=0, sets the value of qtr{i} to zero after each iteration of the first DO loop. Without the assignment statement, the values of Qtr1, Qtr2, Qtr3, and Qtr4 would accumulate across iterations of the DATA step due to the qtr{i}+m{i,j} sum statement within the DO loop.

```
data finance.quarters(drop=i j);
   set finance.monthly;
   array m{4,3} month1-month12;
   array Qtr{4};
   do i=1 to 4;
     qtr{i}=0;
      do j=1 to 3;
         qtr{i}+m{i,j};
      end;
   end;
run;
```

The second DO loop executes the same number of times as the second dimension of the m array (that is, the number of columns in each row of the m array).

```
data finance.quarters(drop=i j);
   set finance.monthly;
   array m{4,3} month1-month12;
   array Qtr{4};
   do i=1 to 4;
     qtr{i}=0;
      do j=1 to 3;
         qtr{i}+m{i,j};
      end;
   end;
run;
```

To see how the nested DO loop processes these arrays, let's examine the execution of this DATA step.

When this DATA step is compiled, the program data vector is created. The PDV contains the variables Year, Month1 through Month12, and the new variables Qtr1 through Qtr4. (Only the beginning and ending portions of the program data vector are represented here.)

```
data finance.quarters(drop=i j);
   set finance.monthly;
   array m{4,3} month1-month12;
   array Qtr{4};
   do i=1 to 4;
     qtr{i}=0;
      do j=1 to 3;
         qtr{i}+m{i,j};
      end;
   end;
```

run;

N	Year	Month1	Month2	Month3		Qtr1	Qtr2	Qtr3	Qtr4	i	j
.	.	.	.	.		.	.	.	.	.	.

During the first execution of the DATA step, the values of the first observation of Finance.Monthly are read into the program data vector. When the first DO loop executes the first time, the index variable i is set to 1.

```
data finance.quarters(drop=i j);
  set finance.monthly;
  array m{4,3} month1-month12;
  array Qtr{4};
  do i=1 to 4;        i=1
   qtr{i}=0;
    do j=1 to 3;
      qtr{i}+m{i,j};
    end;
  end;
run;
```

N	Year	Month1	Month2	Month3		Qtr1	Qtr2	Qtr3	Qtr4	i	j
1	1989	23000	21500	24600		.	.	.	.	1	.

During the first iteration of the nested DO loop, the value of Month1, which is referenced by m(i,j), is added to Qtr1.

```
data finance.quarters(drop=i j);
  set finance.monthly;
  array m{4,3} month1-month12;
  array Qtr{4};
  do i=1 to 4;        i=1
   qtr{i}=0;
  > do j=1 to 3;      j=1
      qtr(1)+m(1,1);
    end;
  end;
run;
```

N	Year	Month1	Month2	Month3		Qtr1	Qtr2	Qtr3	Qtr4	i	j
1	1989	23000	21500	24600		23000	.	.	.	1	1

During the second iteration of the nested DO loop, the value of Month2, which is referenced by m (i,j), is added to Qtr1.

```
data finance.quarters(drop=i j);
  set finance.monthly;
  array m{4,3} month1-month12;
  array Qtr{4};
  do i=1 to 4;        i=1
   qtr{i}=0;
   > do j=1 to 3;      j=2
      qtr{1}+m{1,2};
   end;
  end;
run;
```

Program Data Vector

N	Year	Month1	Month2	Month3		Qtr1	Qtr2	Qtr3	Qtr4	i	j
1	1989	23000	21500	24600		44500	•	•	•	1	2

The nested DO loop continues to execute until the index variable j exceeds the stop value, **3**. When the nested DO loop completes execution, the total sales for the first quarter, Qtr1, have been computed.

```
data finance.quarters(drop=i j);
  set finance.monthly;
  array m{4,3} month1-month12;
  array Qtr{4};
  do i=1 to 4;        i=1
   qtr{i}=0;
   > do j=1 to 3;      j=3
      qtr{1}+m{1,3};
   end;
  end;
run;
```

Program Data Vector

N	Year	Month1	Month2	Month3		Qtr1	Qtr2	Qtr3	Qtr4	i	j
1	1989	23000	21500	24600		69100	•	•	•	1	4

The outer DO loop increments i to 2, and the process continues for the array element Qtr2 and the m array elements Month4 through Month6.

```
data finance.quarters(drop=i j);
  set finance.monthly;
  array m{4,3} month1-month12;
  array Qtr{4};
```

```
> do i=1 to 4;        i=2
    qtr{i}=0;
     do j=1 to 3;      j=1
       qtr{i}+m{i,j};
     end;
  end;
run;
```

Program Data Vector

N		Month2	Month3	Month4		Qtr1	Qtr2	Qtr3	Qtr4	i	j
1		21500	24600	23300		69100	23300	•	•	2	1

After the outer DO loop completes execution, the end of the DATA step is reached, and the first observation is written to the data set Finance.Quarters.

```
data finance.quarters(drop=i j);
   set finance.monthly;
   array m{4,3} month1-month12;
   array Qtr{4};
 > do i=1 to 4;        i=5 (loop ends)
     qtr{i}=0;
      do j=1 to 3;
        qtr{i}+m{i,j};
      end;
   end;
run;
```

Program Data Vector

N		Month2	Month3	Month4		Qtr1	Qtr2	Qtr3	Qtr4	i	j
1		21500	24600	23300		69100	64400	69200	71800	5	4

What you have seen so far represents the first iteration of the DATA step. All observations in the data set Finance.Monthly are processed in the same manner. Below is a portion of the resulting data set, which contains the sales figures grouped by quarters.

SAS Data Set Finance.Quarters (Partial Listing)

Year	Qtr1	Qtr2	Qtr3	Qtr4
1989	69100	64400	69200	71800
1990	73100	72000	83200	82800
1991	73400	81800	85200	87800

Overview

Introduction

To program effectively using SAS, you need to understand basic concepts about SAS programs and the SAS files that they process. In particular, you need to be familiar with SAS data sets.

In this chapter, you'll examine a simple SAS program and see how it works. You'll learn details about SAS data sets (which are files that contain data that is logically arranged in a form that SAS can understand). You'll see how SAS data sets are stored temporarily or permanently in SAS libraries. Finally, you'll learn how to use SAS windows to manage your SAS session and to process SAS programs.

SAS Library with SAS Data Sets and Data Files

Objectives

In this chapter, you learn about

the structure and components of SAS programs

the steps involved in processing SAS programs

SAS libraries and the types of SAS files that they contain

temporary and permanent SAS libraries

the structure and components of SAS data sets

the SAS windowing environment.

Chapter Summary

Text Summary

Accumulating Totals

Use a sum statement to add the result of an expression to an accumulator variable.

Initializing and Retaining Variables

You can use the RETAIN statement to assign an initial value to a variable whose value is assigned by a sum statement.

Assigning Values Conditionally

To perform an action conditionally, use an IF-THEN statement. The IF-THEN statement executes a SAS statement when the condition in the IF expression is true. You can include comparison and logical operators; logical comparisons that are enclosed in parentheses are evaluated as true or false before other expressions are evaluated. Use the ELSE statement to specify an alternative action when the condition in an IF-THEN statement is false.

Specifying Lengths for Variables

When creating a new character variable, SAS allocates as many bytes of storage space as there are characters in the first value that it encounters for that variable at compile time. This can result in truncated values. You can use the LENGTH statement to specify a length before the variable's first value is referenced in the DATA step.

Subsetting Data

To omit observations as you read data, include the DELETE statement in an IF-THEN statement. If you need to read and process variables that you don't want to keep in the data set, use the DROP= and KEEP= data set options or the DROP and KEEP statements.

Assigning Permanent Labels and Formats

You can use LABEL and FORMAT statements in DATA steps to permanently assign labels and formats. These do not affect how data is stored in the data set, only how it appears in output.

Assigning Values Conditionally Using SELECT Groups

As an alternative to IF-THEN/ELSE statements, you can use SELECT groups in DATA steps to perform conditional processing.

Grouping Statements Using DO Groups

You can execute a group of statements as a unit with DO groups in DATA steps. You can use DO groups in IF-THEN/ELSE statements and SELECT groups to perform many statements as part of the conditional action.

Syntax

LIBNAME *libref 'SAS-data-library'*;

FILENAME *fileref 'filename'*;

DATA *SAS-data-set*(**DROP**=*variable(s)*|**KEEP**=*variable(s)*);

INFILE *file-specification* <OBS=*n*>;
INPUT *variable* <$> *startcol-endcol...*;

DROP *variable(s)*;
KEEP *variable(s)*;
RETAIN *variable initial-value*;
variable+expression;
LENGTH *variable(s) <$> length*;
IF *expression***THEN** *statement*;
ELSE *statement*;
IF *expression***THEN DELETE**;
LABEL *variable1='label1' variable2='label2' ...*;
FORMAT *variable(s) format-name*;
SELECT *<(select-expression)>*;
WHEN-1 (*when-expression-1 <..., when-expression-n>*) *statement*;
WHEN-n (*when-expression-1 <..., when-expression-n>*) *statement*;
<OTHERWISEstatement;>
END;

RUN;

PROC PRINT DATA=*SAS-data set* **LABEL**;

RUN;

Sample Program

```
data clinic.stress;
   infile tests;
   input ID $ 1-4 Name $ 6-25 RestHR 27-29 MaxHR 31-33
        RecHR 35-37 TimeMin 39-40 TimeSec 42-43
        Tolerance $ 45;
   if tolerance='D'and resthr ge 70 then delete;
   drop timemin timesec;
   TotalTime=(timemin*60)+timesec;
   retain SumSec 5400;
   sumsec+totaltime;
   length TestLength $ 6;
   if totaltime>800 then testlength='Long';
   else if 750<=totaltime<=800 then testlength='Normal';
   else if totaltime<750 then TestLength='Short';
   label sumsec='Cumulative Total Seconds (+5,400)';
   format sumsec comma6.;
run;
```

Points to Remember

Like the assignment statement, the sum statement does not contain a keyword.

If the expression in a sum statement produces a missing value, the sum statement ignores it.
  (Remember, however, that assignment statements assign a missing value if the expression produces a missing value.)

Using ELSE statements with IF-THEN statements can save resources. For greater efficiency, construct your IF-THEN/ELSE statements with conditions of decreasing probability.

Make sure the LENGTH statement appears before any other reference to the variable in the DATA step. If the variable has been created by another statement, a later use of the LENGTH statement will not change its length.

Labels and formats do not affect how data is stored in the data set, only how it appears in output. You assign labels and formats temporarily in PROC steps and permanently in DATA steps.

Appending

Overview

Another way to combine SAS data sets is to append one data set to another using the APPEND procedure. Although appending and concatenating are similar, there are some important differences between the two methods. Whereas the DATA step creates an entirely new data set when concatenating, PROC APPEND simply adds the observations of one data set to the end of a "master" (or BASE) data set. SAS does not create a new data set nor does it read the base data set when executing the APPEND procedure.

To append SAS data sets, you specify a BASE= data set, which is the data set to which observations are added and then specify a DATA= data set, which is the data set containing the observations that are added to the base data set. The data set specified with DATA= is the only one of the two data sets that SAS actually reads.

General form of the APPEND procedure:

PROC APPEND *BASE=SAS-data-set*

DATA=SAS-data-set;

RUN;

where

BASE= names the data set to which observations are added

DATA= names the data set containing observations that are added to the base data set

For example, the following PROC APPEND statement appends the observations in data set B to the end of data set A:

```
proc append base=A
       data=B;
run;
```

How PROC APPEND Appends Data

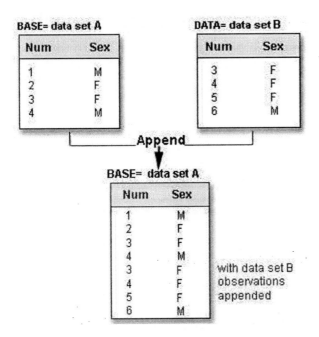

Requirements for the APPEND Procedure

The requirements for appending one data set to another are as follows:

> Only two data sets can be used at a time in one step.

> The observations in the base data set are not read.

> The variable information in the descriptor portion of the base data set cannot change.

Notice that the final data set is the original data set with appended observations and that no new data set was created.

Example

The following PROC APPEND statement appends the data set totals2011 to the base data set totals2005. The two data sets are like-structured data sets: that is, both data sets have the same variable information.

```
proc append base=totals2005 data=totals2011;
run;
```

Below is the listing of totals2005. The first 4 observations already existed in totals2005, and the last 4 observations were read from totals2011 and added to totals2005.

Example: PROC APPEND

Obs	Month	Therapy	NewAdmit	Treadmill
1	01	220	27	11
2	02	209	63	43
3	03	189	11	2
4	04	211	52	36
5	01	210	27	13
6	02	219	63	23
7	03	199	11	21
8	04	251	52	30

Using the FORCE Option with Unlike-Structured Data Sets

In order to use PROC APPEND with data sets that have unmatching variable definitions, you can use the FORCE option in the PROC APPEND statement.

General form of the APPEND procedure with the FORCE option:

PROC APPEND *BASE=SAS-data-set*

DATA=SAS-data-set FORCE;

RUN;

The FORCE option is needed when the DATA= data set contains variables that meet any one of the following criteria:

They are not in the BASE= data set.

They are variables of a different type (for example, character or numeric).

They are longer than the variables in the BASE= data set.

If the length of a variable is longer in the DATA= data set than in the BASE= data set, SAS truncates values from the DATA= data set to fit them into the length that is specified in the BASE= data set.

If the type of a variable in the DATA= data set is different than in the BASE= data set, SAS replaces all values for the variable in the DATA= data set with missing values and keeps the variable type of the variable specified in the BASE= data set.

If the BASE= data set contains a variable that is not in the DATA= data set, the observations are appended, but the observations from the DATA= data set have a missing value for the variable that was not present in the DATA= data set. If the DATA= data set contains a variable that is not in the BASE= data set, the variable is dropped from the output.

Example

For example:

```
proc append  base=sasuser.patients
          data=clinic.append force;
run;
```

Example: PROC APPEND with FORCE Option

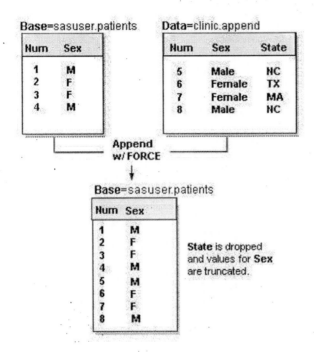

Base=sasuser.patients

Num	Sex
1	M
2	F
3	F
4	M

Data=clinic.append

Num	Sex	State
5	Male	NC
6	Female	TX
7	Female	MA
8	Male	NC

Append w/ FORCE

Base=sasuser.patients

Num	Sex
1	M
2	F
3	F
4	M
5	M
6	F
7	F
8	M

State is dropped and values for **Sex** are truncated.

Specifying Variables in PROC FREQ

Overview

By default, the FREQ procedure creates frequency tables for every variable in your data set. But this isn't always what you want. A variable that has continuous numeric values—such as DateTime—can result in a lengthy and meaningless table. Likewise, a variable that has a unique value for each observation—such as FullName—is unsuitable for PROC FREQ processing. Frequency distributions work best with variables whose values can be described as categorical, and whose values are best summarized by counts rather than by averages.

To specify the variables to be processed by the FREQ procedure, include a TABLES statement.

General form, TABLES statement:

TABLES *variable(s)*;

where *variable(s)* lists the variables to include.

Example

The order in which the variables appear in the TABLES statement determines the order in which they are listed in the PROC FREQ report.

Consider the SAS data set Finance.Loans. The variables Rate and Months are best described as categorical variables, so they are the best choices for frequency tables.

PROC PRINT Report of the Data Set Finance.Loans

Account	Amount	Rate	Months	Payment
101-1092	$22,000	10.00%	60	$467.43
101-1731	$114,000	9.50%	360	$958.57
101-1289	$10,000	10.50%	36	$325.02
101-3144	$3,500	10.50%	12	$308.52
103-1135	$8,700	10.50%	24	$403.47
103-1994	$18,500	10.00%	60	$393.07
103-2335	$5,000	10.50%	48	$128.02
103-3864	$87,500	9.50%	360	$735.75
103-3891	$30,000	9.75%	360	$257.75

```
proc freq data=finance.loans;
  tables rate months;
run;
```

Frequency Tables for Rate and Months

The FREQ Procedure

Rate	Frequency	Percent	Cumulative Frequency	Cumulative Percent
9.50%	2	22.22	2	22.22
9.75%	1	11.11	3	33.33
10.00%	2	22.22	5	55.56
10.50%	4	44.44	9	100.00

Months	Frequency	Percent	Cumulative Frequency	Cumulative Percent
12	1	11.11	1	11.11
24	1	11.11	2	22.22
36	1	11.11	3	33.33
48	1	11.11	4	44.44
60	2	22.22	6	66.67
360	3	33.33	9	100.00

In addition to listing variables separately, you can use a numbered range of variables.

```
proc freq data=perm.survey;
   tables item1-item3;
run;
```

Frequency Tables for Item1–Item3

The FREQ Procedure

Item1	Frequency	Percent	Cumulative Frequency	Cumulative Percent
2	1	25.00	1	25.00
4	2	50.00	3	75.00
5	1	25.00	4	100.00

Item2	Frequency	Percent	Cumulative Frequency	Cumulative Percent
1	1	25.00	1	25.00
3	2	50.00	3	75.00
5	1	25.00	4	100.00

Item3	Frequency	Percent	Cumulative Frequency	Cumulative Percent
4	3	75.00	3	75.00
5	1	25.00	4	100.00

Adding the NOCUM option to your TABLES statement suppresses the display of cumulative frequencies and cumulative percentages in one-way frequency tables and in list output. The syntax for the NOCUM option is shown below.

TABLES variable(s) / NOCUM;

Overview

Introduction

You've learned about creating a SAS data set from raw data. However, you might often want to create a new data set from an existing SAS data set. To create the new data set, you can read a data set using the DATA step. As you read the data set, you can use all the programming features of the DATA step to manipulate your data.

Data Set Diagram

SAS Data Set A

Num	VarA
1	A1
2	A2
3	A3

Read
↓

SAS Data Set B

Num	VarA
1	A1
2	A2
3	A3

This chapter shows you how to use the DATA step to read an existing SAS data set. When you create your new data set, you can choose variables, select observations based on one or more conditions, and assign values conditionally. You can also assign variable attributes such as formats and labels.

You can also merge, concatenate, or interleave two or more data sets. For details, see Creating SAS Data Sets from External Files and Combining SAS Data Sets.

Objectives

In this chapter, you learn to

create a new data set from an existing data set

use BY groups to process observations

read observations by observation number

stop processing when necessary

explicitly write observations to an output data set

detect the last observation in a data set

identify differences in DATA step processing for raw data and SAS data sets.

Creating HTML Output with Options

ODS HTML Statement

To create simple HTML output, you do not have to specify the ODS HTML statement. However, to create HTML output with options specified, you open the HTML destination using the ODS HTML statement.

General form, ODS HTML statement:

ODS HTML BODY=*file-specification*;

ODS HTML CLOSE;

where *file-specification* identifies the file that contains the HTML output. The specification can be

- a quoted string which contains the HTML filename (use only the filename to write the file to your current working directory location, such as **C:\Documents and Settings***username***\My Documents\My SAS Files**) Example: **ODS HTML BODY=***"myreport.html"*;

- a quoted string which contains the complete directory path and HTML filename (include the complete pathname if you want to save the HTML file to a specific location other than your working directory) Example: **ODS HTML BODY=***"c:\reportdir\myreport.html"*;

- a fileref (unquoted file shortcut) that has been assigned to an HTML file using the FILENAME statement Example: **FILENAME MYHTML** *"c:\reportdir\myreport.html"*; **ODS HTML BODY=MYHTML;**

- a SAS catalog entry in the form *entry-name*.html. Note that the catalog name is specified in the PATH= option and the *entry-name*.html value for the BODY= option is unquoted. Example: **ODS HTML PATH=***work.mycat***BODY=***myentry* **BODY=.HTML;**

🖑 **FILE**= can also be used to specify the file that contains the HTML output. FILE= is an alias for BODY=.

🖑 You can also use the **PATH**= option to explicitly specify a directory path for your file. This option will be discussed in an upcoming topic.

Example

The program below creates PROC PRINT output in an HTML file. The BODY= option specifies the file **F:\admit.html** in the Windows operating environment as the file that contains the PROC PRINT results.

```
ods html body='f:\admit.html';
proc print data=clinic.admit label;
   var sex age height weight actlevel;
   label actlevel='Activity Level';
run;
ods html close;
ods html;
```

The HTML file admit.html contains the results of all procedure steps between the ODS HTML statement and ODS HTML CLOSE statement.

HTML Output

Obs	Sex	Age	Height	Weight	Activity Level
1	M	27	72	168	HIGH
2	F	34	66	152	HIGH
3	F	31	61	123	LOW
4	F	43	63	137	MOD
5	M	51	71	158	LOW
6	M	29	76	193	HIGH
7	F	32	67	151	MOD
8	M	35	70	173	MOD
9	M	34	73	154	LOW
10	F	49	64	172	LOW
11	F	44	66	140	HIGH
12	F	28	62	118	LOW
13	M	30	69	147	MOD
14	F	40	69	163	HIGH
15	M	47	72	173	MOD
16	M	60	71	191	LOW
17	F	43	65	123	MOD
18	M	25	75	188	HIGH
19	F	22	63	139	LOW
20	F	41	67	141	HIGH
21	M	54	71	183	MOD

Viewing Your HTML Output

If you're working in the Windows environment, when you submit the program, the body file will automatically appear in the Results Viewer (using the internal browser) or your preferred Web browser, as specified in the **Results** tab of the Preferences window.

In other operating environments, you can double-click the corresponding link in the Results window to view the HTML output in your Web browser. If you don't have a Web browser in your operating environment, you can transfer the HTML files to an operating environment where you can view them.

Creating HTML Output in Enterprise Guide

When you specify a path and filename for your HTML results, SAS Enterprise Guide will allow you to download and display the HTML file. In addition, you can use Windows Explorer to locate the file that you created and then double-click it to open it in your browser.

When you submit a program, two HTML results appear in the Project window. One is the HTML output that is created by SAS Enterprise Guide ODS statements. The other uses the ODS statements from the code that you submitted and creates a temporary file labeled with the path and filename that you designated. It is similar in style to the actual HTML file that is created in the location that you specify.

You can double-click the shortcut to open the HTML results in SAS Enterprise Guide, or you can right-click the shortcut and select **Open with default-browser** to open it in a browser. To see the actual file rather than the temporary file, you can use Windows Explorer to locate the HTML file that you created and then double-click it to open it in your browser.

Creating HTML Output from Multiple Procedures

You can also use the ODS HTML statement to direct the results from multiple procedures to the same HTML file.

The program below generates HTML output for the PRINT and TABULATE procedures. The results for both procedures are saved to the file **C:\Records\data.html** in the Windows environment. A link for each output object (one for each procedure) appears in the Results window.

```
ods html body='c:\records\data.html';
proc print data=clinic.admit label;
   var id sex age height weight actlevel;
   label actlevel='Activity Level';
run;
proc tabulate data=clinic.stress2;
   var resthr maxhr rechr;
   table min mean, resthr maxhr rechr;
run;
ods html close;
```

The following is a representation of the HTML file containing the results from the program above. The results from the TABULATE procedure are appended. The results also show up in the Results window, where you can select the PRINT procedure output or the TABULATE procedure output.

HTML Output

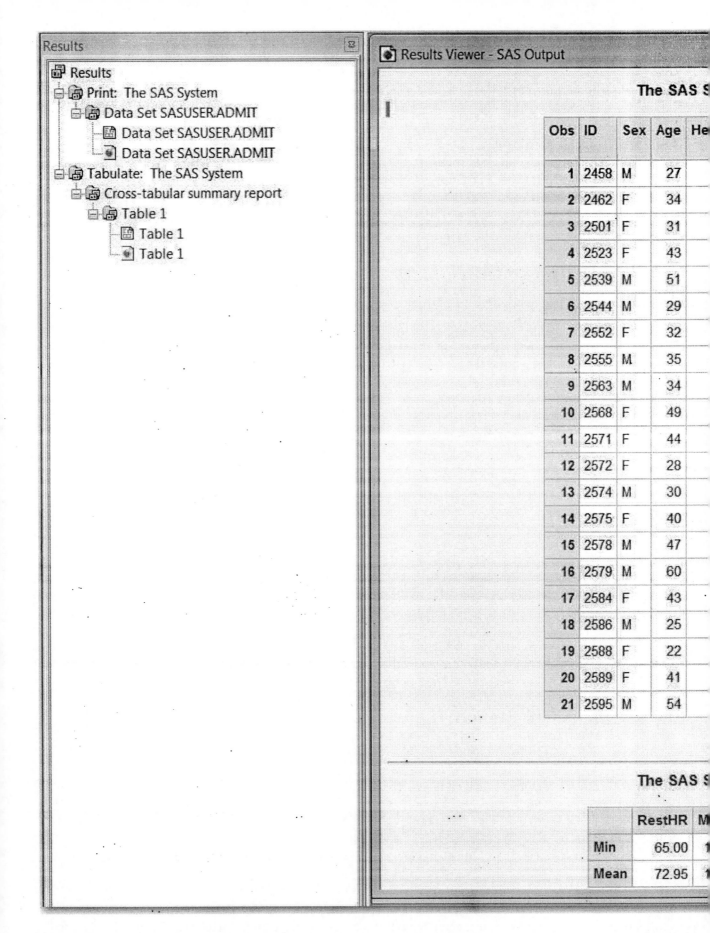

Iteratively Processing Observations from a Data Set

So far, you have seen examples of DATA steps that use DO loops to generate one or more observations from one iteration of the DATA step. Now, let's look at a DATA step that reads a data set to compute the value of a new variable.

The SAS data set Finance.CDRates, shown below, contains interest rates for certificates of deposit (CDs) that are available from several institutions.

SAS Data Set Finance.CDRates

Institution	Rate	Years
MBNA America	0.0817	5
Metropolitan Bank	0.0814	3
Standard Pacific	0.0806	4

Suppose you want to compare how much each CD will earn at maturity with an investment of $5,000. The DATA step below creates a new data set, Work.Compare, that contains the added variable, Investment.

```
data work.compare(drop=i);
   set finance.cdrates;
   Investment=5000;
   do i=1 to years;
      investment+rate*investment;
   end;
run;
```

SAS Data Set Work.Compare

Institution	Rate	Years	Investment

The index variable is used only to execute the DO loop, so it is dropped from the new data set. Notice that the data set variable Years is used as the stop value in the iterative DO statement. As a result, the DO loop executes the number of times specified by the current value of Years.

During each iteration of the DATA step,

an observation is read from Finance.CDRates

the value **5000** is assigned to the variable Investment

the DO loop executes, based on the current value of Years

the value of Investment is incremented (each time that the DO loop executes), using the current value of Rate.

At the bottom of the DATA step, the first observation is written to the Work.Compare data set. Control returns to the top of the DATA step, and the next observation is read from Finance.CDRates. These steps are repeated for each observation in Finance.CDRates. The resulting data set contains the computed values of Investment for all observations that have been read from Finance.CDRates.

SAS Data Set Work.Compare

Institution	Rate	Years	Investment
MBNA America	0.0817	5	7404.64
Metropolitan Bank	0.0814	3	6323.09
Standard Pacific	0.0806	4	6817.57

Reading the Same Number of Repeating Fields

Overview

So far, you have created multiple observations from a single record by executing the DATA step once for each block of data in a record.

Now, look at another file that is organized differently.

Each record in the file Data97 contains a sales representative's ID number, followed by four repeating fields that represent his or her quarterly sales totals for 1997.

You want to pair each employee ID number with one quarterly sales total to produce a single observation. Four observations are generated from each record.

Multiple Fields for the Same ID

Raw Data File Data97

```
1---+-----10---+----20---+----30---+----40
0734 1,323.34 2,472.85 3,276.65 5,345.52
0943 1,908.34 2,560.38 3,472.09 5,290.86
1009 2,934.12 3,308.41 4,176.18 7,581.81
1043 1,295.38 5,980.28 8,876.84 6,345.94
1190 2,189.84 5,023.57 2,794.67 4,243.35
1382 3,456.34 2,065.83 3,139.08 6,503.49
1734 2,345.83 3,423.32 1,034.43 1,942.28
```

ID	Quarter	Sales
0734	1	1323.34
0734	2	2472.85
0734	3	3276.65
0734	4	5345.52
0943	1	1908.34
0943	2	2560.38
0943	3	3472.09
0943	4	5290.86

To accomplish this, you must execute the DATA step once for each record, repetitively reading and writing values in one iteration.

This means that a DATA step must

read the value for ID and hold the current record

create a new variable named Quarter to identify the fiscal quarter for each sales figure

read a new value for Sales and write the values to the data set as an observation

continue reading a new value for Sales and writing values to the data set three more times.

Using the Single Trailing At Sign (@) to Hold the Current Record

First, you need to read the value for ID and hold the record so that subsequent values for Sales can be read.

data perm.sales97;
  infile data97;
  input ID $

Holding a Record

```
                    Raw Data File Data97
1---V----10---+----20---+----30---+----40
0734 1,323.34 2,472.85 3,276.65 5,345.52
0943 1,908.34 2,560.38 3,472.09 5,290.86
1009 2,934.12 3,308.41 4,176.18 7,581.81
```

You are already familiar with the trailing @@, which holds the current record across multiple iterations of the DATA step.

However, in this case, you want to hold the record with the trailing @, so that a second INPUT statement can read the multiple sales values from a single record within the same iteration of the DATA step. Like the trailing @@, the single trailing @

enables the next INPUT statement to continue reading from the same record

releases the current record when a subsequent INPUT statement executes without a line-hold specifier.

It's easy to distinguish between the trailing @@ and the trailing @ by remembering that

the double trailing at sign (@@) holds a record across multiple iterations of the DATA step until the end of the record is reached.

the single trailing at sign (@) releases a record when control returns to the top of the DATA step.

In this example, the first INPUT statement reads the value for ID and uses the trailing @ to hold the current record for the next INPUT statement in the DATA step.

```
data perm.sales97;
  infile data97;
  input ID $ @;
  input Sales : comma. @;
output;
```

Reading the Value for ID

```
                    Raw Data File Data97
1---V----10---+----20---+----30---+----40
0734 1,323.34 2,472.85 3,276.65 5,345.52
0943 1,908.34 2,560.38 3,472.09 5,290.86
1009 2,934.12 3,308.41 4,176.18 7,581.81
```

The second INPUT statement reads a value for Sales and holds the record. The COMMAw.d informat in the INPUT statement reads the numeric value for Sales and removes the embedded commas. An OUTPUT statement writes the observation to the SAS data set, and the DATA step continues processing.

🖐 Notice that the COMMAw.d informat does *not* specify a w value. Remember that list input reads values until the next blank is detected. The default length of numeric variables is 8 bytes, so you don't need to specify a w value to determine the length of a numeric variable.

When all of the repeating fields have been read and output, control returns to the top of the DATA step, and the record is released.

```
data perm.sales97;
   infile data97;
   input ID $ @;
   input Sales : comma. @;
   output;
   input Sales : comma. @;
   output;
   input Sales : comma. @;
   output;
   input Sales : comma. @;
   output;
run;
```

Reading the Value for Sales

```
              Raw Data File Data97
1---+----10--V+--,--20---+----30---,-+----40
0734 1,323.34 2,472.85 3,276.65 5,345.52
0943 1,908.34 2,560.38 3,472.09 5,290.86
1009 2,934.12 3,308.41 4,176.18 7,581.81
```

More Efficient Programming

Each record contains four different values for the variable Sales, so the INPUT statement must execute four times. Rather than writing four INPUT statements, you can execute one INPUT statement repeatedly in an iterative DO loop.

Each time the loop executes, you need to write the values for ID, Quarter, and Sales as an observation to the data set. This is easily accomplished by using the OUTPUT statement.

```
data perm.sales97;
   infile data97;
   input ID $ @;
   do Quarter=1 to 4;
      input Sales : comma. @;
      output;
   end;
run;
```

By default, every DATA step contains an implicit OUTPUT statement at the end of the step. Placing an explicit OUTPUT statement in a DATA step overrides the automatic output, and SAS adds an observation to a data set only when the explicit OUTPUT statement is executed.

Processing a DATA Step That Contains an Iterative DO Loop

Now that the program is complete, let's see how SAS processes a DATA step that contains an iterative DO loop.

```
data perm.sales97;
   infile data97;
   input ID $ @;
   do Quarter=1 to 4;
      input Sales : comma. @;
      output;
   end;
run;
```

During the first iteration, the value for ID is read and Quarter is initialized to **1** as the loop begins to execute.

Reading the Value for ID and Initializing Quarter

Raw Data File Data97

```
>----V----10---+----20---+----30---+----40-
 0734 1,323.34 2,472.85 3,276.65 5,345.52
 0943 1,908.34 2,560.38 3,472.09 5,290.86
 1009 2,934.12 3,308.41 4,176.18 7,581.81
```

Program Data Vector

N	ID	Quarter	Sales
1	0734	1	.

The INPUT statement reads the first repeating field and assigns the value to Sales in the program data vector. The @ holds the current record.

Results of the INPUT Statement

Raw Data File Data97

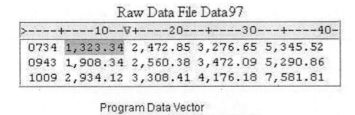

```
>----+----10--V+----20---+----30---+----40-
 0734 1,323.34 2,472.85 3,276.65 5,345.52
 0943 1,908.34 2,560.38 3,472.09 5,290.86
 1009 2,934.12 3,308.41 4,176.18 7,581.81
```

Program Data Vector

N	ID	Quarter	Sales
1	0734	1	1323.34

The OUTPUT statement writes the values in the program data vector to the data set as the first observation.

Results of the OUTPUT Statement

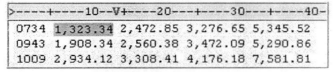

Raw Data File Data97

```
>----+----10--V+----20---+----30---+----40-
 0734 1,323.34 2,472.85 3,276.65 5,345.52
 0943 1,908.34 2,560.38 3,472.09 5,290.86
 1009 2,934.12 3,308.41 4,176.18 7,581.81
```

Program Data Vector

N	ID	Quarter	Sales
1	0734	1	1323.34

SAS Data Set Perm.Sales97

ID	Quarter	Sales
1 0734	1	1323.34

The END statement indicates the bottom of the loop, but control returns to the DO statement, not to the top of the DATA step. Now the value of Quarter is incremented to **2**.

Results of the END Statement

Raw Data File Data97

```
>----+----10---V----20---+----30---+----40-
 0734 1,323.34 2,472.85 3,276.65 5,345.52
 0943 1,908.34.2,560.38 3,472.09 5,290.86
 1009 2,934.12 3,308.41 4,176.18 7,581.81
```

Program Data Vector

N	ID	Quarter	Sales
1	0734	2	1323.34

SAS Data Set Perm.Sales97

ID	Quarter	Sales
1 0734	1	1323.34

The INPUT statement executes again, reading the second repeating field and storing the value for Sales in the program data vector.

Results of the Second Reading of the INPUT Statement

Raw Data File Data97

```
>----+----10---+----20-V-+----30---+----40-
 0734 1,323.34 2,472.85 3,276.65 5,345.52
 0943 1,908.34 2,560.38 3,472.09 5,290.86
 1009 2,934.12 3,308.41 4,176.18 7,581.81
```

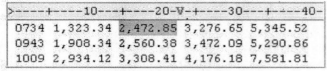

Program Data Vector

N	ID	Quarter	Sales
1	0734	2	2472.85

SAS Data Set Perm.Sales97

·ID	Quarter	Sales
1 0734	1	1323.34

The OUTPUT statement writes the values in the program data vector as the second observation.

Results of the Second Reading of the OUTPUT Statement

Raw Data File Data97

```
>----+----10---+----20-V-+----30---+----40-
 0734 1,323.34 2,472.85 3,276.65 5,345.52
 0943 1,908.34 2,560.38 3,472.09 5,290.86
 1009 2,934.12 3,308.41 4,176.18 7,581.81
```

Program Data Vector

N	ID	Quarter	Sales
1	0734	2	2472.85

SAS Data Set Perm.Sales97

	ID	Quarter	Sales
1	0734	1	1323.34
2	0734	2	2472.85

The loop continues executing while the value for Quarter is **3**, and then **4**. In the process, the third and fourth observations are written.

Writing the Third and Fourth Observations

Raw Data File Data97

```
>----+----10---+----20---+----30---+----4V-
 0734 1,323.34 2,472.85 3,276.65 5,345.52
 0943 1,908.34 2,560.38 3,472.09 5,290.86
 1009 2,934.12 3,308.41 4,176.18 7,581.81
```

Program Data Vector

N	ID	Quarter	Sales
1	0734	4	5345.52

SAS Data Set Perm.Sales97

	ID	Quarter	Sales
1	0734	1	1323.34
2	0734	2	2472.85
3	0734	3	3276.65
4	0734	4	5345.52

After the fourth observation is written, Quarter is incremented to **5** at the bottom of the DO loop and control returns to the top of the loop. The loop does not execute again because the value of Quarter is now greater than **4**.

Raw Data File Data97

```
>----+----10---+----20---+----30---+----4V-
 0734 1,323.34 2,472.85 3,276.65 5,345.52
 0943 1,908.34 2,560.38 3,472.09 5,290.86
 1009 2,934.12 3,308.41 4,176.18 7,581.81
```

Program Data Vector

N	ID	Quarter	Sales
1	0734	5	5345.52

SAS Data Set Perm.Sales97

	ID	Quarter	Sales
1	0734	1	1323.34
2	0734	2	2472.85
3	0734	3	3276.65
4	0734	4	5345.52

Control returns to the top of the DATA step, and the input pointer moves to column 1 of the next record. The variable values in the program data vector are reset to missing.

Returning Control to the Top of the DATA Step

Raw Data File Data97

```
>V---+----10---+----20---+----30---+----40-
 0734 1,323.34 2,472.85 3,276.65 5,345.52
 0943 1,908.34 2,560.38 3,472.09 5,290.86
 1009 2,934.12 3,308.41 4,176.18 7,581.81
```

Program Data Vector

N	ID	Quarter	Sales
2	.	.	.

SAS Data Set Perm.Sales97

	ID	Quarter	Sales
1	0734	1	1323.34
2	0734	2	2472.85
3	0734	3	3276.65
4	0734	4	5345.52

When the execution phase is complete, you can display the data set with the PRINT procedure.

```
proc print data=perm.sales97;
run;
```

Output of PROC PRINT

Obs	ID	Quarter	Sales
1	0734	1	1323.34
2	0734	2	2472.85
3	0734	3	3276.65
4	0734	4	5345.52
5	0943	1	1908.34
6	0943	2	2560.38
7	0943	3	3472.09
8	0943	4	5290.86
9	1009	1	2934.12
10	1009	2	3308.41
11	1009	3	4176.18
12	1009	4	7581.81

Creating Free-Format Data

Overview

Creating SAS Data Sets from External Files explained how the PUT statement can be used with column output to write observations from a SAS data set to a raw data file. The PUT statement can also be used with list output to create free-format raw data files.

List output is similar to list input. With list output, you simply list the names of the variables whose values you want to write. The PUT statement writes a value, leaves a blank, and then writes the next value.

General form, PUT statement using list output:

PUT *variable <: format>*;

where

variable specifies the variable whose value you want to write

: precedes a format

format specifies a format to use for writing the data values.

The following program creates the raw data file Findat, using the SAS data set sasuser.Finance. The DATE*w.* format is used to write the value of Date in the form *DDMMYYYY*.

```
data _null_;
   set sasuser.finance;
   file 'c:\data\findat.txt';
   put ssn name salary date : date9.;
run;
```

SAS Data Set Finance

SAS Data Set Finance

SSN	Name	Salary	Date
074-53-9892	Vincent	35000	05/22/97
776-84-5391	Phillipon	29750	12/15/96
929-75-0218	Gunter	27500	04/30/97
446-93-2122	Harbinger	33900	07/08/96
228-88-9649	Benito	28000	03/04/96
029-46-9261	Rudelich	35000	02/15/95
442-21-8075	Sirignano	5000	11/22/95

Raw Data File Findat

Raw Data File Findat

```
1---+----10---+----20---+----30---+----40
074-53-9892 Vincent 35000 22MAY1997
776-84-5391 Phillipon 29750 15DEC1996
929-75-0218 Gunter 27500 30APR1997
446-93-2122 Harbinger 33900 08JUL1996
228-88-9649 Benito 28000 04MAR1996
029-46-9261 Rudelich 35000 15FEB1995
442-21-8075 Sirignano 5000 22NOV1995
```

Specifying a Delimiter

You can use the DLM= option with a FILE statement to create a character-delimited raw data file.

```
data _null_;
   set sasuser.finance;
   file 'c:\data\findat2' dlm=',';
   put ssn name salary date : date9.;
run;
```

SAS Data Set Finance

SAS Data Set Finance

SSN	Name	Salary	Date
074-53-9892	Vincent	35000	05/22/97
776-84-5391	Phillipon	29750	12/15/96
929-75-0218	Gunter	27500	04/30/97
446-93-2122	Harbinger	33900	07/08/96
228-88-9649	Benito	28000	03/04/96
029-46-9261	Rudelich	35000	02/15/95
442-21-8075	Sirignano	5000	11/22/95

Raw Data File Created by the DLM= Option

```
Raw Data File Findat2
1---+----10---+----20---+----30---+----40
074-53-9892,Vincent,35000,22MAY1997
776-84-5391,Phillipon,29750,15DEC1996
929-75-0218,Gunter,27500,30APR1997
446-93-2122,Harbinger,33900,08JUL1996
228-88-9649,Benito,28000,04MAR1996
029-46-9261,Rudelich,35000,15FEB1995
442-21-8075,Sirignano,5000,22NOV1995
```

For creating a simple raw data file, an alternative to the DATA step is the EXPORT procedure.

General form, PROC EXPORT:

PROC EXPORT DATA=*SAS-data-set*;

OUTFILE=*filename* <DELIMITER=*'delimiter'*>;

RUN;

where

   SAS-data-set names the input SAS data set

   filename specifies the complete path and filename of the output

   delimiter specifies the delimiter to separate columns of data in the output file.

For more information about the EXPORT procedure, see the SAS documentation.

Using the DSD Option

What happens if you need to create a comma-delimited file that requires the use of a format that writes out values using commas?

If you used the following program, the resulting raw data file would contain five fields rather than four.

```
data _null_;
   set sasuser.finance;
   file 'c:\data\findat2' dlm=',';
   put ssn name salary : comma6. date : date9.;
run;
```

SAS Data Set Finance

SAS Data Set Finance

SSN	Name	Salary	Date
074-53-9892	Vincent	35000	05/22/97
776-84-5391	Phillipon	29750	12/15/96
929-75-0218	Gunter	27500	04/30/97
446-93-2122	Harbinger	33900	07/08/96
228-88-9649	Benito	28000	03/04/96
029-46-9261	Rudelich	35000	02/15/95
442-21-8075	Sirignano	5000	11/22/95

Raw Data Created with the DLM Option

Raw Data File Findat2

```
1---+----10---+----20---+----30---+----40
074-53-9892,Vincent,35,000,22MAY1997
776-84-5391,Phillipon,29,750,15DEC1996
929-75-0218,Gunter,27,500,30APR1997
446-93-2122,Harbinger,33,900,08JUL1996
228-88-9649,Benito,28,000,04MAR1996
029-46-9261,Rudelich,35,000,15FEB1995
442-21-8075,Sirignano,5,000,22NOV1995
```

You can use the DSD option in the FILE statement to specify that data values containing commas should be enclosed in quotation marks. Remember that the DSD option uses a comma as a delimiter, so a DLM= option isn't necessary here.

```
data _null_;
   set sasuser.finance;
   file 'c:\data\findat2' dsd;
   put ssn name salary : comma. date : date9.;
run;
```

Raw Data Created with the DSD Option

```
                    Raw Data File Findat2
1---+----10---+----20---+----30---+----40
074-53-9892,Vincent,"35,000",22MAY1997
776-84-5391,Phillipon,"29,750",15DEC1996
929-75-0218,Gunter,"27,500",30APR1997
446-93-2122,Harbinger,"33,900",08JUL1996
228-88-9649,Benito,"28,000",04MAR1996
029-46-9261,Rudelich,"35,000",15FEB1995
442-21-8075,Sirignano,"5,000",22NOV1995
```

Reading Values That Contain Delimiters within a Quoted String

You can also use the DSD option in an INFILE statement to read values that contain delimiters within a quoted string. As shown in the following PROC PRINT output, the INPUT statement correctly interprets the commas within the values for Salary, does not interpret them as delimiters, and removes the quotation marks from the character strings before the value is stored.

```
data work.finance2;
   infile findat2 dsd;
   length SSN $ 11 Name $ 9;
   input ssn name Salary : comma. Date : date9.;
run;
proc print data=work.finance2;
   format date date9.;
run;
```

Raw Data File Findat2

```
                    Raw Data File Findat2
1---+----10---+----20---+----30---+----40
074-53-9892,Vincent,"35,000",22MAY1997
776-84-5391,Phillipon,"29,750",15DEC1996
929-75-0218,Gunter,"27,500",30APR1997
446-93-2122,Harbinger,"33,900",08JUL1996
228-88-9649,Benito,"28,000",04MAR1996
029-46-9261,Rudelich,"35,000",15FEB1995
442-21-8075,Sirignano,"5,000",22NOV1995
```

Output Created with PROC PRINT

Obs	SSN	Name	Salary	Date
1	074-53-9892	Vincent	35000	22MAY1997
2	776-84-5391	Phillipon	29750	15DEC1996
3	929-75-0218	Gunter	27500	30APR1997
4	446-93-2122	Harbinger	33900	08JUL1996
5	228-88-9649	Benito	28000	04MAR1996
6	029-46-9261	Rudelich	35000	15FEB1995
7	442-21-8075	Sirignano	5000	22NOV1995

Additional Features

When you set up your SAS session, you can set SAS system options that affect LISTING output, information written to the SAS log, and much more. Here are some additional system options that you are likely to use with SAS:

Selected System Options and Their Descriptions

FORMCHAR= *'formatting-characters'*	specifies the formatting characters for your output device. Formatting characters are used to construct the outlines of tables as well as dividers for various procedures, such as the FREQ and TABULATE procedures. If you do not specify formatting characters as an option in the procedure, then the default specifications given in the FORMCHAR= system option are used.
FORMDLIM= *'delimit-character'*	specifies a character that is used to delimit page breaks in SAS System output. Normally, the delimit character is null. When the delimit character is null, a new physical page starts whenever a page break occurs.
LABEL|NOLABEL	permits SAS procedures to temporarily replace variable names with descriptive labels. The LABEL system option must be in effect before the LABEL option of any procedure can be used. If NOLABEL is specified, then the LABEL option of a procedure is ignored. The default setting is LABEL.
REPLACE|NOREPLACE	specifies whether permanently stored SAS data sets are replaced. If you specify NOREPLACE, a permanently stored SAS data set cannot be replaced with one that has the same name. This prevents you from inadvertently replacing existing SAS data sets. The default setting is REPLACE.

SOURCE|NOSOURCE   controls whether SAS source statements are written to the SAS log. NOSOURCE specifies not to write SAS source statements to the SAS log. The default setting is SOURCE.

You can also use programming statements to control the result format of each item of procedure output individually. For more information, see Producing HTML Output .

Chapter 7: Creating and Applying User-Defined Formats

If you don't specify the LIBRARY= option on the PROC FORMAT statement, your formats are stored in Work.Formats, and they exist ...

only for the current procedure.

only for the current DATA step.

only for the current SAS session.

permanently.

Correct answer: c

If you do not specify the LIBRARY= option, formats are stored in a default format catalog named Work.Formats. As the libref Work implies, any format that is stored in Work.Formats is a temporary format that exists only for the current SAS session.

Which of the following statements will store your formats in a permanent catalog?

```
libname library 'c:\sas\formats\lib';
proc format lib=library
   ...;
```

```
libname library 'c:\sas\formats\lib';
format lib=library
   ...;
```

```
library='c:\sas\formats\lib';
proc format library
   ...;
```

```
library='c:\sas\formats\lib';
proc library
```

...;

Correct answer: a

To store formats in a permanent catalog, you first write a LIBNAME statement to associate the libref with the SAS data library in which the catalog will be stored. Then add the LIB= (or LIBRARY=) option to the PROC FORMAT statement, specifying the name of the catalog.

When creating a format with the VALUE statement, the new format's name

cannot end with a number

cannot end with a period

cannot be the name of a SAS format, and...

cannot be the name of a data set variable.

must be at least two characters long.

must be at least eight characters long.

must begin with a dollar sign ($) if used with a character variable.

Correct answer: d

The name of a format that is created with a VALUE statement must begin with a dollar sign ($) if it applies to a character variable.

Which of the following FORMAT procedures is written correctly?

```
proc format lib=library
  value colorfmt;
      1='Red'
      2='Green'
      3='Blue'
  run;
```

```
proc format lib=library;
  value colorfmt
      1='Red'
      2='Green'
      3='Blue';
  run;
```

```
proc format lib=library;
  value colorfmt;
```

```
                1='Red'
                2='Green'
                3='Blue'
        run;



        proc format lib=library;
           value colorfmt
                1='Red';
                2='Green';
                3='Blue';
        run;
```

Correct answer: b

A semicolon is needed after the PROC FORMAT statement. The VALUE statement begins with
the keyword VALUE and ends with a semicolon after all the labels have been defined.

Which of these is *false*? Ranges in the VALUE statement can specify...

a single value, such as **24** or **'S'**.

a range of numeric values, such as **0-1500**.

a range of character values, such as **'A'-'M'**.

a list of numeric and character values separated by commas, such as **90,'B',180,'D',270**.

Correct answer: d

You can list values separated by commas, but the list must contain either all numeric values or all
character values. Data set variables are either numeric or character.

How many characters can be used in a label?

40

96

200

256

Correct answer: d

When specifying a label, enclose it in quotation marks and limit the label to 256 characters.

Which keyword can be used to label missing numeric values as well as any values that are not
specified in a range?

LOW

MISS

MISSING

OTHER

Correct answer: d

MISS and MISSING are invalid keywords, and LOW does not include missing numeric values. The keyword OTHER can be used in the VALUE statement to label missing values as well as any values that are not specifically included in a range.

You can place the FORMAT statement in either a DATA step or a PROC step. What happens when you place it in a DATA step?

    You temporarily associate the formats with variables.

    You permanently associate the formats with variables.

    You replace the original data with the format labels.

    You make the formats available to other data sets.

Correct answer: b

By placing the FORMAT statement in a DATA step, you permanently associate the defined format with variables.

The format JOBFMT was created in a FORMAT procedure. Which FORMAT statement will apply it to the variable JobTitle in the program output?

    format jobtitle jobfmt;

    format jobtitle jobfmt.;

    format jobtitle=jobfmt;

    format jobtitle='jobfmt';

Correct answer: b

To associate a user-defined format with a variable, place a period at the end of the format name when it is used in the FORMAT statement.

Which keyword, when added to the PROC FORMAT statement, will display all the formats in your catalog?

    CATALOG

    LISTFMT

    FMTCAT

    FMTLIB

Correct answer: d

Adding the keyword FMTLIB to the PROC FORMAT statement displays a list of all the formats in your catalog, along with descriptions of their values.

Opening and Closing ODS Destinations

ODS Destinations

You use ODS statements to specify destinations for your output. Each destination creates a specific type of formatted output. The table below lists some of the ODS destinations that are currently supported.

This destination . . .	Produces . . .
HTML	output that is formatted in Hypertext Markup Language (HTML). This is the default destination. You do not have to specify the ODS HTML statement to produce basic HTML output.
LISTING	plain text output that is formatted like traditional SAS procedure (LISTING) output
Markup Languages Family	output that is formatted using markup languages such as Extensible Markup Language (XML)
Document	a hierarchy of output objects that enables you to render multiple ODS output without rerunning procedures
Output	SAS data sets
Printer Family	output that is formatted for a high-resolution printer such as PostScript (PS),

RTF   Rich Text Format output for use with Word

In this chapter, we'll primarily work with the LISTING destination and the HTML destination. For information about all ODS destinations, please see the SAS documentation for the Output Delivery System.

Using Statements to Open and Close ODS Destinations

For each type of formatted output that you want to create, you use an ODS statement to open the destination. At the end of your program, you use another ODS statement to close the destination so that you can access your output.

General form, ODS statement to open and close destinations:

ODS *open-destination*;

ODS *close-destination* **CLOSE;**

where

open-destination is a keyword and any required options for the type of output that you want to create, such as

HTML FILE='*html-file-pathname*'

LISTING

close-destination is a keyword for the type of output.

You can issue ODS statements in any order, depending on whether you need to open or close the destination. Most ODS destinations are closed by default. You open them at the beginning of your program and close them at the end. The exception is the HTML destination, which is open by default.

Default ODS Destination

Example

The following program creates HTML output because the HTML destination is open by default. No other ODS destinations are open, so no other output objects are produced.

```
proc print data=sasuser.mydata;
run;
```

The following program produces HTML and LISTING output:

```
ods listing;
proc print data=sasuser.mydata;
run;
ods listing close;
```

This example is meant to demonstrate how you open and close ODS destinations. You learn the specifics of creating HTML output later in this chapter.

Closing the HTML Destination

As you have learned, the HTML destination is open by default. Because open destinations use system resources, it is a good idea to close the HTML destination at the beginning of your program if you don't want to produce HTML output. For example:

```
ods html close;
```

The HTML destination remains closed until you end your current SAS session or until you re-open the destination. It's a good programming practice to reset ODS to HTML output (the default setting) at the end of your programs. For example:

```
ods html;
```

Example

The following program produces only LISTING output:

```
ods html close;
ods listing;
proc print data=sasuser.mydata;
run;
ods listing close;
ods html;
```

Closing Multiple ODS Destinations at Once

You can produce output in multiple formats at once by opening each ODS destination at the beginning of the program.

When you have more than one open ODS destination, you can use the keyword _ALL_ in the ODS CLOSE statement to close all open destinations at once.

Example

The program below opens the RTF and PDF destinations before the PROC step and closes all ODS destinations at the end of the program:

```
ods rtf file='RTF-file-pathname';
ods pdf file='PDF-file-pathname';

proc print data=sasuser.admit;
run;

ods _all_ close;
ods html;
```

Notice that the last ODS statement reopens the HTML destination so that ODS returns to producing HTML output for subsequent DATA or PROC steps in the current session.

Now that you have learned how to open and close ODS destinations, let's look at creating HTML output with options.

Chapter 4: Creating List Reports

Which PROC PRINT step below creates the following output

XisError: altImageDescription Element Should Not Be Blank.

Date	On	Changed	Flight
04MAR99	232	18	219
05MAR99	160	4	219
06MAR99	163	14	219
07MAR99	241	9	219
08MAR99	183	11	219
09MAR99	211	18	219
10MAR99	167	7	219

```
proc print data=flights.laguardia noobs;
  var on changed flight;
  where on>=160;
run;
```

```
proc print data=flights.laguardia;
  var date on changed flight;
  where changed>3;
run;
```

```
proc print data=flights.laguardia label;
  id date;
  var boarded transferred flight;
  label boarded='On' transferred='Changed';
  where flight='219';
run;
```

```
proc print flights.laguardia noobs;
  id date;
  var date on changed flight;
  where flight='219';
run;
```

Correct answer: c

The DATA= option specifies the data set that you are listing, and the ID statement replaces the Obs column with the specified variable. The VAR statement specifies variables and controls the order in which they appear, and the WHERE statement selects rows based on a condition. The LABEL option in the PROC PRINT statement causes the labels specified in the LABEL statement to be displayed.

Which of the following PROC PRINT steps is correct if labels are not stored with the data set?

```
proc print data=allsales.totals label;
  label region8='Region 8 Yearly Totals';
run;
```

```
proc print data=allsales.totals;
  label region8='Region 8 Yearly Totals';
run;
```

```
proc print data allsales.totals label noobs;
run;
```

```
proc print allsales.totals label;
run;
```

Correct answer: a

You use the DATA= option to specify the data set to be printed. The LABEL option specifies that variable labels appear in output instead of variable names.

Which of the following statements selects from a data set only those observations for which the value of the variable Style is **RANCH**, **SPLIT**, or **TWOSTORY**?

```
where style='RANCH' or 'SPLIT' or 'TWOSTORY';
```

```
where style in 'RANCH' or 'SPLIT' or 'TWOSTORY';
```

```
where style in (RANCH, SPLIT, TWOSTORY);
```

```
where style in ('RANCH','SPLIT','TWOSTORY');
```

Correct answer: d

In the WHERE statement, the IN operator enables you to select observations based on several values. You specify values in parentheses and separated by spaces or commas. Character values must be enclosed in quotation marks and must be in the same case as in the data set.

If you want to sort your data and create a temporary data set named Calc to store the sorted data, which of the following steps should you submit?

```
proc sort data=work.calc out=finance.dividend;
run;
```

```
proc sort dividend out=calc;
  by account;
run;
```

```
proc sort data=finance.dividend out=work.calc;
   by account;
run;
```

```
proc sort from finance.dividend to calc;
   by account;
run;
```

Correct answer: c

In a PROC SORT step, you specify the DATA= option to specify the data set to sort. The OUT= option specifies an output data set. The required BY statement specifies the variable(s) to use in sorting the data.

Which options are used to create the following PROC PRINT output?

XisError: altImageDescription Element Should Not Be Blank.

```
                            13:27 Monday, March 22, 1999

   Patient      Arterial      Heart      Cardiac      Urinary

     203           88           95          66          110

      54           83          183          95            0

     664           72          111         332           12

     210           74           97         369            0

     101           80          130         291            0
```

the DATE system option and the LABEL option in PROC PRINT

the DATE and NONUMBER system options and the DOUBLE and NOOBS options in PROC PRINT

the DATE and NONUMBER system options and the DOUBLE option in PROC PRINT

the DATE and NONUMBER system options and the NOOBS option in PROC PRINT

Correct answer: b

The DATE and NONUMBER system options cause the output to appear with the date but without page numbers. In the PROC PRINT step, the DOUBLE option specifies double spacing, and the NOOBS option removes the default Obs column.

Which of the following statements can you use in a PROC PRINT step to create this output?

XisError: altImageDescription Element Should Not Be Blank.

Month	Instructors	AerClass	WalkJogRun	Swim
01	1	37	91	83
02	2	41	102	27
03	1	52	98	19
04	1	61	118	22
05	3	49	88	29
	8	240	497	180

```
var month instructors;
sum instructors aerclass walkjogrun swim;
```

```
var month;
sum instructors aerclass walkjogrun swim;
```

```
var month instructors aerclass;
sum instructors aerclass walkjogrun swim;
```

all of the above

Correct answer: d

You do not need to name the variables in a VAR statement if you specify them in the SUM statement, but you can. If you choose not to name the variables in the VAR statement as well, then the SUM statement determines their order in the output.

What happens if you submit the following program?

```
proc sort data=clinic.diabetes;
run;
proc print data=clinic.diabetes;
   var age height weight pulse;
   where sex='F';
```

The PROC PRINT step runs successfully, printing observations in their sorted order.

The PROC SORT step permanently sorts the input data set.

The PROC SORT step generates errors and stops processing, but the PROC PRINT step runs successfully, printing observations in their original (unsorted) order.

The PROC SORT step runs successfully, but the PROC PRINT step generates errors and stops processing.

Correct answer: c

The BY statement is required in PROC SORT. Without it, the PROC SORT step fails. However, the PROC PRINT step prints the original data set as requested.

If you submit the following program, which output does it create?

```
proc sort data=finance.loans out=work.loans;
  by months amount;
run;
proc print data=work.loans noobs;
  var months;
  sum amount payment;
  where months<360;
run;
```

XisError: altImageDescription Element Should Not Be Blank.

Months	Amount	Payment
12	$3,500	$308.52
24	$8,700	$403.47
36	$10,000	$325.02
48	$5,000	$128.02
	$27,200	$1,165.03

XisError: altImageDescription Element Should Not Be Blank.

Months	Amount	Payment
12	$3,500	$308.52
24	$8,700	$403.47
36	$10,000	$325.02
48	$5,000	$128.02
	27,200	1,165.03

XisError: altImageDescription Element Should Not Be Blank.

Months	Amount	Payment
12	$3,500	$308.52
48	$5,000	$128.02
24	$8,700	$403.47
36	$10,000	$325.02
	$27,200	$1,165.03

XisError: altImageDescription Element Should Not Be Blank.

Months	Amount	Payment
12	$3,500	$308.52
24	$8,700	$403.47
36	$10,000	$325.02
48	$5,000	$128.02
		$1,165.03

Correct answer: a

Column totals appear at the end of the report in the same format as the values of the variables, so b is incorrect. Work.Loans is sorted by Month and Amount, so c is incorrect. The program sums both Amount and Payment, so d is incorrect.

Choose the statement below that selects rows in which

the amount is less than or equal to $5000

the account is 101-1092 or the rate equals 0.095.

where amount <= 5000 and

account='101-1092' or rate = 0.095;

where (amount le 5000 and account='101-1092')
    or rate = 0.095;

where amount <= 5000 and
    (account='101-1092' or rate eq 0.095);

where amount <= 5000 or account='101-1092'
    and rate = 0.095;

Correct answer: c

To ensure that the compound expression is evaluated correctly, you can use parentheses to group

account='101-1092' or rate eq 0.095

XisError: altImageDescription Element Should Not Be Blank.

OBS	Account	Amount	Rate	Months	Payment
1	101-1092	$22,000	10.00%	60	$467.43
2	101-1731	$114,000	9.50%	360.	$958.57
3	101-1289	$10,000	10.50%	36	$325.02
4	101-3144	$3,500	10.50%	12	$308.52
5	103-1135	$8,700	10.50%	24	$403.47
6	103-1994	$18,500	10.00%	60	$393.07
7	103-2335	$5,000	10.50%	48	$128.02
8	103-3864	$87,500	9.50%	360	$735.75
9	103-3891	$30,000	9.75%	360	$257.75

For example, from the data set above, a and b above select observations 2 and 8 (those that have a rate of 0.095); c selects no observations; and d selects observations 4 and 7 (those that have an amount less than or equal to 5000).

What does PROC PRINT display by default?

PROC PRINT does not create a default report; you must specify the rows and columns to be displayed.

PROC PRINT displays all observations and variables in the data set. If you want an additional column for observation numbers, you can request it.

PROC PRINT displays columns in the following order: a column for observation numbers, all character variables, and all numeric variables.

PROC PRINT displays all observations and variables in the data set, a column for observation numbers on the far left, and variables in the order in which they occur in the data set.

Correct answer: d

You can remove the column for observation numbers. You can also specify the variables you want, and you can select observations according to conditions.

Creating a Single Observation from Multiple Records

Using Dates and Times in Calculations

In this chapter so far, you've learned how date and time informats read common date and time expressions in specific forms. Now you will see how converting date and time expressions to numeric SAS date values can be useful, particularly for determining time intervals or performing calculations.

Suppose you work in the billing department of a small community hospital. It's your job to create a SAS data set from the raw data file that is referenced by the fileref Aprdata. A portion of the raw data file below shows data values that represent each patient's

last name

date checked in

date checked out

daily room rate

equipment cost.

Raw Data File Aprdata

```
                Raw Data File Aprdata
1---+----10---+----20---+----30---+----40
Akron      04/05/99 04/09/99 175.00 298.45
Brown      04/12/99 05/01/99 125.00 326.78
Carnes     04/27/99 04/29/99 125.00 174.24
Denison    04/11/99 04/12/99 175.00  87.41
Fields     04/15/99 04/22/99 175.00 378.96
Jamison    04/16/99 04/23/99 125.00 346.28
```

The data set that you create must also include variable values that represent how many days each person stayed in the hospital, the total room charges, and the total of all expenses that each patient incurred. When building the SAS program, you must first name the data set, identify the raw data file Aprdata, and use formatted input to read the data.

⚠ The following example is shown with the YEARCUTOFF= system option. When you work with two-digit year data, remember to check the default value of the YEARCUTOFF= option, and change it if necessary.

```
options yearcutoff=1920;
data perm.aprbills;
  infile aprdata;
  input LastName $8.
```

Notice that the values in the second and third fields are in the form *mmddyy*. To complete the INPUT statement, add instructions to read the values for RoomRate (fourth field) and EquipCost (fifth field), and add a semicolon.

```
options yearcutoff=1920;
data perm.aprbills;
  infile aprdata;
  input LastName $8. @10 DateIn mmddyy8. +1 DateOut
     mmddyy8. +1 RoomRate 6. @35 EquipCost 6.;
```

Now that the INPUT statement is complete, calculate how many days each patient was hospitalized. Because DateIn and DateOut are numeric variables, you can simply subtract to find the difference. But because the dates should be inclusive (patients are charged for both the first and last days), you must add 1 to the difference. Call this new variable Days.

```
options yearcutoff=1920;
data perm.aprbills;
  infile aprdata;
  input LastName $8. @10 DateIn mmddyy8. +1 DateOut
     mmddyy8. +1 RoomRate 6. @35 EquipCost 6.;
  Days=dateout-datein+1;
```

You can calculate a total room charge by multiplying Days times RoomRate.

```
options yearcutoff=1920;
data perm.aprbills;
   infile aprdata;
   input LastName $8. @10 DateIn mmddyy8. +1 DateOut
      mmddyy8. +1 RoomRate 6. @35 EquipCost 6.;
   Days=dateout-datein+1;
   RoomCharge=days*roomrate;
```

Calculating the total cost for each patient is easy. Create a variable named Total whose value is the sum of RoomCharge and EquipCost. Then add a PROC PRINT step and a RUN statement to view the new data.

```
options yearcutoff=1920;
data perm.aprbills;
   infile aprdata;
   input LastName $8. @10 DateIn mmddyy8. +1 DateOut
   mmddyy8. +1 RoomRate 6. @35 EquipCost 6.;
   Days=dateout-datein+1;
   RoomCharge=days*roomrate;
   Total=roomcharge+equipcost;
run;
proc print data=perm.aprbills;
run;
```

Table Created with PROC PRINT

Obs	LastName	DateIn	DateOut	RoomRate	EquipCost	Days	RoomCharge	Total
1	Akron	14339	14343	175	298.45	5	875	1173.45
2	Brown	14346	14365	125	326.78	20	2500	2826.78
3	Carnes	14361	14363	125	174.24	3	375	549.24
4	Denison	14345	14346	175	87.41	2	350	437.41
5	Fields	14349	14356	175	378.96	8	1400	1778.96
6	Jamison	14350	14357	125	346.28	8	1000	1346.28

If the values for DateIn and DateOut look odd to you, remember that these are SAS date values. Applying a format such as MMDDYY displays them as they appeared in Aprdata. You'll work with some other date and time formats later in this chapter.

Follow the execution of the program below. When the DATA step executes, the values for DateIn and DateOut are converted to SAS date values.

```
options yearcutoff=1920;
data perm.aprbills;
   infile aprdata;
```

```
    input LastName $8. @10 DateIn mmddyy8. +1 DateOut
        mmddyy8. +1 RoomRate 6. @35 EquipCost 6.;
    Days=dateout-datein+1;
    RoomCharge=days*roomrate;
    Total=roomcharge+equipcost;
run;
```

Raw Data File Aprdata and Program Data Vector

```
                    Raw Data File Aprdata
1---+----10---+----20---+----30---+----40
Akron      04/05/99 04/09/99 175.00 298.45
Brown      04/12/99 05/01/99 125.00 326.78
Carnes     04/27/99 04/29/99 125.00 174.24
Denison    04/11/99 04/12/99 175.00  87.41
Fields     04/15/99 04/22/99 175.00 378.96
Jamison    04/16/99 04/23/99 125.00 346.28
```

Program Data Vector

LastName	DateIn	DateOut	RoomRate	EquipCost	Days	RoomCharge	Total
Akron	14339	14343	•	•	•	•	•

After the INPUT statement, Days is created by subtracting DateIn from DateOut and adding 1.

```
options yearcutoff=1920;
data perm.aprbills;
    infile aprdata;
    input LastName $8. @10 DateIn mmddyy8. +1 DateOut
        mmddyy8. +1 RoomRate 6. @35 EquipCost 6.;
    Days=dateout-datein+1;
    RoomCharge=days*roomrate;
    Total=roomcharge+equipcost;
run;
```

Program Data Vector

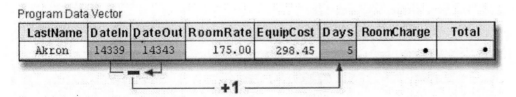

Program Data Vector

LastName	DateIn	DateOut	RoomRate	EquipCost	Days	RoomCharge	Total
Akron	14339	14343	175.00	298.45	5	•	•

The value for RoomCharge is calculated next. RoomCharge is the product of Days and RoomRate.

```
options yearcutoff=1920;
data perm.aprbills;
```

```
  infile aprdata;
  input LastName $8. @10 DateIn mmddyy8. +1 DateOut
    mmddyy8. +1 RoomRate 6. @35 EquipCost 6.;
  Days=dateout-datein+1;
  RoomCharge=days*roomrate;
  Total=roomcharge+equipcost;
run;
```

Raw Data File Aprdata and Program Data Vector

```
                     Raw Data File Aprdata
 1---+----10---+----20---+----30---+----40
Akron     04/05/99 04/09/99 175.00 298.45
Brown     04/12/99 05/01/99 125.00 326.78
Carnes    04/27/99 04/29/99 125.00 174.24
Denison   04/11/99 04/12/99 175.00  87.41
Fields    04/15/99 04/22/99 175.00 378.96
Jamison   04/16/99 04/23/99 125.00 346.28
```

Program Data Vector

LastName	DateIn	DateOut	RoomRate	EquipCost	Days	RoomCharge	Total
Akron	14339	14343	175.00	298.45	5	875.00	•

The value for Total is the final calculation. Total is the sum of EquipCost and RoomCharge.

```
options yearcutoff=1920;
data perm.aprbills;
  infile aprdata;
  input LastName $8. @10 DateIn mmddyy8. +1 DateOut
    mmddyy8. +1 RoomRate 6. @35 EquipCost 6.;
  Days=dateout-datein+1;
  RoomCharge=days*roomrate;
  Total=roomcharge+equipcost;
run;
```

Raw Data File Aprdata and Program Data Vector

Raw Data File Aprdata

```
1---+----10---+----20---+----30---+----40
Akron     04/05/99 04/09/99 175.00 298.45
Brown     04/12/99 05/01/99 125.00 326.78
Carnes    04/27/99 04/29/99 125.00 174.24
Denison   04/11/99 04/12/99 175.00  87.41
Fields    04/15/99 04/22/99 175.00 378.96
Jamison   04/16/99 04/23/99 125.00 346.28
```

Program Data Vector

LastName	DateIn	DateOut	RoomRate	EquipCost	Days	RoomCharge	Total
Akron	14339	14343	175.00	298.45	5	875.00	1173.45

Steps to Create a SAS Data Set from a Raw Data File

Let's look at the steps for creating a SAS data set from a raw data file. In the first part of this chapter, you will follow these steps to create a SAS data set from a raw data file that contains fixed fields.

Before reading raw data from a file, you might need to reference the SAS library in which you will store the data set. Then you can write a DATA step program to read the raw data file and create a SAS data set.

To read the raw data file, the DATA step must provide the following instructions to SAS:

the location or name of the external text file

a name for the new SAS data set

a reference that identifies the external file

a description of the data values to be read.

After using the DATA step to read the raw data, you can use a PROC PRINT step to produce a report that displays the data values that are in the new data set.

The table below outlines the basic statements that are used in a program that reads raw data in fixed fields. Throughout this chapter, you'll see similar tables that show sample SAS statements.

Basic Statements for Reading Raw Data

To do this...	Use this SAS statement...
Reference SAS data library	LIBNAME statement

Reference external file	FILENAME statement
Name SAS data set	DATA statement
Identify external file	INFILE statement
Describe data	INPUT statement
Execute DATA step	RUN statement
Print the data set	PROC PRINT statement
Execute final program step	RUN statement

You can also use additional SAS statements to perform tasks that customize your data for your needs. For example, you may want to create new variables from the values of existing variables.

Creating SAS Data Sets from External Files

Overview

Raw Data Files

Steps to Create a SAS Data Set from a Raw Data File

Referencing a SAS Library

Referencing a Raw Data File

Writing a DATA Step Program

Submitting the DATA Step Program

Creating and Modifying Variables

Subsetting Data

Reading Instream Data

Creating a Raw Data File

Additional Features

Reading Microsoft Excel Data

LIBNAME Statement Options

Creating Excel Worksheets

The IMPORT Wizard

Chapter Summary

Chapter Quiz

Copyright © SAS Institute Inc. All rights reserved.

Specifying Variables in PROC MEANS

By default, the MEANS procedure generates statistics for every numeric variable in a data set. But you'll typically want to focus on just a few variables, particularly if the data set is large. It also makes sense to exclude certain types of variables. The values of ID, for example, are unlikely to yield useful statistics.

To specify the variables that PROC MEANS analyzes, add a VAR statement and list the variable names.

General form, VAR statement:

VAR *variable(s)*;

where *variable(s)* lists numeric variables for which to calculate statistics.

```
proc means data=clinic.diabetes min max maxdec=0;
   var age height weight;
run;
```

Output with Selected Variables Age, Height, and Weight

The MEANS Procedure

Variable	Minimum	Maximum
Age	15	63
Height	61	75
Weight	102	240

In addition to listing variables separately, you can use a numbered range of variables.

```
proc means data=perm.survey mean stderr maxdec=2;
```

```
    var item1-item5;
run;
```

Output with a Range of Variables Selected

The MEANS Procedure

Variable	Mean	Std Error
Item1	3.75	0.63
Item2	3.00	0.82
Item3	4.25	0.25
Item4	3.50	0.65
Item5	3.00	0.82

Copyright © SAS Institute Inc. All rights reserved.

Overview

Introduction

In DATA step programming, you often need to perform the same action on more than one variable. Although you can process variables individually, it is easier to handle them as a group. You can do this by using array processing.

For example, using an array and DO loop, the program below eliminates the need for 365 separate programming statements to convert the daily temperature from Fahrenheit to Celsius for the year.

```
data work.report(drop=i);
  set master.temps;
  array daytemp{365} day1-day365;
  do i=1 to 365;
    daytemp{i}=5*(daytemp{i}-32)/9;
  end;
run;
```

You can use arrays to simplify the code needed to

perform repetitive calculations

create many variables that have the same attributes

read data

rotate SAS data sets by changing variables to observations or observations to variables

compare variables

perform a table lookup.

This chapter teaches you how to define an array and how to reference elements of the array in the DATA step.

Objectives

In this chapter, you learn to

  group variables into one- and two-dimensional arrays

  perform an action on array elements

  create new variables with an ARRAY statement

  assign initial values to array elements

  create temporary array elements with an ARRAY statement.

Chapter Summary

Text Summary

Opening a Stored SAS Program

A SAS program that is stored in an external file can be opened in the code editing window using

  file shortcuts

  My Favorite Folders

  the Open window

  the INCLUDE command.

Editing SAS Programs

SAS programs consist of SAS statements. Although you can write SAS statements in almost any format, a consistent layout enhances readability and enables you to understand the program's purpose.

In the Windows operating environment, the Enhanced Editor enables you to enter and view text and

  select one or more lines of text

  use color-coding to identify code elements

  automatically indent the next line when you press the Enter key

  collapse and expand sections of SAS procedures, DATA steps, and macros

  bookmark lines of code for easy access to different sections of your program.

Using the Editor window, you can also find and replace text, use abbreviations, open multiple views of a file, and set Enhanced Editor options.

The Program Editor window enables you to edit your programs just as you would with a word processing program. You can also use text editor commands and block text editor commands to edit SAS programs. Activating line numbers can make it easier for you to edit your program regardless of your operating environment.

Remember that SAS statements disappear from the Program Editor window when they are submitted. However, you can recall a program to the Program Editor window.

To save your SAS program to an external file, first activate the Program Editor window and select **File** ➡ **Save As**. Then specify the name of your program in the Save As window.

Clearing SAS Programming Windows

Text and output accumulate in the Editor, Program Editor, Log, and Output windows throughout your SAS session. You can clear a window by selecting **Edit** ➡ **Clear All**.

Interpreting Error Messages

When a SAS program that contains errors is submitted, error messages appear in the Log window. SAS can detect three types of errors: syntax, execution-time, and data. This chapter focuses on identifying and resolving common syntax errors.

Correcting Errors

To modify programs that contain errors, you can correct the errors in the code editing window. In the Program Editor window, you need to recall the submitted statements before editing them.

Before resubmitting a revised program, it is a good idea to clear the messages from the Log window so that you don't confuse old messages with the new. You can delete any error-free steps from a revised program before resubmitting it.

Resolving Common Problems

You might need to resolve several types of common problems: missing RUN statements, missing semicolons, unbalanced quotation marks, and invalid options.

Points to Remember

It's a good idea to begin DATA steps, PROC steps, and RUN statements on the left and to indent statements within a step.

End each step with a RUN statement.

Review the messages in the Log window each time you submit a SAS program.

You can delete any error-free steps from a revised program before resubmitting it, or you can submit only the revised steps in a program.

Chapter 19: Creating a Single Observation from Multiple Records

You can position the input pointer on a specific record by using

      column pointer controls.

      column specifications.

      line pointer controls.

      line hold specifiers.

Correct answer: c

Information for one observation can be spread out over several records. You can write one INPUT statement that contains line pointer controls to specify the record(s) from which values are read.

Which pointer control is used to read multiple records sequentially?

      $@n$

      $+n$

      /

      all of the above

Correct answer: c

The forward slash (/) line pointer control is used to read multiple records sequentially. Each time a / pointer is encountered, the input pointer advances to the next line. $@n$ and $+n$ are column pointer controls.

Which pointer control can be used to read records non-sequentially?

      $@n$

      $\#n$

      $+n$

      /

Correct answer: b

The $\#n$ line pointer control is used to read records non-sequentially. The $\#n$ specifies the absolute number of the line to which you want to move the pointer.

Which SAS statement correctly reads the values for Fname, Lname, Address, City, State and Zip in order?

XisError: altImageDescription Element Should Not Be Blank.

```
1---+----10---+----20---
LAWRENCE CALDWELL
1010 LAKE STREET
ANAHEIM CA 94122
RACHEL CHEVONT
3719 OLIVE VIEW ROAD
HARTFORD CT 06183
```

input Fname $ Lname $ /
    Address $20. /
    City $ State $ Zip $;

input Fname $ Lname $ /;
    Address $20. /;
    City $ State $ Zip $;

input / Fname $ Lname $
    / Address $20.
    City $ State $ Zip $;

input / Fname $ Lname $;
    / Address $20.;
    City $ State $ Zip $;

Correct answer: a

The INPUT statement uses the / line pointer control to move the input pointer forward from the first record to the second record, and from the second record to the third record. The / line pointer control only moves the input pointer forward and must be specified after the instructions for reading the values in the current record. You should place a semicolon only at the end of a complete INPUT statement.

Which INPUT statement correctly reads the values for ID in the fourth record, and then returns to the first record to read the values for Fname and Lname?

XisError: altImageDescription Element Should Not Be Blank.

```
1---+----10---+----20---
GEORGE CHESSON
3801 WOODSIDE COURT
GARNER NC 27529
XM065 FLOYD
JAMES COLDWELL
123-A TARBERT
APEX NC 27529
XM065 LAWSON
```

    input #4 ID $5.
       #1 Fname $ Lname $;

    input #4 ID $ 1-5
       #1 Fname $ Lname $;

    input #4 ID $
       #1 Fname $ Lname $;

  all of the above

Correct answer: d

The first #*n* line pointer control enables you to read the values for ID from the fourth record. The second #*n* line pointer control moves back to the first record and reads the values for Fname and Lname. You can use formatted input, column input, or list input to read the values for ID.

How many records will be read for each execution of the DATA step?

XisError: altImageDescription Element Should Not Be Blank.

```
1---+----10---+----20---
SKIRT BLACK
COTTON
036499 $44.98
SKIRT NAVY
LINEN
036899 $51.50
DRESS RED
SILK
037299 $76.98
```


data spring.sportswr;

```
    infile newitems;
    input #1 Item $ Color $
        #3 @8 Price comma6.
        #2 Fabric $
        #3 SKU $ 1-6; run;
```

one

two

three

four

Correct answer: c

The first time the DATA step executes, the first three records are read, and an observation is written to the data set. During the second iteration, the next three records are read, and the second observation is written to the data set. During the third iteration, the last three records are read, and the final observation is written to the data set.

Which INPUT statement correctly reads the values for City, State, and Zip?

XisError: altImageDescription Element Should Not Be Blank.

```
1---+----10---+----20---
DINA   FIELDS
904  MAPLE  CIRCLE
DURHAM  NC  27713
ELIZABETH  GARRISON
1293  OAK  AVENUE
CHAPEL HILL  NC  27614
DAVID  HARRINGTON
2426  ELMWOOD  LANE
RALEIGH  NC  27803
```

input #3 City $ State $ Zip $;

input #3 City #38 $11. State $ Zip $;

input #3 City $11. +2 State $2. + 2 Zip $5.;

all of the above

Correct answer: b

A combination of modified and simple list input can be used to read the values for City, State, and Zip. You need to use modified list input to read the values for City, because one of the values is longer than eight characters and contains an embedded blank. You cannot use formatted input, because the values do not begin and end in the same column in each record.

Which program does *not* read the values in the first record as a variable named Item and the values in the second record as two variables named Inventory and Type?

XisError: altImageDescription Element Should Not Be Blank.

```
1---+----10---+----20---
COLORED PENCILS
12 BOXES
WATERCOLOR PAINT
8 PALETTES
DRAWING PAPER
15 PADS
```

```
data perm.supplies;
   infile instock pad;
   input Item #38 $16. /
        Inventory 2. Type $8.;
run;
```

```
data perm.supplies;
   infile instock pad;
   input Item #38 $16.
        / Inventory 2. Type $8.;
run;
```

```
data perm.supplies;
   infile instock pad;
   input #1 Item #38 $16.
        Inventory 2. Type $8.;
run;
```

```
data perm.supplies;
   infile instock pad;
   input Item #38 $16.
        #2 Inventory 2. Type $8.;
run;
```

Correct answer: c

The values for Item in the first record are read, then the following / or #*n* line pointer control advances the input pointer to the second record, to read the values for Inventory and Type.

Which INPUT statement reads the values for Lname, Fname, Department and Salary (in that order)?

XisError: altImageDescription Element Should Not Be Blank.

```
1---+----10---+----20---
ABRAMS THOMAS
SALES $25,209.03
BARCLAY ROBERT
MARKETING $29,180.36
COURTNEY MARK
PUBLICATIONS $24,006.16
```

    input #1 Lname $ Fname $ /
        Department $12. Salary comma10.;

    input #1 Lname $ Fname $ /
        Department : $12. Salary : comma.;

    input #1 Lname $ Fname $
        #2 Department : $12. Salary : comma.;

    both b and c

Correct answer: d

You can use either the / or #*n* line pointer control to advance the input pointer to the second line, in order to read the values for Department and Salary. The colon (:) modifier is used to read the character values that are longer than eight characters (Department) and the nonstandard data values (Salary).

Which raw data file poses potential problems when you are reading multiple records for each observation?

    XisError: altImageDescription Element Should Not Be Blank.

```
1---+----10---+----20---
LAWRENCE CALDWELL
1010 LAKE STREET
ANAHEIM CA 94122
RACHEL CHEVONT
3719 OLIVE VIEW ROAD
HARTFORD CT 06183
```

XisError: altImageDescription Element Should Not Be Blank.

```
1---+----10---+----20---
SHIRT LT BLUE SOLID
SKU 128699
$38.99
SHIRT DK BLUE STRIPE
SKU 128799
$41.99
```

XisError: altImageDescription Element Should Not Be Blank.

```
1---+----10---+----20---
MARCUS JONES
SR01 $26,134.00
MARY ROBERTSON
COURTNEY NEILS
TWO1 $28,342.00
```

XisError: altImageDescription Element Should Not Be Blank.

```
1---+----10---+----20---
CROCUS MIX
10 CASES
DAFFODIL
12 CASES
HYACINTH BLUE
8 BAGS
```

Correct answer: c

The third raw data file does not contain the same number of records for each observation, so the output from this data set will show invalid data for the ID and salary information in the fourth line.

Opening a Stored SAS Program

Overview

You can open a stored program in the code editing window, where you can edit the program and submit it again.

You can open a program using

file shortcuts

My Favorite Folders

the Open window

the INCLUDE command.

   In operating environments that provide drag-and-drop functionality, you can also open a SAS file by dragging and dropping it into the code editing window.

Code Editor Window

Using File Shortcuts

File shortcuts are available in the SAS Explorer window. To open a program using file shortcuts:

At the top level of the SAS Explorer window, double-click **File Shortcuts**.

Double-click the file shortcut that you want to open, or select **Open** from the pop-up menu for the file.

File Short Cuts

The file opens in a new code editing window, with the filename shown as the window title.

💠 You can select **Submit** from the pop-up menu to execute the file directly from **File Shortcuts**.

💠 Remember that you open **File Shortcuts** with a single-click in the z/OS (z/OS) or CMS operating environments. To open a file, you type

? beside the item to display pop-up menus

S beside the item to simulate a double-click.

Using My Favorite Folders

To view and manage any files in your operating environment, you can use the My Favorite Folders window.

To open a file that is stored in My Favorite Folders:

Select **View ➧ My Favorite Folders**.

Double-click the file, or select **Open** from the pop-up menu for the file.

The file opens in a new code editing window, with the filename shown as the window title.

💠 You can select **Submit** from the pop-up menu to execute the file directly from My Favorite Folders.

Using the Open Window

To use the Open window:

With the code editing window active, select **File ➧ Open** (or **File ➧ Open Program**).

In the Open window, click the file that you want to open (or type the path for the file).

Click **Open** or **OK**.

The Open WIndow

The file opens in a new code editing window, with the filename shown as the window title.

In the Windows environment, you can submit your file directly from the Open window by clicking the **Submit** check box before clicking **Open**.

The appearance of the Open window varies by operating environment. In mainframe operating environments, files are not listed, so you must type the path for the file.

If you're not sure of the name of the file in which your program is stored, you can do either of the following:

use My Favorite Folders to locate the file in your operating environment

issue the **X** command to temporarily suspend your SAS session.

The X command enables you to use operating system facilities without ending your SAS session. When you issue the X command, you temporarily exit SAS and enter the host system.

To resume your SAS session after issuing the X command, issue the appropriate host system command, as shown below.

Resuming a SAS Session

Operating Environment	Host command to resume SAS session
z/OS	RETURN or END
UNIX	exit

Windows	EXIT

Issuing an INCLUDE Command

You can also open a program by issuing an INCLUDE command.

General form, basic INCLUDE command:

INCLUDE *'file-specification'*

where *file-specification* is the physical name by which the host system recognizes the file.

Example

Suppose you want to include the program **D:\Programs\Sas\Myprog1.sas** in the Windows operating environment. To do so, you can issue the following INCLUDE command:

include 'd:\programs\sas\myprog1.sas'

Because this is a command (not a SAS statement), no semicolon is used at the end.

Chapter Summary

Text Summary

Components of SAS Programs

SAS programs consist of two types of steps: DATA steps and PROC (procedure) steps. These two steps, alone or combined, form most SAS programs. A SAS program can consist of a DATA step, a PROC step, or any combination of DATA and PROC steps. DATA steps typically create or modify SAS data sets, but they can also be used to produce custom-designed reports. PROC steps are pre-written routines that enable you to analyze and process the data in a SAS data set and to present the data in the form of a report. They sometimes create new SAS data sets that typically contain the results of the procedure.

Characteristics of SAS Programs

SAS programs consist of SAS statements. A SAS statement usually begins with a SAS keyword and always ends with a semicolon. A DATA step begins with the keyword DATA. A PROC step begins with the keyword PROC. SAS statements are free-format, so they can begin and end anywhere on a line. One statement can continue over several lines, and several statements can be on a line. Blanks or special characters separate "words" in a SAS statement.

Processing SAS Programs

When you submit a SAS program, SAS reads SAS statements and checks them for errors. When it encounters a subsequent DATA, PROC, or RUN statement, SAS executes the previous step in the program.

Each time a step is executed, SAS generates a log of the processing activities and the results of the processing. The SAS log collects messages about the processing of SAS programs and about any errors that occur.

The results of processing can vary. Some SAS programs open an interactive window or invoke procedures that create output in the form of a report. Other SAS programs perform tasks such as sorting and managing data, which have no visible results other than messages in the log.

SAS Libraries

Every SAS file is stored in a SAS library, which is a collection of SAS files such as SAS data sets and catalogs. In the Windows and UNIX environments, a SAS library is typically a group of SAS files in the same folder or directory.

Depending on the libref you use, you can store SAS files in a temporary SAS library or in permanent SAS libraries.

Temporary SAS files that are created during the session are held in a special work space that is assigned the default libref Work. If you don't specify a libref when you create a file (or if you specify Work), the file is stored in the temporary SAS library. When you end the session, the temporary library is deleted.

To store files permanently in a SAS library, you assign it a libref other than the default Work. For example, by assigning the libref sasuser to a SAS library, you specify that files within the library are to be stored until you delete them.

Referencing SAS Files

To reference a SAS file, you use a two-level name, *libref.filename*. In the two-level name, *libref* is the name for the SAS library that contains the file, and *filename* is the name of the file itself. A period separates the libref and filename.

To reference temporary SAS files, you specify the default libref Work, a period, and the filename. Alternatively, you can simply use a one-level name (the filename only) to reference a file in a temporary SAS library. Referencing a SAS file in any library *except Work* indicates that the SAS file is stored permanently.

SAS data set names can be 1 to 32 characters long, must begin with a letter (A-Z, either uppercase or lowercase) or an underscore (_), and can continue with any combination of numerals, letters, or underscores.

SAS Data Sets

For many of the data processing tasks that you perform with SAS, you access data in the form of a SAS data set and use SAS programs to analyze, manage, or present the data. Conceptually, a SAS data set is a file that consists of two parts: a descriptor portion and a data portion. Some SAS data sets also contain one or more indexes, which enable SAS to locate records in the data set more efficiently.

The descriptor portion of a SAS data set contains property information about the data set.

The data portion of a SAS data set is a collection of data values that are arranged in a rectangular table. Observations in the data set correspond to rows or data lines. Variables in the data set correspond to columns. If a data value is unknown for a particular observation, a missing value is recorded in the SAS data set.

Variable Attributes

In addition to general information about the data set, the descriptor portion contains property information for each variable in the data set. The property information includes the variable's name, type, and length. A variable's type determines how missing values for a variable are displayed by SAS. For character variables, a *blank* represents a missing value. For numeric variables, a *period* represents a missing value. You can also specify format, informat, and label properties for variables.

Using the Main SAS Windows

You use the following windows to explore and manage your files, to enter and submit SAS programs, to view messages, and to view and manage your output.

Windows and How They Are Used

Use this window ...	To ...
Explorer	view your SAS files
	create new libraries and SAS files
	perform most file management tasks such as moving, copying, and deleting files
	create shortcuts to files that were not created with SAS
Enhanced Editor (code editing window)	enter, edit, and submit SAS program
	The Enhanced Editor window is available only in the Windows operating environment.
Program Editor (code editing window)	enter, edit, and submit SAS programs
Log	view messages about your SAS session and about any SAS programs that you submit

Output	browse output from SAS programs
Results	navigate and manage output from SAS programs
	view, save, and print individual items of output

Points to Remember

Before referencing SAS files, you must assign a name (libref, or library reference) to the library in which the files are stored (or specify that SAS is to assign the name automatically).

You can store SAS files either temporarily or permanently.

Variable names follow the same rules as SAS data set names. However, your site may choose to restrict variable names to those valid in Version 6 SAS, to uppercase variable names automatically, or to remove all restrictions on variable names.

Chapter Summary

Text Summary

Setting Up

Before you can create a new data set, you must assign a libref to the SAS library that will store the data set.

Reading a Single Data Set

After you have referenced the library in which your data set is stored, you can write a DATA step to name the SAS data set to be created. You then specify the data set to be read in the SET statement.

Selecting Variables

You can select the variables that you want to drop or keep by using the DROP= or KEEP= data set options in parentheses after a SAS data set name. For convenience, use DROP= if more variables are kept than dropped.

BY-Group Processing

Use the BY statement in the DATA step to group observations for processing. When you use the BY statement with the SET statement, the DATA step automatically creates two temporary variables, FIRST. and LAST. When you specify multiple BY variables, a change in the value of a primary BY variable forces LAST.variable to equal **1** for the secondary BY variables.

Reading Observations Using Direct Access

In addition to reading input data sequentially, you can access observations directly by using the POINT= option to go directly to a specified observation. There is no end-of-file condition when you use direct access, so include an explicit OUTPUT statement and then the STOP statement to prevent continuous looping.

Detecting the End of a Data Set

To determine when the last observation in an input data set has been read, use the END= option in the SET statement. The specified variable is initialized to 0, then set to 1 when the SET statement reads the last observation of the data set.

Syntax

LIBNAME *libref* '*SAS-data-library*';

DATA *SAS-data-set*;

SET *SAS-data-set* (**KEEP**= *variable-1* <...*variable-n*>) | (**DROP**= *variable-1* <...variable-n>)
POINT=*variable* | **END**=*variable*;
OUTPUT <*SAS-data-set*>;
STOP;

RUN;

Sample Program

```
proc sort data=company.usa out=work.temp2;
  by manager jobtype;
run;

data company.budget2(keep=manager jobtype payroll);
  set work.temp2;
  by manager jobtype;
  if wagecat='S' then Yearly=wagerate*12;
  else if wagecat='H' then Yearly=wagerate*2000;
  if first.jobtype then Payroll=0;
  payroll+yearly;
  if last.jobtype;
run;

data work.getobs5;
  obsnum=5;
  set company.usa(keep=manager payroll) point=obsnum;
  output;
  stop;
run;

data work.addtoend(drop=timemin timesec);
  set sasuser.stress2(keep=timemin timesec) end=last;
  TotalMin+timemin;
  TotalSec+timesec;
  TotalTime=totalmin*60+totalsec;
  if last;
```

run;

Points to Remember

When you perform BY-group processing, the data sets listed in the SET statement must either be sorted by the values of the BY variable(s), or they must have an appropriate index.

When using direct access to read data, you *must* prevent continuous looping. Add a STOP statement to the DATA step.

Do not specify the END= option with the POINT= option in a SET statement.

Overview

Introduction

Raw data can be organized in several ways.

This external file contains data that is arranged in columns, or fixed fields. You can specify a beginning and ending column for each field.

Raw Data in Columns

```
1---+----10---+----20---+----30--
BIRD FEEDER     LG088    3   20
GLASS MUGS      SB082    6   12
GLASS TRAY      BQ049   12    6
PADDED HANGRS   MN256   15   20
JEWELRY BOX     AJ498   23    0
RED APRON       AQ072    9   12
CRYSTAL VASE    AQ672   27    0
PICNIC BASKET   LS930   21    0
```

By contrast, the following external file contains data that is free-format, meaning data that is not arranged in columns. Notice that the values for a particular field do not begin and end in the same columns.

Raw Data in Free-Format

```
1---+----10---+----20---+----30--
ABRAMS L.MARKETING $18,209.03
BARCLAY M.MARKETING $18,435.71
COURTNEY W.MARKETING $20,006.16
FARLEY J.PUBLICATIONS $21,305.89
HEINS W.PUBLICATIONS $20,539.23
```

How your data is organized determines which input style you should use to read the data. SAS provides three primary input styles: column, formatted, and list input. This chapter teaches you how to use list input to read free-format data that is not arranged in fixed fields.

Objectives

In this chapter, you learn to use the INPUT statement with list input to read

free-format data (data that is not organized in fixed fields)

free-format data that is separated by nonblank delimiters, such as commas

free-format data that contains missing values

character values that exceed eight characters

nonstandard free-format data

character values that contain embedded blanks.

In addition, you learn how to mix column, formatted, and list input styles in a single INPUT statement.

Renaming Variables

Sometimes you might have same-named variables in more than one input data set. In this case, DATA step match-merging overwrites values of the like-named variable in the first data set in which it appears with values of the like-named variable in subsequent data sets.

For example, Clinic.Demog contains the variable Date (date of birth), and Clinic.Visit also contains Date (date of the clinic visit in 1998). The DATA step below overwrites the date of birth with the date of the clinic visit.

```
data clinic.merged;
  merge clinic.demog clinic.visit;
  by id;
run;
proc print data=clinic.merged;
run;
```

The following output shows the effects of overwriting the values of a variable in the Clinic.Merged data set. In most observations, the date is now the date of the clinic visit. In observation 11, the date is still the birth date because Clinic.Visit did not contain a matching ID value and did not contribute to the observation.

Renaming Variables

Obs	ID	Age	Sex	Date	Visit	SysBP	DiasBP	Weight
1	A001	21	m	11/05/98	1	140	85	195
2	A001	21	m	10/13/98	2	138	90	198
3	A001	21	m	07/04/98	3	145	95	200
4	A002	32	m	04/14/98	1	121	75	168
5	A003	24	f	08/12/98	1	118	68	125
6	A003	24	f	08/21/98	2	112	65	123
7	A004	.		03/30/98	1	143	86	204
8	A005	.44	f	02/27/98	1	132	76	174
9	A005	44	f	07/11/98	2	132	78	175
10	A005	44	f	04/16/98	3	134	78	176
11	A007	39	m	11/11/57		.	.	.
12	A008	.		05/22/98	1	126	80	182

You now have a data set with values for Date that mean two different things: date of birth and date of clinic visit. Let's see how to prevent this problem.

To prevent overwriting, you can rename variables by using the RENAME= data set option in the MERGE statement.

General form, RENAME= data set option:

(RENAME=(*old-variable-name=new-variable-name*))

where

the **RENAME=** option, in parentheses, follows the name of each data set that contains one or more variables to be renamed

old-variable-name specifies the variable to be renamed

new-variable-name specifies the new name for the variable.

📖 You can rename any number of variables in each occurrence of the RENAME= option.

You can also use RENAME= to rename variables in the SET statement or in the output data set that is specified in the DATA statement.

In the following example, the RENAME= option renames the variable Date in Clinic.Demog to BirthDate, and it renames the variable Date in Clinic.Visit to VisitDate.

```
data clinic.merged;
  merge clinic.demog (rename=(date=BirthDate))
      clinic.visit (rename=(date=VisitDate));
  by id;
run;
proc print data=clinic.merged;
run;
```

The following output shows the effect of the RENAME= option.

Output for RENAME= Option

Obs	ID	Age	Sex	BirthDate	Visit	SysBP	DiasBP	Weight	VisitDate
1	A001	21	m	05/22/75	1	140	85	195	11/05/98
2	A001	21	m	05/22/75	2	138	90	198	10/13/98
3	A001	21	m	05/22/75	3	145	95	200	07/04/98
4	A002	32	m	06/15/63	1	121	75	168	04/14/98
5	A003	24	f	08/17/72	1	118	68	125	08/12/98
6	A003	24	f	08/17/72	2	112	65	123	08/21/98
7	A004			03/27/69	1	143	86	204	03/30/98
8	A005	44	f	02/24/52	1	132	76	174	02/27/98
9	A005	44	f	02/24/52	2	132	78	175	07/11/98
10	A005	44	f	02/24/52	3	134	78	176	04/16/98
11	A007	39	m	11/11/57					
12	A008				1	126	80	182	05/22/98

Chapter Quiz

Select the best answer for each question. After completing the quiz, you can check your answers using the answer key in the appendix.

If you submit the following program, which variables appear in the new data set?

```
data work.cardiac(drop=age group);
  set clinic.fitness(keep=age weight group);
  if group=2 and age>40;
run;
```

- 2028 -

Weight

Age, Group

Age, Weight, Group

Which of the following programs correctly reads the data set Orders and creates the data set FastOrdr?

```
data catalog.fastordr(drop=ordrtime);
  set july.orders(keep=product units price);
  if ordrtime<4;
  Total=units*price;
run;
```

```
data catalog.orders(drop=ordrtime);
  set july.fastordr(keep=product units price);
  if ordrtime<4;
  Total=units*price;
run;
```

```
data catalog.fastordr(drop=ordrtime);
  set july.orders(keep=product units price
            ordrtime);
  if ordrtime<4;
  Total=units*price;
run;
```

none of the above

Which of the following statements is *false* about BY-group processing?

When you use the BY statement with the SET statement:

The data sets listed in the SET statement must be indexed or sorted by the values of the BY variable(s).

The DATA step automatically creates two variables, FIRST. and LAST., for each variable in the BY statement.

FIRST. and LAST. identify the first and last observation in each BY group, respectively.

FIRST. and LAST. are stored in the data set.

There are 500 observations in the data set Usa. What is the result of submitting the following program?

```
data work.getobs5;
```

```
obsnum=5;
set company.usa(keep=manager payroll) point=obsnum;
stop;
run;
```

an error

an empty data set

continuous loop

a data set that contains one observation

There is no end-of-file condition when you use direct access to read data, so how can your program prevent a continuous loop?

Do not use a POINT= variable.

Check for an invalid value of the POINT= variable.

Do not use an END= variable.

Include an OUTPUT statement.

Assuming that the data set Company.USA has five or more observations, what is the result of submitting the following program?

```
data work.getobs5;
  obsnum=5;
  set company.usa(keep=manager payroll) point=obsnum;
  output;
  stop;
run;
```

an error

an empty data set

a continuous loop

a data set that contains one observation

Which of the following statements is *true* regarding direct access of data sets?

You cannot specify END= with POINT=.

You cannot specify OUTPUT with POINT=.

You cannot specify STOP with END=.

You cannot specify FIRST. with LAST.

What is the result of submitting the following program?

```
data work.addtoend;
   set clinic.stress2 end=last;
   if last;
run;
```

    an error

    an empty data set

    a continuous loop

    a data set that contains one observation

At the start of DATA step processing, during the compilation phase, variables are created in the program data vector (PDV), and observations are set to:

    blank

    missing

    0

    there are no observations.

The DATA step executes:

    continuously if you use the POINT= option and the STOP statement.

    once for each variable in the output data set.

    once for each observation in the input data set.

    until it encounters an OUTPUT statement.

Creating Two-Way Tables

So far, you have used the FREQ procedure to create one-way frequency tables. However, it is often helpful to crosstabulate frequencies of two or more variables. For example, census data is typically crosstabulated with a variable that represents geographical regions.

The simplest crosstabulation is a two-way table. To create a two-way table, join two variables with an asterisk (*) in the TABLES statement of a PROC FREQ step.

General form, TABLES statement for crosstabulation:

TABLES *variable-1* *variable-2 <* ... *variable-n*>;

where (for two-way tables)

    variable-1 specifies table rows

    variable-2 specifies table columns.

When crosstabulations are specified, PROC FREQ produces tables with cells that contain

    cell frequency

    cell percentage of total frequency

    cell percentage of row frequency

    cell percentage of column frequency.

For example, the following program creates the two-way table shown below.

```
proc format;
   value wtfmt low-139='< 140'
           140-180='140-180'
           181-high='> 180';
   value htfmt low-64='< 5"5"'
           65-70='5"5-10"'
           71-high='> 5"10"';
run;
proc freq data=clinic.diabetes;
   tables weight*height;
   format weight wtfmt. height htfmt.;
run;
```

Two-Way Table Created by PROC FREQ

The FREQ Procedure

Frequency Percent Row Pct Col Pct	Table of Weight by Height			
		Height		
Weight	< 5'5"	5'5-10"	> 5'10"	Total
< 140	2	0	0	2
	10.00	0.00	0.00	10.00
	100.00	0.00	0.00	
	28.57	0.00	0.00	
140-180	5	5	0	10
	25.00	25.00	0.00	50.00
	50.00	50.00	0.00	
	71.43	62.50	0.00	
> 180	0	3	5	8
	0.00	15.00	25.00	40.00
	0.00	37.50	62.50	
	0.00	37.50	100.00	
Total	7	8	5	20
	35.00	40.00	25.00	100.00

Note that the first variable, Weight, forms the table rows, and the second variable, Height, forms the columns; reversing the order of the variables in the TABLES statement would reverse their positions in the table. Note also that the statistics are listed in the legend box.

Excluding Unmatched Observations

Overview

By default, DATA step match-merging combines all observations in all input data sets. However, you may want to select only observations that match for two or more specific input data sets.

Excluding Unmatched Observations

Work.Clients

Name	EmpID
ANKERTON, L.	11123
DAVIS, R.	22298
MASTERS, T.	33351
WOLMER, B.	44483

Work.Amounts

Name	Date	Amt
ANKERTON, L.	08OCT96	92
ANKERTON, L.	15OCT96	43
DAVIS, R.	04OCT96	16
MASTERS, T.	13OCT96	18
MASTERS, T.	.	27
THOMAS, A.	21OCT96	15

To exclude unmatched observations from your output data set, you can use the IN= data set option and the subsetting IF statement in your DATA step. In this case, you use the IN= data set option to create and name a variable that indicates whether the data set contributed data to the current observation

the subsetting IF statement to check the IN= values and write to the merged data set only matching observations.

Creating Temporary IN= Variables

Suppose you want to match-merge the data sets Clinic.Demog and Clinic.Visit and select only observations that appear in both data sets.

First, you use IN= to create two temporary variables, indemog and invisit. The IN= variable is a temporary variable that is available to program statements during the DATA step, but it is not included in the SAS data set that is being created.

General form, IN= data set option:

(IN= *variable***)**

where

the **IN=** option, in parentheses, follows the data set name

variable names the variable to be created.

Within the DATA step, the value of the variable is **1** if the data set contributed data to the current observation. Otherwise, its value is **0**.

The DATA step that contains the IN= options appears below. The first IN= creates the temporary variable indemog, which is set to **1** when an observation from Clinic.Demog contributes to the current observation. Otherwise, it is set to **0**. Likewise, the value of invisit depends on whether Clinic.Visit contributes to an observation or not.

```
data clinic.merged;
   merge clinic.demog(in=indemog)
       clinic.visit(in=invisit
               rename=(date=BirthDate));
   by id;
run;
```

When you specify multiple data set options for a given data set, enclose them in a single set of parentheses.

Selecting Matching Observations

Next, to select only observations that appear in both Clinic.Demog and Clinic.Visit, you specify a subsetting IF statement in the DATA step.

In the DATA step below, the subsetting IF statement checks the values of indemog and invisit and continues processing only those observations that meet the condition of the expression. Here the condition is that both Clinic.Demog and Clinic.Visit contribute to the observation. If the condition is met, the new observation is written to Clinic.Merged. Otherwise, the observation is deleted.

```
data clinic.merged;
   merge clinic.demog(in=indemog
              rename=(date=BirthDate))
        clinic.visit(in=invisit
              rename=(date=VisitDate));
      by id;
      if indemog=1 and invisit=1;
run;
proc print data=clinic.merged;
run;
```

In previous examples, Clinic.Merged contained 12 observations. In the output below, notice that only 10 observations met the condition in the IF expression.

Selecting Matching Observations

Obs	ID	Age	Sex	BirthDate	Visit	SysBP	DiasBP	Weight	VisitDate
1	A001	21	m	05/22/75	1	140	85	195	11/05/98
2	A001	21	m	05/22/75	2	138	90	198	10/13/98
3	A001	21	m	05/22/75	3	145	95	200	07/04/98
4	A002	32	m	06/15/63	1	121	75	168	04/14/98
5	A003	24	f	08/17/72	1	118	68	125	08/12/98
6	A003	24	f	08/17/72	2	112	65	123	08/21/98
7	A004	.		03/27/69	1	143	86	204	03/30/98
8	A005	44	f	02/24/52	1	132	76	174	02/27/98
9	A005	44	f	02/24/52	2	132	78	175	07/11/98
10	A005	44	f	02/24/52	3	134	78	176	04/16/98

SAS evaluates the expression within an IF statement to produce a result that is either nonzero, zero, or missing. A nonzero and nonmissing result causes the expression to be true; a zero or missing result causes the expression to be false.

Thus, you can specify the subsetting IF statement from the previous example in either of the following ways. The first IF statement checks specifically for a value of **1**. The second IF statement checks for a value that is neither missing nor **0** (which for IN= variables is always **1**).

```
if indemog=1 and invisit=1;
```

if indemog and invisit;

Chapter 17: Reading Free-Format Data

The raw data file referenced by the fileref Students contains data that is

XisError: altImageDescription Element Should Not Be Blank.

```
Raw Data File Students
1---+----10---+----20---+
FRED JOHNSON 18 USC 1
ASHLEY FERRIS 20 NCSU 3
BETH ROSEMONT 21 UNC 4
```

arranged in fixed fields

free-format

mixed-format

arranged in columns

Correct answer: b

The raw data file contains data that is free-format, meaning that the data is not arranged in columns or fixed fields.

Which input style should be used to read the values in the raw data file that is referenced by the fileref Students?

XisError: altImageDescription Element Should Not Be Blank.

```
Raw Data File Students
1---+----10---+----20---+
FRED JOHNSON 18 USC 1
ASHLEY FERRIS 20 NCSU 3
BETH ROSEMONT 21 UNC 4
```

column

formatted

list

mixed

Correct answer: c

List input should be used to read data that is free-format because you do not need to specify the column locations of the data.

Which SAS program was used to create the raw data file Teamdat from the SAS data set Work.Scores?

XisError: altImageDescription Element Should Not Be Blank.

SAS Data Set Work.Scores

Obs	Name	HighScore	Team
1	Joe	87	Blue Beetles, Durham
2	Dani	79	Raleigh Racers, Raleigh
3	Lisa	85	Sand Sharks, Cary
4	Matthew	76	Blue Beetles, Durham

Raw Data File Teamdat

```
1---+----10---+----20---+----30---+
Joe,87,"Blue Beetles, Durham"
Dani,79,"Raleigh Racers, Raleigh"
Lisa,85,"Sand Sharks, Cary"
Matthew,76,"Blue Beetles, Durham"
```

```
data _null_;
   set work.scores;
   file 'c:\data\teamdat' dlm=',';
   put name highscore team;
run;
```

```
data _null_;
   set work.scores;
   file 'c:\data\teamdat' dlm=' ';
   put name highscore team;
run;
```

```
data _null_;
   set work.scores;
   file 'c:\data\teamdat' dsd;
   put name highscore team;
run;
```

```
data _null_;
   set work.scores;
   file 'c:\data\teamdat';
```

```
        put name highscore team;
    run;
```

Correct answer: c

You can use the DSD option in the FILE statement to specify that data values containing commas should be enclosed in quotation marks. The DSD option uses a comma as the delimiter by default.

Which SAS statement reads the raw data values in order and assigns them to the variables shown below?

Variables: FirstName (character), LastName (character), Age (numeric), School (character), Class (numeric)

XisError: altImageDescription Element Should Not Be Blank.

```
Raw Data File Students
1---+----10---+----20---+
FRED JOHNSON 18 USC 1
ASHLEY FERRIS 20 NCSU 3
BETH ROSEMONT 21 UNC 4
```

```
    input FirstName $ LastName $ Age School $ Class;
```

```
    input FirstName LastName Age School Class;
```

```
    input FirstName $ 1-4 LastName $ 6-12 Age 14-15
        School $ 17-19 Class 21;
```

```
    input FirstName 1-4 LastName 6-12 Age 14-15
        School 17-19 Class 21;
```

Correct answer: a

Because the data is free-format, list input is used to read the values. With list input, you simply name each variable and identify its type.

Which SAS statement should be used to read the raw data file that is referenced by the fileref Salesrep?

XisError: altImageDescription Element Should Not Be Blank.

```
1---+----10---+----20---+----30
ELAINE:FRIEDMAN:WILMINGTON:2102
JIM:LLOYD:20:RALEIGH:38392
JENNIFER:WU:21:GREENSBORO:1436
```

infile salesrep;

infile salesrep ':';

infile salesrep dlm;

infile salesrep dlm=':';

Correct answer: d

The INFILE statement identifies the location of the external data file. The DLM= option specifies the colon (:) as the delimiter that separates each field.

Which of the following raw data files can be read by using the MISSOVER option in the INFILE statement? Spaces for missing values are highlighted with colored blocks.

XisError: altImageDescription Element Should Not Be Blank.

```
1---+----10---+----20---+----
ORANGE SUNNYDALE 20 10
PINEAPPLE ALOHA 7 10
GRAPE FARMFRESH 3  ▉
APPLE FARMFRESH 16 5
GRAPEFRUIT SUNNYDALE 12 8
```

XisError: altImageDescription Element Should Not Be Blank.

```
1---+----10---+----20---+----
ORANGE SUNNYDALE 20 10
PINEAPPLE ALOHA 7 10
GRAPE FARMFRESH ▉ 17
APPLE FARMFRESH 16 5
GRAPEFRUIT SUNNYDALE 12 8
```

XisError: altImageDescription Element Should Not Be Blank.

```
1---+----10---+----20---+----
ORANGE SUNNYDALE 20 10
PINEAPPLE ALOHA 7 10
GRAPE           3 17
APPLE FARMFRESH 16 5
GRAPEFRUIT SUNNYDALE 12 8
```

XisError: altImageDescription Element Should Not Be Blank.

```
1---+----10---+----20---+----
ORANGE SUNNYDALE 20 10
PINEAPPLE ALOHA 7 10
     FARMFRESH 3
APPLE FARMFRESH 16 5
GRAPEFRUIT SUNNYDALE 12 8
```

Correct answer: a

You can use the MISSOVER option in the INFILE statement to read the missing values at the end of a record. The MISSOVER option prevents SAS from moving to the next record if values are missing in the current record.

Which SAS program correctly reads the data in the raw data file that is referenced by the fileref Volunteer?

XisError: altImageDescription Element Should Not Be Blank.

Raw Data File Volunteer
```
1---+----10---+----20---+----30
ARLENE BIGGERSTAFF 19 UNC 2
JOSEPH CONSTANTINO 21 CLEM 2
MARTIN FIELDS 18 UNCG 1
```

```
data perm.contest;
  infile volunteer;
  input FirstName $ LastName $ Age
     School $ Class;
run;
```

```
data perm.contest;
  infile volunteer;
  length LastName $ 11;
  input FirstName $ lastname $ Age
     School $ Class;
run;
```

```
data perm.contest;
   infile volunteer;
   input FirstName $ lastname $ Age
        School $ Class;  length LastName $ 11;
run;
```

```
data perm.contest;
   infile volunteer;
   input FirstName $ LastName $ 11. Age
        School $ Class;
run;
```

Correct answer: b

The LENGTH statement extends the length of the character variable LastName so that it is large enough to accommodate the data. Variable attributes such as length are defined the first time a variable is named in a DATA step. The LENGTH statement should precede the INPUT statement so that the correct length is defined.

Which type of input should be used to read the values in the raw data file that is referenced by the fileref University?

XisError: altImageDescription Element Should Not Be Blank.

```
Raw Data File University
1---+----10---+----20---+----30
UNC ASHEVILLE  2,712
UNC CHAPEL HILL  24,189
UNC CHARLOTTE  15,031
UNC GREENSBORO  12,323
```

column

formatted

list

modified list

Correct answer: d

Notice that the values for School contain embedded blanks, and the values for Enrolled are nonstandard numeric values. Modified list input can be used to read the values that contain embedded blanks and nonstandard values.

Which SAS statement correctly reads the values for Flavor and Quantity? Make sure the length of each variable can accommodate the values shown.

Raw Data File Cookies

```
1---+----10---+----20---+----30
CHOCOLATE CHIP  10,453
OATMEAL  12,187
PEANUT BUTTER  11,546
SUGAR  12,331
```

input Flavor #38 $9. Quantity : comma.;

input Flavor #38 $14. Quantity : comma.;

input Flavor : $14. Quantity #38 comma.;

input Flavor $14. Quantity : comma.;

Correct answer: b

The INPUT statement uses list input with format modifiers and informats to read the values for each variable. The ampersand (#38) modifier enables you to read character values that contain single embedded blanks. The colon (:) modifier enables you to read nonstandard data values and character values that are longer than eight characters, but which contain no embedded blanks.

Which SAS statement correctly reads the raw data values in order and assigns them to these corresponding variables: Year (numeric), School (character), Enrolled (numeric)?

Raw Data File Founding

```
1---+----10---+----20---+----30---+----40
1868 U OF CALIFORNIA BERKELEY  31,612
1906 U OF CALIFORNIA DAVIS  21,838
1965 U OF CALIFORNIA IRVINE  15,874
1919 U OF CALIFORNIA LOS ANGELES  35,730
```

input Year School #38 $27.
    Enrolled : comma.;

input Year 1-4 School #38 $27.

Enrolled : comma.;

input @1 Year 4. +1 School #38 $27.
Enrolled : comma.;

all of the above

Correct answer: d

The values for Year can be read with column, formatted, or list input. However, the values for School and Enrolled are free-format data that contain embedded blanks or nonstandard values. Therefore, these last two variables must be read with modified list input.

Overview

Introduction

You've learned how to create a SAS data set from raw data that is stored in an external file. You've also learned how to subset observations and how to assign values to variables.

This chapter shows you additional techniques for creating and managing variables. In this chapter, you learn how to retain and accumulate values, assign variable values conditionally, select variables, and assign permanent labels and formats to variables.

Variables Displayed in a Data Set

Obs	ID	Name	RestHR	MaxHR	RecHR	Tolerance	TotalTime	SumSec	TestLength
1	2458	Murray, W	72	185	128	D	758	6,158	Normal
2	2539	LaMance, K	75	168	141	D	706	6,864	Short
3	2572	Oberon, M	74	177	138	D	731	7,595	Short
4	2574	Peterson, V	80	164	137	D	849	8,444	Long
5	2584	Takahashi, Y	76	163	135	D	967	9,411	Long

Objectives

In this chapter, you learn how to

create variables that accumulate variable values

initialize retained variables

assign values to variables conditionally

specify an alternative action when a condition is false

specify lengths for variables

delete unwanted observations

select variables

assign permanent labels and formats.

Grouping Statements Using DO Groups

Overview

So far in this chapter, you've seen examples of conditional processing (IF-THEN/ELSE statements and SELECT groups) that execute only a single SAS statement when a condition is true. However, you can also execute a group of statements as a unit by using DO groups.

To construct a DO group, you use the DO and END statements along with other SAS statements.

General form, simple DO group:

DO;

SAS statements

END;

where

the **DO** statement begins DO group processing

SAS statements between the DO and END statements are called a DO group and execute as a unit

the **END** statement terminates DO group processing.

You can nest DO statements within DO groups.

You can use DO groups in IF-THEN/ELSE statements and SELECT groups to execute many statements as part of the conditional action.

Examples

In this simple DO group, the statements between DO and END are performed only when TotalTime is greater than 800. If TotalTime is less than or equal to 800, statements in the DO group do not execute, and the program continues with the assignment statement that follows the appropriate ELSE statement.

```
data clinic.stress;
   infile tests;
   input ID $ 1-4 Name $ 6-25 RestHR 27-29 MaxHR 31-33
```

```
      RecHR 35-37 TimeMin 39-40 TimeSec 42-43
      Tolerance $ 45;
  TotalTime=(timemin*60)+timesec;
  retain SumSec 5400;
  sumsec+totaltime;
  length TestLength $ 6 Message $ 20;
  if totaltime>800 then
    do;
      testlength='Long';
      message='Run blood panel';
    end;
  else if 750<=totaltime<=800 then testlength='Normal';
  else if totaltime<750 then TestLength='Short';
run;
```

In the SELECT group below, the statements between DO and END are performed only when the value of Payclass is **hourly**. Notice that an IF-THEN statement appears in the DO group; the PUT statement executes only when Hours is greater than **40**. The second END statement in the program closes the SELECT group.

```
data payroll;
  set salaries;
  select(payclass);
  when ('monthly') amt=salary;
  when ('hourly')
    do;
      amt=hrlywage*min(hrs,40);
      if hrs>40 then put 'CHECK TIMECARD';
    end;
  otherwise put 'PROBLEM OBSERVATION';
  end;
run;
```

Indenting and Nesting DO Groups

You can nest DO groups to any level, just like you nest IF-THEN/ELSE statements. (The memory capabilities of your system may limit the number of nested DO statements that you can use. For details, see the SAS documentation about how many levels of nested DO statements your system's memory can support.)

The following is an example of nested DO groups:

```
do;
  statements;
    do;
        statements ;
          do;
              statements;
          end;
    end;
```

end;

It is good practice to indent the statements in DO groups, as shown in the preceding statements, so that their position indicates the levels of nesting.

There are three other forms of the DO statement:

The iterative DO statement executes statements between DO and END statements repetitively based on the value of an index variable. The iterative DO statement can contain a WHILE or UNTIL clause.

The DO UNTIL statement executes statements in a DO loop repetitively until a condition is true, checking the condition after each iteration of the DO loop.

The DO WHILE statement executes statements in a DO loop repetitively while a condition is true, checking the condition before each iteration of the DO loop.

You can learn about these forms of the DO statement in <u>Generating Data with DO Loops</u>.

Chapter 11: Reading SAS Data Sets

If you submit the following program, which variables appear in the new data set?

```
data work.cardiac(drop=age group);
  set clinic.fitness(keep=age weight group);
  if group=2 and age>40;
run;
```

Weight

Age, Group

Age, Weight, Group

Correct answer: b

The variables Age, Weight, and Group are specified using the KEEP= option in the SET statement. After processing, Age and Group are dropped in the DATA statement.

Which of the following programs correctly reads the data set Orders and creates the data set FastOrdr?

```
data catalog.fastordr(drop=ordrtime);
  set july.orders(keep=product units price);
  if ordrtime<4;
  Total=units*price;
```

```
                run;


        data catalog.orders(drop=ordrtime);
          set july.fastordr(keep=product units price);
          if ordrtime<4;
          Total=units*price;
        run;



        data catalog.fastordr(drop=ordrtime);
          set july.orders(keep=product units price
                      ordrtime);
          if ordrtime<4;
          Total=units*price;
        run;
```

none of the above

Correct answer: c

You specify the data set to be created in the DATA statement. The DROP= data set option prevents variables from being written to the data set. Because you use the variable OrdrTime when processing your data, you cannot drop OrdrTime in the SET statement. If you use the KEEP= option in the SET statement, then you must list OrdrTime as one of the variables to be kept.

Which of the following statements is *false* about BY-group processing?

When you use the BY statement with the SET statement:

> The data sets listed in the SET statement must be indexed or sorted by the values of the BY variable(s).

> The DATA step automatically creates two variables, FIRST. and LAST., for each variable in the BY statement.

> FIRST. and LAST. identify the first and last observation in each BY group, respectively.

> FIRST. and LAST. are stored in the data set.

Correct answer: d

When you use the BY statement with the SET statement, the DATA step creates the temporary variables FIRST. and LAST. They are not stored in the data set.

There are 500 observations in the data set Usa. What is the result of submitting the following program?

```
data work.getobs5;
  obsnum=5;
```

```
set company.usa(keep=manager payroll) point=obsnum;
  stop;
run;
```

an error

an empty data set

continuous loop

a data set that contains one observation

Correct answer: b

The DATA step outputs observations at the end of the DATA step. However, in this program, the STOP statement stops processing before the end of the DATA step. An explicit OUTPUT statement is needed in order to produce an observation.

There is no end-of-file condition when you use direct access to read data, so how can your program prevent a continuous loop?

Do not use a POINT= variable.

Check for an invalid value of the POINT= variable.

Do not use an END= variable.

Include an OUTPUT statement.

Correct answer: b

To avoid a continuous loop when using direct access, either include a STOP statement or use programming logic that executes a STOP statement when the data step encounters an invalid value of the POINT= variable. If SAS reads an invalid value of the POINT= variable, it sets the automatic variable _ERROR_ to 1. You can use this information to check for conditions that cause continuous looping.

Assuming that the data set Company.USA has five or more observations, what is the result of submitting the following program?

```
data work.getobs5;
  obsnum=5;
  set company.usa(keep=manager payroll) point=obsnum;
  output;
  stop;
run;
```

an error

an empty data set

a continuous loop

a data set that contains one observation

Correct answer: d

By combining the POINT= option with the OUTPUT and STOP statements, your program can output a single observation.

Which of the following statements is *true* regarding direct access of data sets?

You cannot specify END= with POINT=.

You cannot specify OUTPUT with POINT=.

You cannot specify STOP with END=.

You cannot specify FIRST. with LAST.

Correct answer: a

The END= option and POINT= option are incompatible in the same SET statement. Use one or the other in your program.

What is the result of submitting the following program?

```
data work.addtoend;
  set clinic.stress2 end=last;
  if last;
run;
```

an error

an empty data set

a continuous loop

a data set that contains one observation

Correct answer: d

This program uses the END= option to name a temporary variable that contains an end-of-file marker. That variable — last — is set to 1 when the SET statement reads the last observation of the data set.

At the start of DATA step processing, during the compilation phase, variables are created in the program data vector (PDV), and observations are set to:

blank

missing

0

there are no observations.

Correct answer: d

At the bottom of the DATA step, the compilation phase is complete, and the descriptor portion of the new SAS data set is created. There are no observations because the DATA step has not yet executed.

The DATA step executes:

continuously if you use the POINT= option and the STOP statement.

once for each variable in the output data set.

once for each observation in the input data set.

until it encounters an OUTPUT statement.

Correct answer: c

The DATA step executes once for each observation in the input data set. You use the POINT= option with the STOP statement to prevent continuous looping.

Specifying Lengths for Variables

Overview

Previously, you added IF-THEN and ELSE statements to a DATA step in order to create the variable TestLength. Values for TestLength were assigned conditionally, based on the value for TotalTime.

```
data clinic.stress;
   infile tests;
   input ID $ 1-4 Name $ 6-25 RestHR 27-29 MaxHR 31-33
       RecHR 35-37 TimeMin 39-40 TimeSec 42-43
       Tolerance $ 45;
   TotalTime=(timemin*60)+timesec;
   retain SumSec 5400;
   sumsec+totaltime;
   if totaltime>800 then TestLength='Long';
   else if 750<=totaltime<=800 then TestLength='Normal';
   else if totaltime<750 then TestLength='Short';
run;
```

But look what happens when you submit this program.

During compilation, when creating a new character variable in an assignment statement, SAS allocates as many bytes of storage space as there are characters in the first value that it encounters for that variable. In this case, the first value for TestLength occurs in the IF-THEN statement, which specifies a four-character value (**Long**). So TestLength is assigned a length of 4, and any longer values (**Normal** and **Short**) are truncated.

Truncated Variable Values

Variable TestLength
(Partial Listing)

TestLength
Norm
Shor
Shor
Shor
Norm
Shor
Long
...

The example above assigns a character constant as the value of the new variable. You can also see other examples of the default type and length that SAS assigns when the type and length of a variable are not explicitly set.

You can use a LENGTH statement to specify a length (the number of bytes) for TestLength before the first value is referenced elsewhere in the DATA step.

General form, LENGTH statement:

LENGTH *variable(s)* <$> *length*;

where

   variable(s) names the variable(s) to be assigned a length

   $ is specified if the variable is a character variable

   length is an integer that specifies the length of the variable.

Examples:

```
length Type $ 8;
length Address1 Address2 Address3
```

$200;
length FirstName $12 LastName
$16;

Within your program, you include a LENGTH statement to assign a length to accommodate the longest
value of the variable TestLength. The longest value is **Normal**, which has six characters. Because
TestLength is a character variable, you must follow the variable name with a dollar sign ($).

```
data clinic.stress;
   infile tests;
   input ID $ 1-4 Name $ 6-25 RestHR 27-29 MaxHR 31-33
       RecHR 35-37 TimeMin 39-40 TimeSec 42-43
       Tolerance $ 45;
   TotalTime=(timemin*60)+timesec;
   retain SumSec 5400;
   sumsec+totaltime;
   length TestLength $ 6;
   if totaltime>800 then testlength='Long';
   else if 750<=totaltime<=800 then testlength='Normal';
   else if totaltime<750 then TestLength='Short';
run;
```

Make sure the LENGTH statement appears before any other reference to the variable in the DATA
step. If the variable has been created by another statement, then a later use of the LENGTH statement will
not change its length.

Now that you have added the LENGTH statement to your program, the values of TestLength are no longer
truncated.

Variable Values That Are Not Truncated.

Variable TestLength
(Partial Listing)

TestLength
Normal
Short
Short
Short
Normal
Short
Long
...

Chapter Summary

Text Summary

Purpose of DO Loops

DO loops process groups of SAS statements repeatedly, reducing the number of statements required in repetitive calculations.

Syntax of Iterative DO Loops

To construct an iterative DO loop, specify an index variable and the conditions that will execute the loop. These conditions include a start value for the index variable, a stop value, and an increment value. Start, stop, and increment values can be any number, numeric variable, or SAS expression that results in a number.

DO Loop Execution

During each iteration of a DO loop, statements within the loop execute. Once the loop's index value exceeds the stop value, the DO loop stops, and processing continues with the following DATA step statement.

Generating Observations with DO Loops

Include an OUTPUT statement within the DO loop to write an observation for each iteration. This overrides the automatic generation of output at the end of the DATA step.

Decrementing DO Loops

You can decrement a DO loop by specifying a negative value for the BY clause. The start value must be greater than the stop value.

Specifying a Series of Items

You can specify how many times a DO loop executes by listing items in a series; the DO loop will execute once for each item, with the index variable equal to the value of each item. A series can consist of all numeric values, all character values (enclosed in quotation marks), or all variable names (without quotation marks).

Nesting DO Loops

DO loops can run within DO loops, as long as you assign a unique index variable to each loop and terminate each DO loop with its own END statement.

Iteratively Processing Observations from a Data Set

You can use a DO loop to read a data set and compute the value of a new variable. DO loop start and stop values, for example, can be read from a data set.

Conditionally Executing DO Loops

The DO UNTIL statement executes a DO loop until a condition becomes true. Because the expression is not evaluated until the bottom of the loop, a DO UNTIL loop will execute at least once. The DO WHILE statement is used to execute a DO loop while a condition is true. Because the DO WHILE statement is evaluated at the top of the DO loop, if the expression is initially false, the DO loop never executes.

Using Conditional Clauses with the Iterative DO Statement

DO WHILE and DO UNTIL statements can be used within iterative DO loops to combine conditional and unconditional execution.

Creating Samples

DO loops provide an efficient way to create samples from data sets. Enclose the SET statement in a DO loop, using the start, stop, and increment values to select the observations. Add the POINT= option to the SET statement, setting it equal to the index variable of the DO loop. Then add a STOP statement to prevent DATA step looping, and add an OUTPUT statement to write observations.

Syntax

DO *index-variable=start* **TO** *stop* **BY** *increment*;

SAS statements

END;

DO UNTIL(*expression***);**

DO WHILE(*expression***);**

DO *index-variable=start* **TO** *stop* **BY** *increment* **UNTIL(***expression***);**

DO *index-variable=start* **TO** *stop* **BY** *increment* **WHILE(***expression)***;**

Sample Programs

Simple DO Loop

```
data work.earn;
  Value=2000;
  do year=1 to 20;
    Interest=value*.075;
    value+interest;
  end;
run;
```

Nested DO Loops

```
data work.earn;
  do year=1 to 20;
```

```
      Capital+2000;
      do month=1 to 12;
          Interest=capital*(.075/12);
          capital+interest;
      end;
   end;
run;
```

Conditional Clause

```
data work.invest;
   do year=1 to 10 until(Capital>=50000);
      capital+2000;
      capital+capital*.10;
   end;
   if year=11 then year=10;
.run;
```

Creating Samples

```
data work.subset;
   do sample=10 to 5000 by 10;
      set factory.widgets point=sample;
      output;
   end;
    stop;
run;
```

Points to Remember

If you do not specify a BY clause, the increment value for DO loops is **1**.

In most cases, the index variable is needed only for processing the DO loop and can be dropped from the data set.

The index variable is always incremented by one value beyond the stop value unless you terminate the DO loop in some other manner.

It's easier to manage nested DO loops if you indent the statements in each loop.

General Form of SAS Functions

Arguments, Variable Lists, Arrays

To use a SAS function, specify the function name followed by the function arguments, which are enclosed in parentheses.

General form, SAS function:

function-name*(argument-1<,argument-n>)***;**

where *arguments* can be

variables, mean(*x,y,z*)

constants, mean(*456,502,612,498*)

expressions, mean(37*2,192/5,*mean*(*22,34,56*))

⚠ Even if the function does not require arguments, the function name must still be followed by parentheses (for example, *function-name()*).

When a function contains more than one argument, the arguments are usually separated by commas.

function-name(argument-1,argument-2,argument-n)

However, for some functions, variable lists and arrays can also be used as arguments, as long as the list or the array is preceded by the word OF. (You can learn about arrays in Processing Variables with Arrays.)

Example

Here is an example of a function that contains multiple arguments. Notice that the arguments are separated by commas.

mean(x1,x2,x3)

The arguments for this function can also be written as a variable list.

mean(of x1-x3)

Or, the variables can be referenced by an array.

mean(of newarray{*})

When specifying function arguments with a variable list or an array, be sure to precede the list or the array with the word OF. If you omit the word OF, the function arguments might not be interpreted as you expect. For example, the function below returns X1 minus X3, not the average of the variables X1, X2, and X3.

mean(x1-x3)

Target Variables

Now that you are familiar with the purpose and general form of SAS functions, let's think about target variables. A target variable is the variable to which the result of a function is assigned. For example, in the statement below, the variable AvgScore is the target variable.

AvgScore=mean(exam1,exam2,exam3);

Unless the length of the target variable has been previously defined, a default length is assigned. The default length depends on the function; the default for character functions can be as long as 200.

Default lengths could cause character variables to use more space than necessary in your data set. So, when using SAS functions, consider the appropriate length for any character target variables. If necessary, add a LENGTH statement to specify a length for the character target variable before the statement that creates the values of that variable.

Chapter Quiz

Select the best answer for each question. After completing the quiz, you can check your answers using the answer key in the appendix.

How many observations and variables does the data set below contain?

Name	Sex	Age
Picker	M	32
Fletcher		28
Romano	F	.
Choi	M	42

3 observations, 4 variables

3 observations, 3 variables

4 observations, 3 variables

can't tell because some values are missing

How many program steps are executed when the program below is processed?

```
data user.tables;
   infile jobs;
   input date yyddmm8. name $ job $;
run;
proc sort data=user.tables;
   by name;
run;
```

```
proc print data=user.tables;
run;
```

three

four

five

six

What type of variable is the variable AcctNum in the data set below?

AcctNum	Gender
3456_1	M
2451_2	
Romano	F
Choi	M

numeric

character

can be either character or numeric

can't tell from the data shown

What type of variable is the variable Wear in the data set below?

Brand	Wear
Acme	43
Ajax	34
Atlas	.

numeric

character

can be either character or numeric

can't tell from the data shown

Which of the following variable names is valid?

4BirthDate

$Cost

Items

Tax-Rate

Which of the following files is a permanent SAS file?

Sashelp.PrdSale

Sasuser.MySales

Profits.Quarter1

all of the above

In a DATA step, how can you reference a temporary SAS data set named Forecast?

Forecast

Work.Forecast

Sales.Forecast (after assigning the libref Sales)

only a and b above

What is the default length for the numeric variable Balance?

Name	Balance
Adams	105.73
Geller	107.89
Martinez	97.45
Noble	182.50

5

6

7

8

How many statements does the following SAS program contain?

proc print data=new.prodsale

```
        label double;
   var state day price1 price2; where state='NC';
   label state='Name of State'; run;
```

three

four

five

six

What is a SAS library?

collection of SAS files, such as SAS data sets and catalogs

in some operating environments, a physical collection of SAS files

a group of SAS files in the same folder or directory

all of the above

Double Spacing LISTING Output

If you are generating SAS LISTING output, one way to control the layout is to double space it. To do so, specify the DOUBLE option in the PROC PRINT statement. For example,

```
proc print data=clinic.stress double;
   var resthr maxhr rechr;
   where tolerance='I';
run;
```

Double spacing does not apply to HTML output.

To generate SAS LISTING output, you must select **Tools ⟶ Options ⟶ Preferences**. Select the **Results** tab. Select the **Create listing** option.

Double-Spaced LISTING Output

SAS Output

OBS	RestHR	MaxHR	RecHR
2	68	171	133
3	78	177	139
8	70	167	122
11	65	181	141
14	74	152	113
15	75	158	108
20	78	189	138

Creating and Applying User-Defined Formats

Overview

Introduction to PROC FORMAT

Defining a Unique Format

Associating User-Defined Formats with Variables

Chapter Summary

Chapter Quiz

Using Informats

Overview

Remember that the general form of the INPUT statement for formatted input is:

INPUT *<pointer-control> variable informat.*;

An informat is an instruction that tells SAS how to read raw data. SAS provides many informats for reading standard and nonstandard data values. Here is a small sample.

Selected Informats for Reading Data

PERCENT*w.d*	DATE*w*.	NENGO*w*.
$BINARY*w*.	DATETIME*w*.	PD*w.d*
$VARYING*w*.	HEX*w*.	PERCENT*w*.
$*w*.	JULIAN*w*.	TIME*w*.
COMMA*w.d*	MMDDYY*w*.	*w.d*

Note that

each informat contains a *w* value to indicate the width of the raw data field

each informat also contains a period, which is a required delimiter

for some informats, the optional *d* value specifies the number of implied decimal places

informats for reading character data always begin with a dollar sign ($).

For a complete list of informats, see the SAS documentation.

Reading Character Values

The $*w*. informat enables you to read character data. The *w* represents the field width of the data value (the total number of columns that contain the raw data field).

In the example below, the $ indicates that FirstName is a character variable, the 5 indicates a field width of five columns, and a period ends the informat.

```
input @9 FirstName $5.;
```

```
        12345
1---+---V10---+----20---+---
EVANS    DONNY 112 29,996.63
HELMS    LISA  105 18,567.23
HIGGINS  JOHN  111 25,309.00
LARSON   AMY   113 32,696.78
MOORE    MARY  112 28,945.89
POWELL   JASON 103 35,099.50
RILEY    JUDY  111 25,309.00
RYAN     NEAL  112 28,180.00
WILSON   HENRY 113 31,875.46
WOODS    CHIP  105 17,098.71
```

Reading Standard Numeric Data

The informat for reading standard numeric data is the *w.d* informat.

The *w* specifies the field width of the raw data value, the period serves as a delimiter, and the *d* optionally specifies the number of implied decimal places for the value. The *w.d* informat ignores any specified *d* value if the data already contains a decimal point.

For example, the raw data value shown below contains 6 digits (4 are decimals) and 1 decimal point. Therefore, the *w.* informat requires a field width of only 7 to correctly read the raw data value.

Raw Data Value		w. Informat		Variable Value
34.0008	▶	7.	▶	34.0008

In the example shown below, the values for JobTitle in columns 15-17 contain only numbers. Remember that standard numeric data values can contain only numbers, decimal points, scientific notation, and plus and minus signs.

A *d* value is not necessary to read the values for JobTitle. Simply move the column pointer forward 7 spaces to column 15, name the variable, and specify a field width of 3.

input @9 FirstName $5. @1 LastName $7. +7 JobTitle 3.;

```
             123
1---+----10---V----20---+---
EVANS    DONNY 112 29,996.63
HELMS    LISA  105 18,567.23
HIGGINS  JOHN  111 25,309.00
LARSON   AMY   113 32,696.78
MOORE    MARY  112 28,945.89
POWELL   JASON 103 35,099.50
RILEY    JUDY  111 25,309.00
```

- 2063 -

⚠️ Be certain to specify the period in the informat name.

Reading Nonstandard Numeric Data

The COMMA*w.d* informat is used to read numeric values and to remove embedded

blanks

commas

dashes

dollar signs

percent signs

right parentheses

left parentheses, which are interpreted as minus signs.

The COMMA*w.d* informat has three parts:

1. the informat name   COMMA

2. a value that specifies the width of the field to be read (including dollar signs, decimal   *w.*
   places, or other special characters), followed by a period

3. an optional value that specifies the number of implied decimal places for a value (not   *d*
   necessary if the value already contains decimal places).

In the example below, the values for Salary contain commas, which means that they are nonstandard numeric values.

The values for Salary begin in column 19, so use the @*n* or +*n* pointer control to point to column 19, and then name the variable.

```
data sasuser.empinfo;
  infile empdata;
  input @9 FirstName $5. @1 LastName $7. +7 JobTitle 3.
     @19 Salary;
```

```
1---+----10---+---v20---+---
EVANS     DONNY 112 29,996.63
HELMS     LISA  105 18,567.23
HIGGINS   JOHN  111 25,309.00
LARSON    AMY   113 32,696.78
MOORE     MARY  112 28,945.89
POWELL    JASON 103 35,099.50
RILEY     JUDY  111 25,309.00
```

Now add the COMMA*w.d* informat and specify the field width. The values end in column 27, so the field width is 9 columns. Add a RUN statement to complete the DATA step.

```
data sasuser.empinfo;
   infile empdata;
   input @9 FirstName $5. @1 LastName $7. +7 JobTitle 3.
       @19 Salary comma9.;
run;
```

```
                      123456789
1---+----10---+---v20---+-v-
EVANS     DONNY 112 29,996.63
HELMS     LISA  105 18,567.23
HIGGINS   JOHN  111 25,309.00
LARSON    AMY   113 32,696.78
MOORE     MARY  112 28,945.89
POWELL    JASON 103 35,099.50
RILEY     JUDY  111 25,309.00
```

If you use PROC PRINT to display the data set, the commas are removed from the values for Salary in the resulting output.

```
data sasuser.empinfo;
   infile empdata;
   input @9 FirstName $5. @1 LastName $7. +7 JobTitle 3.
       @19 Salary comma9.;
run;
proc print data=sasuser.empinfo;
run;
```

Output from the PRINT Procedure

Obs	FirstName	LastName	JobTitle	Salary
1	DONNY	EVANS	112	29996.63
2	ALISA	HELMS	105	18567.23
3	JOHN	HIGGINS	111	25309.00
4	AMY	LARSON	113	32696.78
5	MARY	MOORE	112	28945.89
6	JASON	POWELL	103	35099.50
7	JUDY	RILEY	111	25309.00

Thus, the COMMA$w.d$ informat does more than simply read the raw data values. It removes special characters such as commas from numeric data and stores only numeric values in a SAS data set.

DATA Step Processing of Informats

Let's place our INPUT statement in a DATA step and submit it for processing. Remember that after the DATA step is submitted, it is compiled and then executed.

```
data sasuser.empinfo;
  infile empdata;
  input @9 FirstName $5. @1 LastName $7. +7 JobTitle 3.
     @19 Salary comma9.;
run;
```

During the compile phase, the character variables in the program data vector are defined with the exact length specified by the informat. But notice that the lengths that are defined for JobTitle and Salary in the program data vector are different from the lengths that are specified by their informats.

```
                123  123456789
1---+----10---V-V-V20---+-V-
EVANS     DONNY 112 29,996.63
HELMS     LISA  105 18,567.23
HIGGINS   JOHN  111 25,309.00
```

Program Data Vector

N	ERROR	FirstName	LastName	JobTitle	Salary
		$5.	$7.	8.	8.
		DONNY	EVANS	112	29996.6

Remember, by default, SAS stores numeric values (no matter how many digits the value contains) as floating-point numbers in 8 bytes of storage. The length of a stored numeric variable is not affected by an informat's width nor by other column specifications in an INPUT statement.

However, it is still necessary to specify the actual width of a raw data field in an INPUT statement. Otherwise, if you specify a default field width of 8 for all numeric values, SAS will read inappropriate variable values when the program executes.

In the following example, the values for JobTitle would contain embedded blanks, which represent invalid numeric values.

```
data sasuser.empinfo;
   infile empdata;
   input @9 FirstName $5. @1 LastName $7.
      +7 JobTitle 8. @19 Salary comma8.;
run;
```

```
            12345678
                12345678
┌──────────────────────────────┐
│1---+----10---V---V20V--+V--   │
│EVANS     DONNY 112 29,996.63  │
│HELMS     LISA  105 18,567.23  │
│HIGGINS  JOHN  111 25,309.00   │
└──────────────────────────────┘
```

Program Data Vector

N	ERROR	FirstName	LastName	JobTitle	Salary
		$5.	$7.	8.	8.
		DONNY	EVANS	•	29996.6

Remember that the w value of the informat represents the width of the field in the raw data file. The values for JobTitle have a width of only 3 in the raw data file. However, because they are numeric values, SAS stores them with a default length of 8.

Editing SAS Programs

Now that you know how to open a SAS program, let's review the characteristics of SAS statements and look at enhancing the readability of your SAS programs.

SAS Program Structure

Remember that SAS programs consist of SAS statements. Consider the SAS program that is shown in a code editing window below.

An Example SAS Program

SAS statements...

...usually begin with a SAS keyword.

...always end with a semicolon.

...can begin anywhere on a line.

...contain blanks or special characters to separate words.

...can be combined on one line.

...can continue over several lines.

```
data perm.vansales;
    infile vandata;
    input @1 Region $9. @13 Quarter 1.
          @16 TotalSales comma11.;
run;
proc print data=perm.vansales; run;
```

Although you can write SAS statements in almost any format, a consistent layout enhances readability and helps you understand the program's purpose. It's a good idea to

begin DATA and PROC steps in column one

indent statements within a step

begin RUN statements in column one

include a RUN statement after every DATA step or PROC step.

```
data sashelp.prdsale;
   infile jobs;
   input date name $ job $;
run;
proc print data=sashelp.prdsale;
run;
```

Now let's look at the Enhanced Editor window features that you can use to edit your SAS programs.

If you are running SAS in an operating environment other than Windows, you can skip theEnhanced Editor window section and see Program Editor Features instead.

Using the Enhanced Editor

When you edit SAS programs in the Enhanced Editor, you can take advantage of a number of useful features. The following section shows you how to

use color-coding to identify code elements

automatically indent the next line when you press the **Enter** key

collapse and expand sections of SAS procedures, DATA steps, and macros

bookmark lines of code for easy access to different sections of your program

open multiple views of a file.

Enhanced Editor Window

You can also

- save color-coding settings in a color scheme

- create macros that record and play back program editing commands

- create shortcuts for typing in text using abbreviations

- customize keyboard shortcuts for most Enhanced Editor commands

- create and format your own keywords

- automatically reload modified disk files

- access Help for SAS procedures by placing the insertion point within the procedure name and pressing F1.

Entering and Viewing Text

The Enhanced Editor uses visual aides such as color coding and code sections to help you write and debug your SAS programs.

You can use the margin on the left side of the Editor window to

- select one or more lines of text

- expand and collapse code sections

- display bookmarks.

Finding and Replacing Text

To find text in the Editor window, select **Edit** ➡ **Find** or press Ctrl+F. You can set commonly used find options, including specifying that the text string is a regular expression. You can also specify whether to search in the code only, in the comments only, or in both the code and comments.

The Find Window

Using Abbreviations

You can define a character string so that when you type it and then press the Tab key or the Enter key, the string expands to a longer character string.

For example, you could define the abbreviation myv7sasfiles, which would expand to **'c:\winnt\profiles\myid\personal\mysasfiles\v7';**. Abbreviations are actually macros that insert one or more lines of text.

To create an abbreviation,

Select **Tools ➧ Add Abbreviation**.

For **Abbreviation**, type the name of the abbreviation.

For **Text to insert for abbreviation**, type the text that the abbreviation will expand into.

Click **OK**.

To use an abbreviation, type the abbreviation. When an abbreviation is recognized, a tooltip displays the expanded text. Press the Tab key or Enter key to accept the abbreviation.

You can modify or delete abbreviations that you create.

Opening Multiple Views of a File

When you use the Enhanced Editor, you can see different parts of the same file simultaneously by opening multiple views of the same file. While you are working with multiple views, you are working with only *one file*, not multiple copies of the same file.

To open multiple views of the same file,

make the file the active window.

select **Window ➧ New Window**.

The filename in the title bar is appended with a colon and a view number. Changes that you make to a file in one view, such as changing text or bookmarking a line, occur in all views simultaneously. Actions such as scroll bar movement, text selection, and expanding or contracting a section of code occur only in the active window.

Setting Enhanced Editor Options

You can customize the Enhanced Editor by setting Enhanced Editor options. To open the Enhanced Editor Options window, activate an Editor window and select **Tools** ➧ **Options** ➧ **Enhanced Editor**.

Click the tabs that are located along the top of the window to navigate to the settings that you want to change, and then select the options that you want.

For example, **Show line numbers** specifies whether to display line numbers in the margin. When line numbers are displayed, the current line number is red. **Insert spaces for tabs** specifies whether to insert the space character or the tab character when you press the Tab key. If it is selected, the space character is used. If it is not selected, the tab character is used.

When you are finished, click **OK**.

Enhanced Editor Options Window

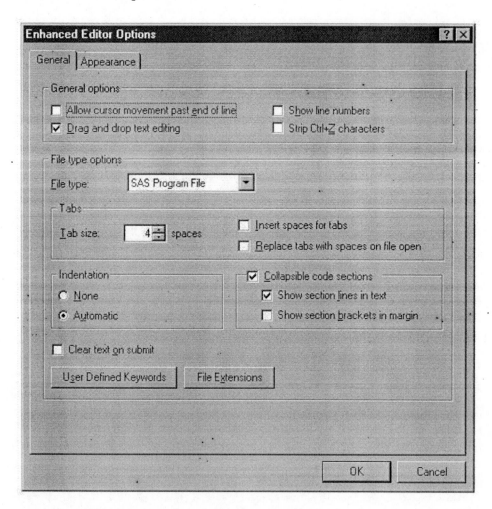

For more information about setting options in the Enhanced Editor, select **Help** ➧ **Using This Window** from an Enhanced Editor window.

Program Editor Features

You use the Program Editor window to submit SAS programs. You can also enter and edit SAS programs in this window, or you can open existing SAS programs that you created in another text editor.

To edit SAS programs in the Program Editor window, you can display line numbers. Then you can use text editor line commands and block text editor line commands within the line numbers to insert, delete, move, and copy lines within the Program Editor window.

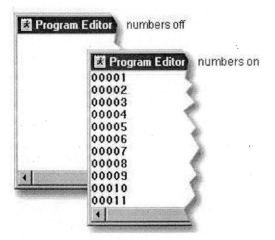 In all operating environments, you can use line numbers, text editor line commands, and block text editor line commands. Depending on your operating environment, you can also use features such as dragging and dropping text, inserting lines with the Enter key, or marking and deleting text. For information about these features, see the SAS documentation for your operating environment.

Line Numbers

In some operating environments, line numbers appear in the Program Editor window by default. In other systems, the use of line numbers is optional. Activating line numbers can make it easier for you to edit your program regardless of your operating environment.

Line Numbers

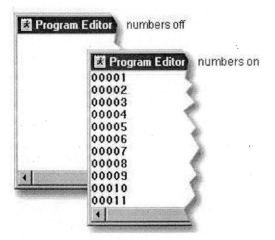

To turn on line numbers, use the NUMS command. Type nums on the command line or in the command box and press Enter. To turn line numbers off, enter the NUMS command again. Line numbers activated using the NUMS command will remain in effect for the duration of your SAS session.

To permanently display line numbers, select **Tools** ➜ **Options** ➜ **Program Editor**. Select the **Editing** tab. Select the **Display line numbers** option. Click **OK**.

Text Editor Line Commands

Text editor line commands enable you to delete, insert, move, copy, and repeat text. You enter these commands in the line number area in the Program Editor window.

The table below summarizes the basic text editing line commands.

Text Editor Line Commands

Command   Action

C*n*	copies *n* lines (where *n* = a number up to 9999)
D*n*	deletes *n* lines
I*n*	inserts *n* blank lines
M*n*	moves *n* lines
R*n*	repeats current line *n* times
A	after (used with C, I, and M)
B	before (used with C, I, and M)

You can use text editor line commands to perform actions like these:

Results from Using Text Editor Line Commands

Command	Action
00001	inserts 3 lines after line 00002
i3002	
00003	
0**ib**01	inserts 1 line before line 00001
00002	
00003	
0**ib4**1	inserts 4 lines before line 00001

00002

00003

000**c2**   copies 2 lines (00001 and 00002) after line 00003

00002

0**a**003

00001   deletes 3 lines (00002, 00003, and 00004)

0**d3**02

00003

00**b**01   moves 1 line (00003) before line 00001

00002

00**m**03

Example 1

In the example below, a PROC PRINT statement and a RUN statement need to be inserted after line 00004.

Incomplete Program

```
Program Editor - Program 1.sas
00001 data clinic.admitfee;
00002     infile feedata;
00003     input name $ 1-20 fee 22-27;
00004 run;
00005 proc tabulate data=clinic.admitfee;
00006     var fee;
00007     table fee,mean;
00008 run;
```

To insert the PROC PRINT and RUN statements in the program,

     Type **i2** anywhere in the line number area for line 00004 in the Program Editor window. Two blank lines are inserted, and the cursor is positioned on the first new line.

     Type the PROC PRINT statement on line 00005.

     Type a RUN statement on line 00006.

Complete Program

```
┌─────────────────────────────────────────────┐
│ ▣ Program Editor - Program 1.sas              │
├─────────────────────────────────────────────┤
│ 00001 data clinic.admitfee;                   │
│ 00002     infile feedata;                     │
│ 00003     input name $ 1-20 fee 22-27;        │
│ 0ı204 run;                                     │
│ 00 ┌────────────────────────────────────────┐│
│ 00 │ ▣ Program Editor - Program 1.sas        ││
│ 00 ├────────────────────────────────────────┤│
│ ◄  │00001 data clinic.admitfee;              ││
│    │00002     infile feedata;                ││
│    │00003     input name $ 1-20 fee 22-27;   ││
│    │00004 run;                               ││
│    │00005                                    ││
│    │00006                                    ││
│ 00 │00 ┌─────────────────────────────────────┐│
│ 00 │00 │ ▣ Program Editor - Program 1.sas     ││
│ 00 │00 ├─────────────────────────────────────┤│
│  ◄ │   │00001 data clinic.admitfee;          ││
│    │   │00002     infile feedata;            ││
│    │   │00003     input name $ 1-20 fee 22-27;││
│    │   │00004 run;                           ││
│    │   │00005 proc print data=clinic.admitfee;││
│    │   │00006 run;                           ││
│    │   │00007 proc tabulate data=clinic.admitfee;││
│    │   │00008     var fee;                   ││
│    │   │00009     table fee,mean;            ││
│    │   │00010 run;                           ││
│    │   ├─────────────────────────────────────┤│
│    │   │◄                                    ││
│    │   └─────────────────────────────────────┘│
└─────────────────────────────────────────────┘
```

Block Text Editor Line Commands

Block text editor line commands enable you to delete, repeat, copy, and move multiple lines in the Program Editor window.

The block text editor line commands include the following:

Block Text Editor Line Commands

Command	Action
DD	deletes a block of lines
CC	copies a block of lines
MM	moves a block of lines
RR	repeats multiple lines
A	after (used with CC and MM commands)

B   before (used with CC and MM commands)

To use a block command, specify the command on the first line affected and on the final line affected, and then press Enter.

Example 1

In the program below, the PROC TABULATE step needs to be deleted.

Original Program

```
Program Editor - Program 1.sas
00001 data clinic.admitfee;
00002     infile feedata;
00003     input name $ 1-20 fee 22-27;
00004 run;
00005 proc print data=clinic.admitfee;
00006 run;
00007 proc tabulate data=clinic.admitfee;
00008     var fee;
00009     table fee,mean;
00010 run;
```

You can use the DD block command to remove the step. To use the DD command:

Type **DD** anywhere in the line number area for line 00007 to mark the first line affected.

Type **DD** anywhere in the line number area for line 00010 to mark the final line affected.

Press Enter to delete lines 00007-00010.

Edited Program

Example 2

In the example below, the PROC TABULATE step needs to be moved to the line after the PROC PRINT step.

Original Program

```
Program Editor - Program2.sas
00001 data clinic.admitfee;
00002      infile feedata;
00003      input name $ 1-20  fee 22-27;
00004 run;
00005 proc tabulate data=clinic.admitfee;
00006     var fee;
00007     table fee,mean;
00008 run;
00009 proc print data=clinic.admitfee;
00010 run;
00011
```

You can use the MM block command with the A or B command to move a block of code to a specific location. The MM is used to mark the block to be moved and the A or B is used to mark where you want the block to go. You use the A if you want to move the block after the line, and you use b if you want to move the block before the line.

To use the MM command:

Type **MM** anywhere in the line number area for line 00005 to mark the first line affected.

Type **MM** anywhere in the line number area for line 00008 to mark the last line affected.

Type **A** anywhere in the line number area for line 00010 to move the block after line 00010.

Press Enter to move lines 00005-00008 to line 00010.

Edited Program

Recalling SAS Programs

SAS statements disappear from the Program Editor window when you submit them. However, you can recall a program to the Program Editor by selecting **Run** ➤ **Recall Last Submit**.

The area in which submitted SAS code is stored is known as the recall buffer. Program statements accumulate in the recall buffer each time you submit a program. The recall buffer is last-in/first-out (the most recently submitted statements are recalled first).

For example, if you submit two programs, you will need to select **Run** ➤ **Recall Last Submit** two times to recall the first program to the Program Editor window. You can recall statements any time during your SAS session.

Recalled Programs

Saving SAS Programs

To save your SAS program to an external file, first activate the code editing window and select **File** ➤ **Save As**. Then specify the name of your program in the Save As window. It's good practice to assign the extension .SAS to your SAS programs to distinguish them from other types of SAS files (such as .LOG for log files and .DAT for raw data files).

To save a SAS program as an external file in the z/OS operating environment, select **File** ➤ **Save As** ➤ **Write to File**, and then specify the name of your program in the Save As dialog box. You can specify SAS as the last level of the filename.

Save as WIndow

You can also save a SAS program by issuing a FILE command.

General form, basic FILE command:

FILE *'file-specification'*

where *file-specification* is the name of the file to be saved.

Example

Suppose you want to save a program as **D:\Programs\Sas\Newprog.Sas** in the Windows operating environment. To do so, you can issue the following FILE command:

file 'd:\programs\sas\newprog.sas'

Record Formats

The record format of an external file might affect how data is read with column input and formatted input. A record format specifies how records are organized in a file. Two common record formats are fixed-length records and variable-length records.

Fixed-Length Records

External files that have a fixed-length record format have an end-of-record marker after a predetermined number of columns. A typical record length is 80 columns.

```
123456789..........................................80
< field1 >< field2 >< field3 >..unused space      record 1
123456789..........................................80
< field1 >< field2 >< field3 >< field4 >....       record 2
123456789..........................................80
< field1 >< field2 >.... unused space ......        record 3
```

Variable-Length Records

Files that have a variable-length record format have an end-of-record marker after the last field in each record.

As you can see, the length of each record varies.

```
123456789.....................*
< field1 >< field2 >< field3 >    record 1
123456789...............................*
< field1 >< field2 >< field3 >< field4 >    record 2
123456789.........*
< field1 >< field2 >    record 3
```

Reading Variable-Length Records

When you work with variable-length records that contain fixed-field data, you might have values that are shorter than others or that are missing. This can cause problems when you try to read the raw data into your SAS data set.

For example, notice that the following INPUT statement specifies a field width of 8 columns for Receipts. In the third record, the input pointer encounters an end-of-record marker before the 8th column.

input Dept $ 1-11 @13 Receipts comma8.;

The asterisk symbolizes the end-of-record marker and is not part of the data.

```
                    12345678
1---+----10---+---V20--
BED/BATH      1,354.93*
HOUSEWARES    2,464.05*
GARDEN         923.34*
GRILL          598.34*
SHOES         1,345.82*
SPORTS*
TOYS          6,536.53*
```

The input pointer moves down to the next record in an attempt to complete the value for Receipts. However, **GRILL** is a character value, and Receipts is a numeric variable. Thus, an invalid data error occurs, and Receipts is set to missing.

```
V---+----10---+-----20--
BED/BATH      1,354.93*
HOUSEWARES    2,464.05*
GARDEN         923.34*
GRILL          598.34*
SHOES         1,345.82*
SPORTS*
TOYS          6,536.53*
```

The PAD Option

When reading variable-length records that contain fixed-field data, you can avoid problems by using the PAD option in the INFILE statement. The PAD option pads each record with blanks so that all data lines have the same length.

infile receipts pad;

```
1---+----10---+----20--
BED/BATH      1,354.93
HOUSEWARES    2,464.05
GARDEN        923.34
GRILL         598.34
SHOES         1,345.82
SPORTS
TOYS          6,536.53
```

When you use column input or formatted input to read fixed-field data in variable-length records, remember to determine whether or not you need to use the PAD option. For more information about the PAD option, see the SAS documentation.

⚠ The PAD option is useful only when missing data occurs at the end of a record or when SAS encounters an end-of-record marker before all fields are completely read.

The default value of the maximum record length is determined by your operating system. If you encounter unexpected results when reading many variables, you might need to change the maximum record length by specifying the LRECL=option in the INFILE statement. For more information about the LRECL= option, see the SAS documentation for your operating environment.

Assigning Descriptive Labels

Temporarily Assigning Labels to Variables

You can also enhance your PROC PRINT report by labeling columns with more descriptive text. To label columns, you use

- the LABEL statement to assign a descriptive label to a variable

- the LABEL option in the PROC PRINT statement to specify that the labels be displayed.

General form, LABEL statement:

LABEL *variable1='label1'*

variable2='label2'
... ;

Labels can be up to 256 characters long. Enclose the label in quotation marks.

🗒 The LABEL statement applies only to the PROC step in which it appears.

Example

In the PROC PRINT step below, the variable name WalkJogRun is displayed with the label Walk/Jog/Run. Note the LABEL option in the PROC PRINT statement. Without the LABEL option in the PROC PRINT statement, PROC PRINT would use the name of the column heading **walkjogrun** even though you specified a value for the variable.

```
proc print data=clinic.therapy label;
   label walkjogrun=Walk/Jog/Run;
run;
```

Output Created Without the LABEL Option

Obs	Date	AerClass	Walk/Jog/Run	Swim
6	JUN1999	61	114	67
7	JUL1999	67	102	72
8	AUG1999	64	76	77
9	SEP1999	78	77	54
10	OCT1999	81	62	47
11	NOV1999	84	31	52
16	APR2000	61	118	22
20	AUG2000	63	65	53
22	OCT2000	78	70	41
23	NOV2000	82	44	58
24	DEC2000	93	57	47

Using Single or Multiple LABEL Statements

You can assign labels in separate LABEL statements . . .

```
proc print data=clinic.admit label;
   var age height;
   label age='Age of Patient';
   label height='Height in Inches';
run;
```

. . . or you can assign any number of labels in a single LABEL statement.

```
proc print data=clinic.admit label;
   var actlevel height weight;
   label actlevel='Activity Level'
         height='Height in Inches'
         weight='Weight in Pounds';
```

run;

Using Date and Time Formats

Overview

Remember that when Perm.Aprbills is printed, the values for DateIn and DateOut appear as SAS date values.

```
            Raw Data File Aprdata
1---+----10---+----20---+----30---+----40
Akron     04/05/99 04/09/99 175.00 298.45
Brown     04/12/99 05/01/99 125.00 326.78
Carnes    04/27/99 04/29/99 125.00 174.24
Denison   04/11/99 04/12/99 175.00  87.41
Fields    04/15/99 04/22/99 175.00 378.96
Jamison   04/16/99 04/23/99 125.00 346.28
```

```
options yearcutoff=1920;
data perm.aprbills;
   infile aprdata;
   input LastName $8. @10 DateIn mmddyy8. +1 DateOut
      mmddyy8. +1 RoomRate 6. @35 EquipCost 6.;
   Days=dateout-datein+1;
   RoomCharge=days*roomrate;
   Total=roomcharge+equipcost;
run;
proc print data=perm.aprbills;
run;
```

PROC PRINT Output for the above Example

Obs	LastName	DateIn	DateOut	RoomRate	EquipCost	Days	RoomCharge	Total
1	Akron	14339	14343	175	298.45	5	875	1173.45
2	Brown	14346	14365	125	326.78	20	2500	2826.78
3	Carnes	14361	14363	125	174.24	3	375	549.24
4	Denison	14345	14346	175	87.41	2	350	437.41
5	Fields	14349	14356	175	378.96	8	1400	1778.96
6	Jamison	14350	14357	125	346.28	8	1000	1346.28

SAS provides many specialized date and time formats that enable you to specify how date and time values are displayed. Let's look at two date formats: WEEKDATE*w*. and WORDDATE*w*.

- 2084 -

The WEEKDATEw. Format

You can use the WEEKDATEw. format to write date values in a format that displays the day of the week, month, day, and year.

General form, WEEKDATEw. format:

WEEKDATEw.

The WEEKDATEw. format writes date values in the form *day-of-week, month-name dd, yy* (or *yyyy*).

where

   dd is an integer between 01 and 31, representing the day

   yy or *yyyy* is an integer that represents the year.

   Tip XisError: altImageDescription Element Should Not Be Blank.   If the *w* value is too small to write the complete day of the week and month, SAS abbreviates as needed.

```
proc print data=perm.aprbills;
   format datein dateout weekdate17.;
run;
```

PROC PRINT Output for the above Example

Obs	LastName	DateIn	DateOut	RoomRate	EquipCost	Days	RoomCharge	Total
1	Akron	Mon, Apr 5, 1999	Fri, Apr 9, 1999	175	298.45	5	875	1173.45
2	Brown	Mon, Apr 12, 1999	Sat, May 1, 1999	125	326.78	20	2500	2826.78
3	Carnes	Tue, Apr 27,1999	Thu, Apr 29, 1999	125	174.24	3	375	549.24
4	Denison	Sun, Apr 11, 1999	Mon, Apr 12, 1999	175	87.41	2	350	437.41
5	Fields	Thu, Apr 15, 1999	Thu, Apr 22, 1999	175	378.96	8	1400	1778.96
6	Jamison	Fri, Apr 16, 1999	Fri, Apr 23, 1999	125	346.28	8	1000	1346.28

You can vary the results by changing the w value in the format.

FORMAT Statement   Result

                             Mon

format datein weekdate3.;

Monday

format datein weekdate6.;

Mon, Apr 5, 1999

format datein weekdate17.;

Monday, April 5, 1999

format datein weekdate21.;

The WORDDATEw. Format

The WORDDATEw. format is similar to the WEEKDATEw. format, but it does not display the day of the week or the two-digit year values.

General form, WORDDATEw. format:

WORDDATEw.

The WORDDATEw. format writes date values in the form *month-name dd, yyyy*.

where

   dd is an integer between 01 and 31, representing the day

   yyyy is an integer that represents the year.

   Tip XisError: altImageDescription Element Should Not Be Blank.   If the *w* value is too small to write the complete month, SAS abbreviates as needed.

```
proc print data=perm.aprbills;
   format datein dateout worddate12.;
run;
```


PROC PRINT Output for the above Example

Obs	LastName	DateIn	DateOut	RoomRate	EquipCost	Days	RoomCharge	Total
1	Akron	Apr 5, 1999	Apr 9, 1999	175	298.45	5	875	1173.45
2	Brown	Apr 12, 1999	May 1, 1999	125	326.78	20	2500	2826.78
3	Carnes	Apr 27, 1999	Apr 29, 1999	125	174.24	3	375	549.24
4	Denison	Apr 11, 1999	Apr 12, 1999	175	87.41	2	350	437.41
5	Fields	Apr 15, 1999	Apr 22, 1999	175	378.96	8	1400	1778.96
6	Jamison	Apr 16, 1999	Apr 23, 1999	125	346.28	8	1000	1346.28

You can vary the results by changing the *w* value in the format.

FORMAT Statements and Corresponding Results

FORMAT Statement	Result
format datein worddate3.;	Apr
format datein worddate5.;	April
format datein worddate14.;	April 15, 1999

Remember that you can permanently assign a format to variable values by including a FORMAT statement in the DATA step.

```
options yearcutoff=1920;
data work.aprbills;
   infile aprdata;
   input LastName $8. @10 DateIn mmddyy8. +1 DateOut
      mmddyy8. +1 RoomRate 6. @35 EquipCost 6.;
   Days=dateout-datein+1;
   RoomCharge=days*roomrate;
   Total=roomcharge+equipcost;
   format datein dateout worddate12.;
run;
proc print data=work.aprbills;
run;
```

Creating a Raw Data File

Overview

Look at the SAS program and SAS data set that you created earlier in this chapter.

```
data sasuser.stress;
   infile tests;
   input ID $ 1-4 Name $ 6-25 RestHR 27-29 MaxHR 31-33
       RecHR 35-37 TimeMin 39-40 TimeSec 42-43
       Tolerance $ 45;
   if tolerance='D';
   TotalTime=(timemin*60)+timesec;
run;
```

SAS Data Set sasuser.stress Output

SAS Data Set Sasuser.Stress

ID	Name	RestHR	MaxHR	RecHR	TimeMin	TimeSec	Tolerance	TotalTime
2458	Murray, W	72	185	128	12	38	D	758
2539	LaMance, K	75	168	141	11	46	D	706
2552	Reberson, P	69	158	139	15	41	D	941
2572	Oberon, M	74	177	138	12	11	D	731
2574	Peterson, V	80	164	137	14	9	D	849
2584	Takahashi, Y	76	163	135	16	7	D	967

As you can see, the data set has been modified with SAS statements. If you wanted to write the new observations to a raw data file, you could reverse the process that you've been following and write out the observations from a SAS data set as records or lines to a new raw data file.

Using the _NULL_ Keyword

Because the goal of your SAS program is to create a raw data file and not a SAS data set, it is inefficient to print a data set name in the DATA statement. Instead, use the keyword _NULL_, which enables you to use the DATA step without actually creating a SAS data set. A SET statement specifies the SAS data set that you want to read from.

```
data _null_;
   set sasuser.stress;
```

The next step is to specify the output file.

Specifying the Raw Data File

You use the FILE and PUT statements to write the observations from a SAS data set to a raw data file, just as you used the INFILE and INPUT statements to create a SAS data set. These two sets of statements work almost identically.

When writing observations to a raw data file, use the FILE statement to specify the output file.

General form, FILE statement:

FILE *file-specification* *<options>* *<operating-environment-options>*;

where

> *file-specification* can take the form *fileref* to name a previously defined file reference or *'filename'* to point to the actual name and location of the file
>
> *options* names options that are used in creating the output file
>
> *operating-environment-options* names options that are specific to an operating environment (for more information, see the SAS documentation for your operating environment).

For example, if you want to read the Sasuser.Stress.data set and write it to a raw data file that is referenced by the fileref Newdat, you would begin your program with the following SAS statements.

```
data _null_;
  set sasuser.stress;
  file newdat;
```

Instead of identifying the raw data file with a SAS fileref, you can choose to specify the entire filename and location in the FILE statement. For example, the following FILE statement points directly to the **C:\Clinic\Patients\Stress.dat** file. Note that the path specifying the filename and location must be enclosed in quotation marks.

```
data _null_;
  set sasuser.stress;
  file 'c:\clinic\patients\stress.dat';
```

Describing the Data

Whereas the FILE statement specifies the output raw data file, the PUT statement describes the lines to write to the raw data file.

General form, PUT statement using column output:

PUT *variable startcol-endcol...*;

where

variable is the name of the variable whose value is written

startcol indicates where in the line to begin writing the value

endcol indicates where in the line to end the value.

In general, the PUT statement mirrors the capabilities of the INPUT statement. In this case you are working with column output. Therefore, you need to specify the variable name, starting column, and ending column for each field that you want to create. Because you are creating raw data, you don't need to follow character variable names with a dollar sign ($).

```
data _null_;
  set sasuser.stress;
  file 'c:\clinic\patients\stress.dat';
  put id $ 1-4 name 6-25 resthr 27-29 maxhr 31-33
      rechr 35-37 timemin 39-40 timesec 42-43
      tolerance 45 totaltime 47-49;
run;
```

SAS Data Set sasuser.stress Output with PUT Statement

SAS Data Set Sasuser.Stress

ID	Name	RestHR	MaxHR	RecHR	TimeMin	TimeSec	Tolerance	TotalTime
2458	Murray, W	72	185	128	12	38	D	758
2539	LaMance, K	75	168	141	11	46	D	706
2552	Reberson, P	69	158	139	15	41	D	941
2572	Oberon, M	74	177	138	12	11	D	731
2574	Peterson, V	80	164	137	14	9	D	849
2584	Takahashi, Y	76	163	135	16	7	D	967

The resulting raw data file would look like this.

Creating a Raw Data File

Raw Data File Stress.Dat

```
1---+----10---+----20---+----30---+----40---+----50---+
2458 Murray, W          72   185 128 12 38 D 758
2539 LaMance, K         75   168 141 11 46 D 706
2552 Reberson, P        69   158 139 15 41 D 941
2572 Oberon, M          74   177 138 12 11 D 731
2574 Peterson, V        80   164 137 14 9  D 849
2584 Takahashi, Y       76   163 135 16 7  D 967
```

In later chapters you'll learn how to use INPUT and PUT statements to read and write raw data in other forms and record types.

If you do not execute a FILE statement before a PUT statement in the current iteration of the DATA step, SAS writes the lines to the SAS log. If you specify the PRINT fileref in the FILE statement, before the PUT statement, SAS writes the lines to the procedure output file.

Detecting the End of a Data Set

Overview

Instead of reading specific observations, you might want to determine when the last observation in an input data set has been read, so that you can perform specific processing. For example, you might want to output only one observation that contains grand totals for numeric variables.

To create a temporary numeric variable whose value is used to detect the last observation, you can use the END= option in the SET statement.

General form, END= option:

END=_variable_

where _variable_ creates and names a temporary variable that contains an end-of-file marker. The variable, which is initialized to 0, is set to 1 when the SET statement reads the last observation of the data set.

This variable is _not_ added to the data set.

Do not specify END= with POINT=. POINT= reads only a specific observation, so the last observation in the data set is not encountered.

Example

Suppose you want to sum the number of seconds for treadmill stress tests. If you submit the following program, you produce a new data set that contains cumulative totals for each of the values of TotalTime.

```
data work.addtoend(drop=timemin timesec);
  set sasuser.stress2(keep=timemin timesec);
  TotalMin+timemin;
  TotalSec+timesec;
  TotalTime=totalmin*60+totalsec;
run;
proc print data=work.addtoend noobs;
run;
```

Data Set with Cumulative Totals for Each of the Values of TotalTime

TotalMin	TotalSec	TotalTime
12	38	758
22	43	1363
33	56	2036
42	98	2618
53	144	3324
65	170	4070
80	211	5011
93	224	5804
103	246	6426
119	295	7435
134	297	8337
146	308	9068
160	317	9917
171	343	10603
185	370	11470
198	389	12269
214	396	13236
231	431	14291
246	472	15232
260	529	16129
272	539	16859

But what if you want only the *final* total (the last observation) in the new data set? The following program uses the END= variable last to select only the last observation of the data set. You specify END= in the SET statement and last wherever you need it in processing (here, in the subsetting IF statement).

```
data work.addtoend(drop=timemin timesec);
   set sasuser.stress2(keep=timemin timesec) end=last;
   TotalMin+timemin;
   TotalSec+timesec;
   TotalTime=totalmin*60+totalsec;
   if last;
run;
proc print data=work.addtoend noobs;
run;
```

Now the new data set has one observation:

Data Set with One Observation

TotalMin	TotalSec	TotalTime
272	539	16859

Understanding How Data Sets Are Read

In a previous chapter, you learned about the compilation and execution phases of the DATA step as they pertain to reading raw data. DATA step processing for reading existing SAS data sets is very similar. The main difference is that while reading an existing data set with the SET statement, SAS retains the values of existing variables from one observation to the next.

Let's briefly look at the compilation and execution phases of DATA steps that use a SET statement. In this example, the DATA step reads the data set Finance.Loans, creates the variable Interest, and creates the new data set Finance.DueJan.

```
data finance.duejan;
   set finance.loans;
   Interest=amount*(rate/12);
run;
```

New Data Set Finance.DueJan

SAS Data Set Finance.Loans

Account	Amount	Rate	Months	Payment
101-1092	22000	0.100	60	467.43
101-1731	114000	0.095	360	958.57
101-1289	10000	0.105	36	325.02
101-3144	3500	0.105	12	308.52

Compilation Phase

The program data vector is created and contains the automatic variables _N_ and _ERROR_.

program data vector with Automatic Variables

Program Data Vector

N	ERROR	
1	0	

SAS also scans each statement in the DATA step, looking for syntax errors.

When the SET statement is compiled, a slot is added to the program data vector for each variable in the input data set. The input data set supplies the variable names, as well as attributes such as type and length.

Program Data Vector

N	ERROR	Account	Amount	Rate	Months	Payment

Any variables that are created in the DATA step are also added to the program data vector. The attributes of each of these variables are determined by the expression in the statement.

Program Data Vector

N	ERROR	Account	Amount	Rate	Months	Payment	Interest

At the bottom of the DATA step, the compilation phase is complete, and the descriptor portion of the new SAS data set is created. There are no observations because the DATA step has not yet executed.

When the compilation phase is complete, the execution phase begins.

Execution Phase

The DATA step executes once for each observation in the input data set. For example, this DATA step will execute four times because there are four observations in the input data set Finance.Loans.

At the beginning of the execution phase, the value of _N_ is **1**. Because there are no data errors, the value of _ERROR_ is **0**. The remaining variables are initialized to missing. Missing numeric values are represented by a period, and missing character values are represented by a blank.

```
data finance.duejan;
    set finance.loans;
    Interest=amount*(rate/12);
run;
```

SAS Data Set Finance.Loans

Account	Amount	Rate	Months	Payment
101-1092	22000	0.1000	60	467.43
101-1731	114000	0.0950	360	958.57
101-1289	10000	0.1050	36	325.02
101-3144	3500	0.1050	12	308.52

Program Data Vector

N	ERROR	Account	Amount	Rate	Months	Payment	Interest
1	0			.	.	.	.	.

Character Value — Numeric Values

SAS Data Set Finance.Duejan

Account	Amount	Rate	Months	Payment	Interest

The SET statement reads the first observation from the input data set into the program data vector.

XisError: altImageDescription Element Should Not Be Blank.

Then, the assignment statement executes to compute the value for Interest.

XisError: altImageDescription Element Should Not Be Blank.

At the end of the first iteration of the DATA step, the values in the program data vector are written to the new data set as the first observation.

XisError: altImageDescription Element Should Not Be Blank.

```
data finance.duejan;
   set finance.loans;
   Interest=amount*(rate/12);
run;
```

SAS Data Set Finance.Loans

Account	Amount	Rate	Months	Payment
101-1092	22000	0.1000	60	467.43
101-1731	114000	0.0950	360	958.57
101-1289	10000	0.1050	36	325.02
101-3144	3500	0.1050	12	308.52

Program Data Vector

N	ERROR	Account	Amount	Rate	Months	Payment	Interest
1	0	101-1092	22000	0.1000	60	467.43	183.333

SAS Data Set Finance.Duejan

Account	Amount	Rate	Months	Payment	Interest
101-1092	22000	0.1000	60	467.43	183.333

The value of _N_ increments from **1** to **2**, and control returns to the top of the DATA step. Remember, the automatic variable _N_ keeps track of how many times the DATA step has begun to execute.

XisError: altImageDescription Element Should Not Be Blank.

```
data finance.duejan;
   set finance.loans;
   Interest=amount*(rate/12);
run;
```

SAS Data Set Finance.Loans

Account	Amount	Rate	Months	Payment
101-1092	22000	0.1000	60	467.43
101-1731	114000	0.0950	360	958.57
101-1289	10000	0.1050	36	325.02
101-3144	3500	0.1050	12	308.52

Program Data Vector

N	ERROR	Account	Amount	Rate	Months	Payment	Interest
2	0	101-1092	22000	0.1000	60	467.43	183.333

SAS Data Set Finance.Duejan

Account	Amount	Rate	Months	Payment	Interest
101-1092	22000	0.1000	60	467.43	183.333

SAS retains the values of variables that were read from a SAS data set with the SET statement, or that were created by a sum statement. All other variable values, such as the values of the variable Interest, are set to missing.

XisError: altImageDescription Element Should Not Be Blank.

```
data finance.duejan;
    set finance.loans;
    Interest=amount*(rate/12);
run;
```

SAS Data Set Finance.Loans

Account	Amount	Rate	Months	Payment
101-1092	22000	0.1000	60	467.43
101-1731	114000	0.0950	360	958.57
101-1289	10000	0.1050	36	325.02
101-3144	3500	0.1050	12	308.52

Program Data Vector

N	ERROR	Account	Amount	Rate	Months	Payment	Interest
2	0	101-1092	22000	0.1000	60	467.43	•

Values Retained — Reset to Missing

SAS Data Set Finance.Duejan

Account	Amount	Rate	Months	Payment	Interest
101-1092	22000	0.1000	60	467.43	183.333

When SAS reads raw data, the situation is different. In that case, SAS sets the value of each variable in the DATA step to missing at the beginning of each iteration, with these exceptions:

variables named in a RETAIN statement

variables created in a sum statement

data elements in a _TEMPORARY_ array

any variables created by using options in the FILE or INFILE statements

automatic variables.

At the beginning of the second iteration, the value of _ERROR_ is reset to **0**.

XisError: altImageDescription Element Should Not Be Blank.

```
data finance.duejan;
   set finance.loans;
   Interest=amount*(rate/12);
run;
```

SAS Data Set Finance.Loans

Account	Amount	Rate	Months	Payment
101-1092	22000	0.1000	60	467.43
101-1731	114000	0.0950	360	958.57
101-1289	10000	0.1050	36	325.02
101-3144	3500	0.1050	12	308.52

Program Data Vector

N	ERROR	Account	Amount	Rate	Months	Payment	Interest
2	0	101-1092	22000	0.1000	60	467.43	.

SAS Data Set Finance.Duejan

Account	Amount	Rate	Months	Payment	Interest
101-1092	22000	0.1000	60	467.43	183.333

As the SET statement executes, the values from the second observation are read into the program data vector.

XisError: altImageDescription Element Should Not Be Blank.

```
data finance.duejan;
   set finance.loans;
   Interest=amount*(rate/12);
run;
```

SAS Data Set Finance.Loans

Account	Amount	Rate	Months	Payment
101-1092	22000	0.1000	60	467.43
101-1731	114000	0.0950	360	958.57
101-1289	10000	0.1050	36	325.02
101-3144	3500	0.1050	12	308.52

Program Data Vector

N	ERROR	Account	Amount	Rate	Months	Payment	Interest
2	0	101-1731	114000	0.0950	360	958.57	.

SAS Data Set Finance.Duejan

Account	Amount	Rate	Months	Payment	Interest
101-1092	22000	0.1000	60	467.43	183.333

The assignment statement executes again to compute the value for Interest for the second observation.

XisError: altImageDescription Element Should Not Be Blank.

```
data finance.duejan;
   set finance.loans;
   Interest=amount*(rate/12);
run;
```

SAS Data Set Finance.Loans

Account	Amount	Rate	Months	Payment
101-1092	22000	0.1000	60	467.43
101-1731	114000	0.0950	360	958.57
101-1289	10000	0.1050	36	325.02
101-3144	3500	0.1050	12	308.52

Program Data Vector

N	ERROR	Account	Amount	Rate	Months	Payment	Interest
2	0	101-1731	114000	0.0950	360	958.57	902.5

SAS Data Set Finance.Duejan

Account	Amount	Rate	Months	Payment	Interest
101-1092	22000	0.1000	60	467.43	183.333

At the bottom of the DATA step, the values in the program data vector are written to the data set as the second observation.

XisError: altImageDescription Element Should Not Be Blank.

```
data finance.duejan;
   set finance.loans;
   Interest=amount*(rate/12);
run;
```

SAS Data Set Finance.Loans

Account	Amount	Rate	Months	Payment
101-1092	22000	0.1000	60	467.43
101-1731	114000	0.0950	360	958.57
101-1289	10000	0.1050	36	325.02
101-3144	3500	0.1050	12	308.52

Program Data Vector

N	ERROR	Account	Amount	Rate	Months	Payment	Interest
2	0	101-1731	114000	0.0950	360	958.57	902.5

SAS Data Set Finance.Duejan

Account	Amount	Rate	Months	Payment	Interest
101-1092	22000	0.1000	60	467.43	183.333
101-1731	114000	0.0950	360	958.57	902.5

The value of _N_ increments from **2** to **3**, and control returns to the top of the DATA step. SAS retains the values of variables that were read from a SAS data set with the SET statement, or that were created by a sum statement. All other variable values, such as the values of the variable Interest, are set to missing.

XisError: altImageDescription Element Should Not Be Blank.

```
data finance.duejan;
    set finance.loans;
    Interest=amount*(rate/12);
run;
```

SAS Data Set Finance.Loans

Account	Amount	Rate	Months	Payment
101-1092	22000	0.1000	60	467.43
101-1731	114000	0.0950	360	958.57
101-1289	10000	0.1050	36	325.02
101-3144	3500	0.1050	12	308.52

Program Data Vector

N	ERROR	Account	Amount	Rate	Months	Payment	Interest
3	0	101-1731	114000	0.0950	360	958.57	•

Values Retained ⟷ Reset to Missing

SAS Data Set Finance.Duejan

Account	Amount	Rate	Months	Payment	Interest
101-1092	22000	0.1000	60	467.43	183.333
101-1731	114000	0.0950	360	958.57	902.5

This process continues until all of the observations are read.

Creating Multiple Observations from a Single Record

Overview

Reading Repeating Blocks of Data

Reading the Same Number of Repeating Fields

Reading a Varying Number of Repeating Fields

Chapter Summary

Chapter Quiz

Manipulating Data

Overview

In the previous example, you read in the data set **admit** and used the WHERE statement in the DATA step to subset the data. For any data set you read in, you can use any of the programming features of the DATA step to manipulate your data.

For example, you can use any of the statements and data set options that you learned in previous chapters.

Manipulating Data Using the DATA Step

To do this...	Use this type of statement...
Subset data	
	if resthr<70 then delete; if tolerance='D';
Drop unwanted variables	
	drop timemin timesec;
Create or modify a variable	
	TotalTime=(timemin*60)+timesec;
Initialize and retain a variable Accumulate values	
	retain SumSec 5400; sumsec+totaltime;
Specify a variable's length	
	length TestLength $ 6;
Execute statements conditionally	

	if totaltime>800 then TestLength='Long';
	else if 750<=totaltime<=800
	    then TestLength='Normal';
	else if totaltime<750
	    then TestLength='Short';

Label a variableFormat a variable

label sumsec='Cumulative Total Seconds';
format sumsec comma6.;

Example

The following DATA step reads the data set lab23.drug1h, selects observations and variables, and creates new variables.

```
data lab23.drug1h(drop=placebo uric);
  set research.cltrials(drop=triglyc);
    if sex='M' then delete;
    if placebo='YES';
    retain TestDate='22MAY1999'd;
    retain Days 30;
    days+1;
    length Retest $ 5;
    if cholesterol>190 then retest='YES';
      else if 150<=cholesterol<=190 then retest='CHECK';
      else if cholesterol<150 then retest='NO';
  label retest='Perform Cholesterol Test 2?';
  format enddate mmddyy10.;
run;
```

Where to Specify the DROP= and KEEP= Data Set Options

You've learned that you can specify the DROP= and KEEP= data set options anywhere you name a SAS data set. You can specify DROP= and KEEP= in either the DATA statement or the SET statement, depending on whether you want to drop variables onto output or input:

If you never reference certain variables and you don't want them to appear in the new data set, use a DROP= option in the SET statement.

In the DATA step shown below, the DROP= or KEEP= option in the SET statement prevents the variables Triglycerides and UricAcid from being read. These variables won't appear in the Lab23.Drug1H data set.

```
data lab23.drug1h(drop=placebo);
  set research.cltrials(drop=triglycerides uricacid);
    if placebo='YES';
  run;
```

If you do need to reference a variable in the original data set (in a subsetting IF statement, for example), you can specify the variable in the DROP= or KEEP= option in the DATA statement. Otherwise, the statement that references the variable uses a missing value for that variable.

This DATA step uses the variable Placebo to select observations. To drop Placebo from the new data set, the DROP= option must appear in the DATA statement.

```
data lab23.drug1h(drop=placebo);
  set research.cltrials(drop=triglycerides uricacid);
  if placebo='YES';
run;
```

When used in the DATA statement, the DROP= option simply drops the variables from the new data set. However, they are still read from the original data set and are available within the DATA step.

Chapter 18: Reading Date and Time Values

SAS date values are the number of days since which date?

January 1, 1900

January 1, 1950

January 1, 1960

January 1, 1970

Correct answer: c

A SAS date value is the number of days from January 1, 1960, to the given date.

A great advantage of storing dates and times as SAS numeric date and time values is that

they can easily be edited.

they can easily be read and understood.

they can be used in text strings like other character values.

they can be used in calculations like other numeric values.

Correct answer: d

In addition to tracking time intervals, SAS date and time values can be used in calculations like other numeric values. This lets you calculate values that involve dates much more easily than in other programming languages.

SAS does not automatically make adjustments for daylight saving time, but it *does* make adjustments for:

    leap seconds

    leap years

    Julian dates

    time zones

Correct answer: b

SAS automatically makes adjustments for leap years.

An input data file has date expressions in the form 10222001. Which SAS informat should you use to read these dates?

    DATE6.

    DATE8.

    MMDDYY6.

    MMDDYY8.

Correct answer: d

The SAS informat MMDDYYw. reads dates such as 10222001, 10/22/01, or 10-22-01. In this case, the field width is eight.

The minimum width of the TIMEw. informat is:

    4

    5

    6

    7

Correct answer: b

The minimum acceptable field width for the TIMEw. informat is five. If you specify a *w* value less than five, you will receive an error message in the SAS log.

Shown below are date and time expressions and corresponding SAS datetime informats. Which date and time expression *cannot* be read by the informat that is shown beside it?

    30May2000:10:03:17.2 **DATETIME20.**

    0May00 10:03:17.2 **DATETIME18.**

30May2000/10:03 **DATETIME15.**

30May2000/1003 **DATETIME14.**

Correct answer: d

In the time value of a date and time expression, you must use delimiters to separate the values for hour, minutes, and seconds.

What is the default value of the YEARCUTOFF= system option?

1920

1910

1900

1930

Correct answer: a

The default value of YEARCUTOFF= is **1920**. This enables you to read two-digit years from 00-19 as the years 2000 through 2019.

Suppose your input data file contains the date expression 13APR2009. The YEARCUTOFF= system option is set to 1910. SAS will read the date as:

13APR1909

13APR1920

13APR2009

13APR2020

Correct answer: c

The value of the YEARCUTOFF= system option does not affect four-digit year values. Four-digit values are always read correctly.

Suppose the YEARCUTOFF= system option is set to 1920. An input file contains the date expression 12/08/1925, which is being read with the MMDDYY8. informat. Which date will appear in your data?

08DEC1920

08DEC1925

08DEC2019

08DEC2025

Correct answer: c

The *w* value of the informat MMDDYY8. is too small to read the entire value, so the last two digits of the year are truncated. The last two digits thus become 19 instead of 25. Because the YEARCUTOFF= system option is set to 1920, SAS interprets this year as 2019. To avoid such errors, be sure to specify an informat that is wide enough for your date expressions.

Suppose your program creates two variables from an input file. Both variables are stored as SAS date values: FirstDay records the start of a billing cycle, and LastDay records the end of that cycle. The code for calculating the total number of days in the cycle would be:

TotDays=lastday-firstday;

TotDays=lastday-firstday+1;

TotDays=lastday/firstday;

You cannot use date values in calculations.

Correct answer: b

To find the number of days spanned by two dates, subtract the first day from the last day and add one. Because SAS date values are numeric values, they can easily be used in calculations.

Conditionally Executing DO Loops

Overview

The iterative DO statement specifies a fixed number of iterations for the DO loop. However, there are times when you want to execute a DO loop until a condition is reached or while a condition exists, but you don't know how many iterations are needed.

Suppose you want to calculate the number of years required for an investment to reach $50,000. In the DATA step below, using an iterative DO statement is inappropriate because you are trying to determine the number of iterations required for Capital to reach $50,000.

```
data work.invest;
  do year=1 to ? ;
    Capital+2000;
    capital+capital*.10;
  end;
run;
```

The DO WHILE and DO UNTIL statements enable you to execute DO loops based on whether a condition is true or false.

Using the DO UNTIL Statement

The DO UNTIL statement executes a DO loop until the expression becomes true.

General form, DO UNTIL statement:

DO UNTIL(*expression*);

SAS statements

END;

where *expression* is a valid SAS expression enclosed in parentheses.

The expression is not evaluated until the bottom of the loop, so a DO UNTIL loop always executes at least once. When the expression is evaluated as true, the DO loop stops.

Assume you want to know how many years it will take to earn $50,000 if you deposit $2,000 each year into an account that earns 10% interest. The DATA step below uses a DO UNTIL statement to perform the calculation until $50,000 is reached. Each iteration of the DO loop represents one year.

```
data work.invest;
   do until(Capital>=50000);
      capital+2000;
      capital+capital*.10;
      Year+1;
   end;
run;
```

During each iteration of the DO loop,

   2000 is added to the value of Capital to reflect the annual deposit of $2,000

   10% interest is added to Capital

   the value of Year is incremented by 1.

Because there is no index variable in the DO UNTIL statement, the variable Year is created in a sum statement to count the number of iterations of the DO loop. This program produces a data set that contains the single observation shown below. To accumulate more than $50,000 in capital requires 13 years (and 13 iterations of the DO loop).

SAS Data Set Work.Invest

Capital	Year
53949.97	13

Using the DO WHILE Statement

Like the DO UNTIL statement, the DO WHILE statement executes DO loops conditionally. You can use the DO WHILE statement to execute a DO loop **while** the expression is true.

General form, DO WHILE statement:

DO WHILE(*expression*)**;**

SAS statements

END;

where *expression* is a valid SAS expression enclosed in parentheses.

An important difference between the DO UNTIL and DO WHILE statements is that the DO WHILE expression is evaluated at the top of the DO loop. If the expression is false the first time it is evaluated, the DO loop never executes. For example, in the following program, because the value of Capital is initially zero, which is less than **50,000**, the DO loop does not execute.

```
data work.invest;
  do while(Capital>=50000);
    capital+2000;
    capital+capital*.10;
    Year+1;
  end;
run;
```

More about SAS Date and Time Values

As you use SAS date and time values, remember that

SAS date values are based on the Gregorian calendar, and they are valid for dates from A.D. 1582 through A.D. 20,000. Use caution when working with historical dates. Most of Europe started to use the Gregorian calendar in 1582. Great Britain and the American colonies adopted it in 1752. Check the adoption date for other parts of the world before making important calculations.

SAS makes adjustments for leap years but ignores leap seconds.

SAS does not make adjustments for daylight saving time.

Chapter Summary

Text Summary

Creating a Basic Report

To list the information in a SAS data set, you can use PROC PRINT. You use the PROC PRINT statement to invoke the PRINT procedure and to specify the data set that you are listing. Include the DATA= option to specify the data set that you are using. By default, PROC PRINT displays all observations and variables in the data set, includes a column for observation numbers on the far left, and displays observations and variables in the order in which they occur in the data set. If you use a LABEL statement with PROC PRINT, you must specify the LABEL option in the PROC PRINT statement.

To refine a basic report, you can

    select which variables and observations are processed

    sort the data

    generate column totals for numeric variables.

Selecting Variables

You can select variables and control the order in which they appear by using a VAR statement in your PROC PRINT step. To remove the Obs column, you can specify the NOOBS option in the PROC PRINT statement. As an alternative, you can replace the Obs column with one or more variables by using the ID statement.

Selecting Observations

The WHERE statement enables you to select observations that meet a particular condition in the SAS data set. You use comparison operators to express a condition in the WHERE statement. You can also use the CONTAINS operator to express a condition in the WHERE statement. To specify a condition based on the value of a character variable, you must enclose the value in quotation marks, and you must write the value with lower and uppercase letters exactly as it appears in the data set. You can also use the WHERE statement to select a subset of observations based on multiple conditions. To link a sequence of expressions into compound expressions, you use logical operators. When you test for multiple values of the same variable, you specify the variable name in each expression. You can use the IN operator as a convenient alternative. To control how compound expressions are evaluated, you can use parentheses.

Sorting Data

To display your data in sorted order, you use PROC SORT to sort your data before using PROC PRINT to create reports. By default, PROC SORT sorts the data set specified in the DATA= option permanently. If you do not want your data to be sorted permanently, you must create an output data set that contains the data in sorted order. The OUT= option in the PROC SORT statement specifies an output data set. If you need sorted data to produce output for only one SAS session, you should specify a temporary SAS data set as the output data set. The BY statement, which is required with PROC SORT, specifies the variable(s) whose values are used to sort the data.

Generating Column Totals

To total the values of numeric variables, use the SUM statement in the PROC PRINT step. You do not need to specify the variables in a VAR statement if you specify them in the SUM statement. Column totals appear at the end of the report in the same format as the values of the variables. To produce subtotals, add both the SUM statement and the BY statement to your PROC PRINT step. To show BY variable headings only once, use an ID and BY statement together with the SUM statement. As another enhancement to your report, you can request that each BY group be printed on a separate page by using the PAGEBY statement.

Double Spacing Output

To double space your SAS LISTING output, you can specify the DOUBLE option in the PROC PRINT statement.

Specifying Titles

To make your report more meaningful and self-explanatory, you can associate up to 10 titles with procedure output by using TITLE statements anywhere within or preceding the PROC step. After you define a title, it remains in effect until you modify it, cancel it, or end your SAS session. Redefining a title line cancels any higher-numbered title lines. To cancel all previous titles, specify a null TITLE statement (a TITLE statement with no number or text).

Specifying Footnotes

To add footnotes to your output, you can use the FOOTNOTE statement. Like TITLE statements, FOOTNOTE statements are global. Footnotes appear at the bottom of each page of procedure output, and footnote lines are *pushed up* from the bottom. The FOOTNOTE statement that has the largest number appears on the bottom line. After you define a footnote, it remains in effect until you modify it, cancel it, or end your SAS session. Redefining a footnote line cancels any higher-numbered footnote lines. To cancel all previous footnotes, specify a null FOOTNOTE statement (a FOOTNOTE statement with no number or text).

Assigning Descriptive Labels

To label the columns in your report with more descriptive text, you use the LABEL statement, which assigns a descriptive label to a variable. To display the labels that were assigned in a LABEL statement, you must specify the LABEL option in the PROC PRINT statement.

Formatting Data Values

To make data values more understandable when they are displayed in your procedure output, you can use the FORMAT statement, which associates formats with variables. The FORMAT statement remains in effect only for the PROC step in which it appears. Formats affect only how the data values appear in output, not the actual data values as they are stored in the SAS data set. All SAS formats can specify the total field width (w) that is used for displaying the values in the output. For numeric variables you can also specify the number of decimal places (d), if any, to be displayed in the output.

Using Permanently Assigned Labels and Formats

You can take advantage of permanently assigned labels or formats without adding LABEL or FORMAT statements to your PROC step.

Syntax

LIBNAME *libref 'SAS-data-library'*;

OPTIONS *options*;

PROC SORT DATA=*SAS-data-set* **OUT**=*SAS-data-set*;

BY *variable(s)*;

RUN;

TITLE<*n* > *'text'*;

FOOTNOTE<*n*>*'text'*;

PROC PRINT DATA=*SAS-data-set*

BY<DESCENDING>*BY-variable-1*<...<DESCENDING><*BY-variable-n*>>
<NOTSORTED>;
PAGEBY*BY-variable*;
NOOBS LABEL DOUBLE;
ID *variable(s)*;
VAR *variable(s)*;
WHERE *where-expression*;
SUM *variable(s)*;
LABEL *variable1='label1' variable2='label2' ...*;
FORMAT *variable(s) format-name;*

RUN;

Sample Program

```
libname clinic 'c:\stress\labdata';
options nodate number pageno=15;
proc sort data=clinic.stress out=work.maxrates;
   by maxhr;
   where tolerance='I' and resthr>60;
run;
title 'August Admission Fees';
footnote 'For High Activity Patients';
proc print data=work.maxrates label double noobs;
   id name;
   var resthr maxhr rechr;
   label rechr='Recovery HR';
run;

proc print data=clinic.admit label;
   var actlevel fee;
   where actlevel='HIGH';
   label fee='Admission Fee';
   sum fee;
   format fee dollar4.;
run;
```

Points to Remember

VAR, WHERE, SUM, FORMAT and LABEL statements remain in effect only for the PROC step in which they appear.

If you don't use the OUT= option, PROC SORT permanently sorts the data set specified in the DATA= option.

TITLE and FOOTNOTE statements remain in effect until you modify them, cancel them, or end your SAS session.

Be sure to match the quotation marks that enclose the text in TITLE, FOOTNOTE, and LABEL statements.

To display labels in PRINT procedure output, remember to add the LABEL option to the PROC PRINT statement.

To permanently assign labels or formats to data set variables, place the LABEL or FORMAT statement inside the DATA step.

Chapter Summary

Text Summary

Purpose of PROC MEANS

The MEANS procedure provides an easy way to compute descriptive statistics. Descriptive statistics such as the mean, minimum, and maximum provide useful information about numeric data.

Specifying Statistics

By default, PROC MEANS computes the n-count (the number of non-missing values), the mean, the standard deviation, and the minimum and maximum values for variables. To specify statistics, list their keywords in the PROC MEANS statement.

Limiting Decimal Places

Because PROC MEANS uses the BEST. format by default, procedure output can contain unnecessary decimal places. To limit decimal places, use the MAXDEC= option and set it equal to the length that you prefer.

Specifying Variables in PROC MEANS

By default, PROC MEANS computes statistics for all numeric variables. To specify the variables to include in PROC MEANS output, list them in a VAR statement.

Group Processing Using the CLASS Statement

Include a CLASS statement, specifying variable names, to group PROC MEANS output by variable values of classes.

Group Processing Using the BY Statement

Include a BY statement, specifying variable names, to group PROC MEANS output by variable values. Your data must be sorted according to those variables. Statistics are not computed for the BY variables.

Creating a Summarized Data Set Using PROC MEANS

You can create an output data set that contains summarized variables by using the OUTPUT statement in PROC MEANS. When you use the OUTPUT statement without specifying the statistic-keyword= option, the summary statistics N, MEAN, STD, MIN, and MAX are produced for all of the numeric variables or for all of the variables that are listed in a VAR statement.

Creating a Summarized Data Set Using PROC SUMMARY

You can also create a summarized output data set by using PROC SUMMARY. The PROC SUMMARY code for producing an output data set is exactly the same as the code for producing an output data set with PROC MEANS. The difference between the two procedures is that PROC MEANS produces a report by default, whereas PROC SUMMARY produces an output data set by default.

The FREQ Procedure

The FREQ Procedure is a descriptive procedure as well as a statistical procedure that produces one-way and n-way frequency tables. It describes your data by reporting the distribution of variable values.

Specifying Variables

By default, the FREQ procedure creates frequency tables for every variable in your data set. To specify the variables to analyze, include them in a TABLES statement.

Creating Two-Way Tables

When a TABLES statement contains two variables joined by an asterisk (*), PROC FREQ produces crosstabulations. The resulting table displays values for

cell frequency

cell percentage of total frequency

cell percentage of row frequency

cell percentage of column frequency.

Creating N-Way Tables

Crosstabulations can include more than two variables. When three or more variables are joined in a TABLES statement, the result is a series of two-way tables that are grouped by the values of the first variables listed.

Creating Tables in List Format

To reduce the bulk of n-way table output, add a slash (/) and the LIST option to the end of the TABLES statement. PROC FREQ then prints compact, multi-column lists instead of a series of tables. Beginning in SAS®9, you can use the CROSSLIST option to format your tables in ODS column format.

Suppressing Table Information

You can suppress the display of specific statistics by adding one or more options to the TABLES statement:

NOFREQ suppresses cell frequencies

NOPERCENT suppresses cell percentages

NOROW suppresses row percentages

NOCOL suppresses column percentages.

Syntax

PROC MEANS <DATA=*SAS-data-set*>

<*statistic-keyword(s)*> <*option(s)*>;
<VAR*variable(s)*>;
<CLASS*variable(s)*>;
<BY*variable(s)*>;
<OUTPUT*out=SAS-data-set statistic=variable(s)*>;

RUN;

PROC SUMMARY <DATA=*SAS-data-set*>

<*statistic-keyword(s)*> <*option(s)*>;
<VAR*variable(s)*>;
<CLASS*variable(s)*>;
<BY*variable(s)*>;
<OUTPUT*out=SAS-data-set*>;

RUN;

PROC FREQ <DATA=*SAS-data-set*>;

TABLES *variable-1 *variable-2 <* ... variable-n>*
/ <NOFREQ|NOPERCENT|NOROW|NOCOL|CROSSLIST>;

RUN;

Sample Programs

```
proc means data=clinic.heart min max maxdec=1;
   var arterial heart cardiac urinary;
   class survive sex;
run;

proc summary data=clinic.diabetes;
   var age height weight;
   class sex;
   output out=work.sum_gender
     mean=AvgAge AvgHeight AvgWeight;
```

```
run;

proc freq data=clinic.heart;
  tables sex*survive*shock / nopercent list;
run;
```

Points to Remember

In PROC MEANS, use a VAR statement to limit output to relevant variables. Exclude statistics for variables such as dates.

By default, PROC MEANS prints the full width of each numeric variable. Use the MAXDEC= option to limit decimal places and improve legibility.

Data must be sorted for BY group processing. You might need to run PROC SORT before using PROC MEANS with a BY statement.

PROC MEANS and PROC SUMMARY produce the same results; however, the default output is different. PROC MEANS produces a report, whereas PROC SUMMARY produces an output data set.

If you do not include a TABLES statement, PROC FREQ produces statistics for every variable in the data set. Variables that have continuous numeric values can create a large amount of output. Use a TABLES statement to exclude such variables, or group their values by applying a FORMAT statement.

Using Formatted Input

The General Form of Formatted Input

Formatted input is a very powerful method for reading both standard and nonstandard data in fixed fields.

General form, INPUT statement using formatted input:

INPUT *<pointer-control> variable informat.*;

where

pointer-control positions the input pointer on a specified column

variable is the name of the variable

informat is the special instruction that specifies how SAS reads the raw data.

In this chapter, you'll work with two column pointer controls.

The @*n* moves the input pointer to a specific column number.

The +*n* moves the input pointer forward to a column number that is relative to the current position.

Let's first look at the @*n* column pointer control.

Using the @n Column Pointer Control

The @*n* is an absolute pointer control that moves the input pointer to a specific column number. The @ moves the pointer to column *n*, which is the first column of the field that is being read.

General form, INPUT statement using formatted input and the @*n* pointer control:

INPUT @*n variable informat.*;

    variable is the name of the variable

    informat is a special instruction that specifies how SAS reads the raw data.

Let's use the @*n* pointer control to locate variable values in the external file Empdata. As you can see, the values for LastName begin in column 1. We could start with the @1 pointer control.

input @1 LastName $7.

However, the default column pointer location is column 1, so you do not need to use a column pointer control to read the first field.

input LastName $7.

```
V---+----10---+----20---+---
EVANS    DONNY 112 29,996.63
HELMS    LISA  105 18,567.23
HIGGINS  JOHN  111 25,309.00
LARSON   AMY   113 32,696.78
MOORE    MARY  112 28,945.89
POWELL   JASON 103 35,099.50
RILEY    JUDY  111 25,309.00
```

Next, the values for FirstName begin in column 9. To point to column 9, use an @ sign and the column number in the INPUT statement:

input LastName $7. @9 FirstName $5.

```
1---+---v10---+----20---+---
EVANS    DONNY 112 29,996.63
HELMS    LISA  105 18,567.23
HIGGINS  JOHN  111 25,309.00
LARSON   AMY   113 32,696.78
MOORE    MARY  112 28,945.89
POWELL   JASON 103 35,099.50
RILEY    JUDY  111 25,309.00
```

The $7. and $5. informats are explained later in this chapter.

Reading Columns in Any Order

Column pointer controls are very useful. For example, you can use the @*n* to move a pointer forward or backward when reading a record.

In this INPUT statement, the value for FirstName is read first, starting in column 9.

input @9 FirstName $5.

```
1---+---v10---+----20---+---
EVANS    DONNY 112 29,996.63
HELMS    LISA  105 18,567.23
HIGGINS  JOHN  111 25,309.00
```

Now let's read the values for LastName, which begin in the first column. Here you must use the @*n* pointer control to move the pointer back to column 1.

input @9 FirstName $5. @1 LastName $7.

```
v---+----10---+----20---+---
EVANS    DONNY 112 29,996.63
HELMS    LISA  105 18,567.23
HIGGINS  JOHN  111 25,309.00
```

The rest of the INPUT statement specifies the column locations of the raw data value for JobTitle and Salary.

input @9 FirstName $5. @1 LastName $7. @15 JobTitle 3.
    @19 Salary comma9.;

```
1---+----10---v----v20---+---
EVANS    DONNY 112 29,996.63
HELMS    LISA  105 18,567.23
HIGGINS  JOHN  111 25,309.00
```

The $5., $7., 3., and comma9. informats are explained later in this chapter.

The +n Pointer Control

The +*n* pointer control moves the input pointer forward to a column number that is relative to the current position. The + moves the pointer forward *n* columns.

General form, INPUT statement using formatted input and the +*n* pointer control:

INPUT +*n* *variable informat.*;

    variable is the name of the variable

    informat is a special instruction that specifies how SAS reads the raw data.

In order to count correctly, it is important to understand where the column pointer is located after each data value is read. Let's look at an example.

Suppose you want to read the data from Empdata in the following order: LastName, FirstName, Salary, JobTitle. Because the values for LastName begin in column 1, a column pointer control is not needed.

input LastName $7.

```
v---+----10---+----20---+---
EVANS    DONNY 112 29,996.63
HELMS    LISA  105 18,567.23
HIGGINS  JOHN  111 25,309.00
```

With formatted input, the column pointer moves to the first column following the field that was just read. In this example, after LastName is read, the pointer moves to column 8.

```
1---+--v-10---+----20---+---
EVANS    DONNY 112 29,996.63
HELMS    LISA  105 18,567.23
HIGGINS  JOHN  111 25,309.00
```

To start reading FirstName, which begins in column 9, you move the column pointer ahead 1 column with +1.

input LastName $7. +1 FirstName $5.

```
1---+---v10---+----20---+---
EVANS    DONNY 112 29,996.63
HELMS    LISA  105 18,567.23
HIGGINS  JOHN  111 25,309.00
```

After reading FirstName, the column pointer moves to column 14. Now you want to skip over the values for JobTitle and read the values for Salary, which begin in column 19. So you move the column pointer ahead 5 columns from column 14.

input LastName $7. +1 FirstName $5. +5 Salary comma9.

```
             12345
1---+----10---v---v20---+---
EVANS    DONNY 112 29,996.63
HELMS    LISA  105 18,567.23
HIGGINS  JOHN  111 25,309.00
```

The last field to be read contains the values for JobTitle. You can use the @n column pointer control to return to column 15.

input LastName $7. +1 FirstName $5. +5 Salary comma9.
    @15 JobTitle 3.;

```
1---+----10---v-----20---+---
EVANS    DONNY 112 29,996.63
HELMS    LISA  105 18,567.23
HIGGINS  JOHN  111 25,309.00
```

The $7., $5., comma9., and 3. informats are explained later in this chapter.

You can use the notation +(-n) to move the +n pointer backwards. For more information about the +(-n) notation, see the SAS documentation.

Chapter Summary

Text Summary

Invoking PROC FORMAT

The FORMAT procedure enables you to substitute descriptive text for the values of variables. The LIBRARY= option stores the new formats in a specified format catalog; otherwise, they are stored in a default catalog named Work.Formats. The keyword FMTLIB displays the formats and values that are currently stored in the catalog. The VALUE statement defines a new format for the values of a variable.

Defining a Unique Format

Formats can be specified for a single value, a range of values, or a list of unique values. Unique values must be separated by commas. When character values are specified, the values must be enclosed in quotation marks, and the format name must begin with a dollar sign ($). You can specify non-inclusive numeric ranges by using the less than sign (<). The keywords HIGH, LOW, and OTHER can be used to label values that are not specifically addressed in a range.

Associating User-Defined Formats with Variables

To access the permanent, user-defined formats in a format catalog, you'll need to use a LIBNAME statement to reference the catalog library. To associate user-defined formats with variables in the FORMAT statement, use the same format names in both the FORMAT and VALUE statements, but place a period at the end of the format name when it is used in the FORMAT statement.

Syntax

LIBNAME *libref 'SAS-data-library'*;

PROC FORMAT LIBRARY=*libref* **FMTLIB;**

VALUE *format-name*
range1='label1'
range2 'label2'
...;

RUN;

DATA *SAS-data-set;*

INFILE *data-file;*
INPUT *pointer variable-name informat.;*
FORMAT *variable(s) format-name.;*

RUN;

Sample Programs

```
libname library 'c:\sas\formats\lib';
proc format library=library fmtlib;
   value jobfmt
       103='manager'
       105='text processor';
run;

data perm.empinfo;
   infile empdata;
```

```
input @9 FirstName $5. @1 LastName $7.
    +7 JobTitle 3. @19 Salary comma9.;
format salary comma9.2 jobtitle jobfmt.;
run;
```

Points to Remember

Formats—even permanently associated ones—do not affect the values of variables in a SAS data set. Only the appearance of the values is altered.

A user-defined format name must begin with a dollar sign ($) when it is assigned to character variables. A format name cannot end with a number.

Use two single quotation marks when you want an apostrophe to appear in a label.

Place a period at the end of the format name when you use the format name in the FORMAT statement.

Chapter Quiz

Select the best answer for each question. After completing the quiz, check your answers using the answer key in the appendix.

Which program will combine Brothers.One and Brothers.Two to produce Brothers.Three?

XisError: altImageDescription Element Should Not Be Blank.

Brothers.One			Brothers.Two			Brothers.Three		
VarX	VarY	+	VarX	VarZ	=	VarX	VarY	VarZ
1	Groucho		2	Chico		2	Groucho	Chico
3	Harpo		4	Zeppo		4	Harpo	Zeppo
5	Karl							

```
data brothers.three;
   set brothers.one;
   set brothers.two;
run;
```

```
data brothers.three;
   set brothers.one brothers.two;
run;
```

```
data brothers.three;
    set brothers.one brothers.two;
    by varx;
run;
```

```
data brothers.three;
    merge brothers.one brothers.two;
    by varx;
run;
```

Which program will combine Actors.Props1 and Actors.Props2 to produce Actors.Props3?

XisError: altImageDescription Element Should Not Be Blank.

```
data actors.props3;
    set actors.props1;
    set actors.props2;
run;
```

```
data actors.props3;
    set actors.props1 actors.props2;
run;
```

```
data actors.props3;
    set actors.props1 actors.props2;
    by actor;
run;
```

```
data actors.props3;
    merge actors.props1 actors.props2;
```

```
        by actor;
    run;
```

If you submit the following program, which new data set is created?

XisError: altImageDescription Element Should Not Be Blank.

Work.Dataone

Career	Supervis	Finance
72	26	9
63	76	7
96	31	7
96	98	6
84	94	6

Work.Datatwo

Variety	Feedback	Autonomy
10	11	70
85	22	93
83	63	73
82	75	97
36	77	97

```
data work.jobsatis;
  set work.dataone work.datatwo;
run;
```

XisError: altImageDescription Element Should Not Be Blank.

Career	Supervis	Finance	Variety	Feedback	Autonomy
72	26	9	.	.	.
63	76	7	.	.	.
96	31	7	.	.	.
96	98	6	.	.	.
84	94	6	.	.	.
.	.	.	10	11	70
.	.	.	85	22	93
.	.	.	83	63	73
.	.	.	82	75	97
.	.	.	36	77	97

XisError: altImageDescription Element Should Not Be Blank.

Career	Supervis	Finance	Variety	Feedback	Autonomy
72	26	9	10	11	70
63	76	7	85	22	93
96	31	7	83	63	73
96	98	6	82	75	97
84	94	6	36	77	97

XisError: altImageDescription Element Should Not Be Blank.

Career	Supervis	Finance
72	26	9
63	76	7
96	31	7
96	98	6
84	94	6
10	11	70
85	22	93
83	63	73
82	75	97
36	77	97

none of the above

If you concatenate the data sets below in the order shown, what is the value of Sale in observation 2 of the new data set?

XisError: altImageDescription Element Should Not Be Blank.

Sales.Reps

ID	Name
1	Nay Rong
2	Kelly Windsor
3	Julio Meraz
4	Richard Krabill

Sales.Close

ID	Sale
1	$28,000
2	$30,000
2	$40,000
3	$15,000
3	$20,000
3	$25,000
4	$35,000

Sales.Bonus

ID	Bonus
1	$2,000
2	$4,000
3	$3,000
4	$2,500

missing

$30,000

$40,000

you cannot concatenate these data sets

What happens if you merge the following data sets by the variable SSN?

XisError: altImageDescription Element Should Not Be Blank.

1st

SSN	Age
029-46-9261	39
074-53-9892	34
228-88-9649	32
442-21-8075	12
446-93-2122	36
776-84-5391	28
929-75-0218	27

2nd

SSN	Age	Date
029-46-9261	37	02/15/95
074-53-9892	32	05/22/97
228-88-9649	30	03/04/96
442-21-8075	10	11/22/95
446-93-2122	34	07/08/96
776-84-5391	26	12/15/96
929-75-0218	25	04/30/97

The values of Age in the 1st data set overwrite the values of Age in the 2nd data set.

The values of Age in the 2nd data set overwrite the values of Age in the 1st data set.

The DATA step fails because the two data sets contain same-named variables that have different values.

The values of Age in the 2nd data set are set to missing.

Suppose you merge data sets Health.Set1 and Health.Set2 below:

XisError: altImageDescription Element Should Not Be Blank.

Health.Set1		
ID	Sex	Age
1129	F	48
1274	F	50
1387	F	57
2304	F	16
2486	F	63
4425	F	48
4759	F	60
5438	F	42
6488	F	59
9012	F	39
9125	F	56

Health.Set2		
ID	Height	Weight
1129	61	137
1387	64	142
2304	61	102
5438	62	168
6488	64	154
9012	63	157
9125	64	159

Which output does the following program create?

```
data work.merged;
   merge health.set1(in=in1) health.set2(in=in2);
   by id;
   if in1 and in2;
run;
proc print data=work.merged;
run;
```

XisError: altImageDescription Element Should Not Be Blank.

- 2126 -

Obs	ID	Sex	Age	Height	Weight
1	1129	F	48	61	137
2	1274	F	50	.	.
3	1387	F	57	64	142
4	2304	F	16	61	102
5	2486	F	63	.	.
6	4425	F	48	.	.
7	4759	F	60	.	.
8	5438	F	42	62	168
9	6488	F	59	64	154
10	9012	F	39	63	157
11	9125	F	56	64	159

XisError: altImageDescription Element Should Not Be Blank.

Obs	ID	Sex	Age	Height	Weight
1	1129	F	48	61	137
2	1387	F	50	64	142
3	2304	F	57	61	102
4	5438	F	16	62	168
5	6488	F	63	64	154
6	9012	F	48	63	157
7	9125	F	60	64	159
8	5438	F	42	.	
9	6488	F	59	.	
10	9012	F	39	.	
11	9125	F	56	.	

XisError: altImageDescription Element Should Not Be Blank.

Obs	ID	Sex	Age	Height	Weight
1	1129	F	48	61	137
2	1387	F	57	64	142
3	2304	F	16	61	102
4	5438	F	42	62	168
5	6488	F	59	64	154
6	9012	F	39	63	157
7	9125	F	56	64	159

none of the above

The data sets Ensemble.Spring and Ensemble.Sum both contain a variable named Blue. How do you prevent the values of the variable Blue from being overwritten when you merge the two data sets?

```
data ensemble.merged;
   merge ensemble.spring(in=blue)
          ensemble.summer;
      by fabric;
   run;
```

```
data ensemble.merged;
   merge ensemble.spring(out=blue)
          ensemble.summer;
      by fabric;
   run;
```

```
data ensemble.merged;
   merge ensemble.spring(blue=navy)
          ensemble.summer;
      by fabric;
   run;
```

```
data ensemble.merged;
   merge ensemble.spring(rename=(blue=navy))
          ensemble.summer;
      by fabric;
   run;
```

What happens if you submit the following program to merge Blood.Donors1 and Blood.Donors2, shown below?

```
data work.merged;
  merge blood.donors1 blood.donors2;
  by id;
run
```

XisError: altImageDescription Element Should Not Be Blank.

Blood.Donors1				Blood.Donors2		
ID	Type	Units		ID	Code	Units
2304	O	16		6488	65	27
1129	A	48		1129	63	32
1129	A	50		5438	62	39
1129	A	57		2304	61	45
2486	B	63		1387	64	67

The Merged data set contains some missing values because not all observations have matching observations in the other data set.

The Merged data set contains eight observations.

The DATA step produces errors.

Values for Units in Blood.Donors2 overwrite values of Units in Blood.Donors1.

If you merge Company.Staff1 and Company.Staff2 below by ID, how many observations does the new data set contain?

XisError: altImageDescription Element Should Not Be Blank.

Company.Staff1				Company.Staff2		
ID	Name	Dept	Project	ID	Name	Hours
000	Miguel	A12	Document	111	Fred	35
111	Fred	B45	Survey	222	Diana	40
222	Diana	B45	Document	777	Steve	0
888	Monique	A12	Document	888	Monique	37
999	Vien	D03	Survey			

4

5

6

9

If you merge data sets Sales.Reps, Sales.Close, and Sales.Bonus by ID, what is the value of Bonus in the third observation in the new data set?

XisError: altImageDescription Element Should Not Be Blank.

Sales.Reps	
ID	Name
1	Nay Rong
2	Kelly Windsor
3	Julio Meraz
4	Richard Krabill

Sales.Close	
ID	Sale
1	$28,000
2	$30,000
2	$40,000
3	$15,000
3	$20,000
3	$25,000
4	$35,000

Sales.Bonus	
ID	Bonus
1	$2,000
2	$4,000
3	$3,000
4	$2,500

$4,000

$3,000

missing

can't tell from the information given

Introduction to PROC FORMAT

Overview

Sometimes variable values are stored according to a code. For example, when the PRINT procedure displays the data set Perm.Employee, notice that the values for JobTitle are coded, and they are not easily interpreted.

Perm.Employee Data Set

	FirstName	LastName	JobTitle	Salary
1	Donny,	Evans	112	29996.63
2	Lisa	Helms	105	18567.23
3	John	Higgins	111	25309.24
4	Amy	Larson	113	32696.78
5	Mary	Moore	112	28945.89
6	Jason	Powell	103	35099.55
7	Judy	Riley	111	25309.37
8	Neal	Ryan	112	28180.85

You can display more descriptive values for these variables. Here is how a report that contains formatted values for the variable JobTitle might look. The predefined SAS formats cannot help here.

Perm.Employee Data Set with Formatted Values for JobTitle

	FirstName	LastName	JobTitle	Salary
1	Donny	Evans	technical writer	29996.63
2	Lisa	Helms	text processor	18567.23
3	John	Higgins	assoc. technical writer	25309.24
4	Amy	Larson	senior technical writer	32696.78
5	Mary	Moore	technical writer	28945.89
6	Jason	Powell	manager	35099.55
7	Judy	Riley	assoc. technical writer	25309.37
8	Neal	Ryan	technical writer	28180.85

However, you can use the FORMAT procedure to define your own formats for displaying values of variables.

Invoking PROC FORMAT

To begin a PROC FORMAT step, you use a PROC FORMAT statement.

General form, PROC FORMAT statement:

PROC FORMAT <*options*>;

where *options* include

> **LIBRARY=**_libref_ specifies the libref for a SAS data library to contain a permanent catalog of user-defined formats

> **FMTLIB** displays a list of all of the formats in your catalog, along with descriptions of their values.

Any time you use PROC FORMAT to create a format, the format is stored in a format catalog. If the SAS data library does not already contain a format catalog, SAS automatically creates one. If you do not specify the LIBRARY= option, the formats are stored in a default format catalog named Work.Formats.

As the libref Work implies, any format that is stored in Work.Formats is a temporary format that exists only for the current SAS session. At the end of the current session, the catalog is erased.

Permanently Storing Your Formats

You can store your formats in a permanent format catalog named Formats when you specify the LIBRARY= option in the PROC FORMAT statement.

PROC FORMAT LIBRARY=libref;

But first, you need a LIBNAME statement that associates the libref with the permanent SAS data library in which the format catalog is to be stored.

```
libname library 'c:\sas\formats\lib';
```

When you associate a permanent format with a variable in a subsequent DATA or PROC step, you would then use the Library libref to reference the location of the format catalog.

We'll discuss the use of permanent user-defined formats later, after you learn how to create them.

Now, any format that you create in this PROC FORMAT step is stored in a permanent format catalog called Library.Formats.

```
libname library 'c:\sas\formats\lib';
proc format library=library;
   ... ;
run;
```

In the program above, the catalog Library.Formats is located in the SAS data library **C:\Sas\Formats\Lib**, which is referenced by the libref Library.

Notice that LIB= is an acceptable abbreviation for the LIBRARY= option.

```
proc format lib=library;
```

Also notice that you can specify a catalog name in the LIBRARY= option, and you can store formats in any catalog. The catalog name must conform to SAS naming conventions.

```
proc format lib=library.catalog;
```

Now that you know how to store your own formats, let's see how to create them.

Reading Multiple Records Sequentially

The Forward Slash (/) Line Pointer Control

Use the forward slash (/) line pointer control to read multiple records sequentially. The / advances the input pointer to the next record. The / line pointer control moves the input pointer forward only and must be specified *after* the instructions for reading the values in the current record.

The single INPUT statement below reads the values for Lname and Fname in the first record, followed by the values for Department and JobCode in the second record. Then the value for Salary is read in the third record.

```
input Lname $ 1-8 Fname $ 10-15 /
```

Department $ 1-12 JobCode $ 15-19 /
Salary comma10.;

Multiple Records Comprising Each Observation

```
1---+----10---+----
ABRAMS    THOMAS
MARKETING      SR01
$25,209.03
BARCLAY   ROBERT
EDUCATION      IN01
$24,435.71
COURTNEY MARK
PUBLICATIONS   TW01
$24,006.16
```

Using the / Line Pointer Control

Look at the forward slash (/) line pointer control in the following example.

The raw data file Memdata contains the mailing list of a professional organization. Your task is to combine the information for each member into a single observation. We'll begin by reading each member's name, followed by the street address, and finally the city, state, and zip code.

As you write the instructions to read the values for Fname and Lname, notice that not all of the values for Lname begin in the same column. So, you should use standard list input to read these values.

```
data perm.members;
   infile memdata;
   input Fname $ Lname $
```

Raw Data File Memdata

```
1---+----10---+----20
LEE ATHNOS
1215 RAINTREE CIRCLE
PHOENIX   AZ 85044
HEIDIE BAKER
1751 DIEHL ROAD
VIENNA   VA 22124
MYRON BARKER
131 DONERAIL DRIVE
ATLANTA   GA 30363
JOYCE BENEFIT
85 MAPLE AVENUE
MENLO PARK   CA 94025
```

Now you want to read the values for Address from the second record. The / line pointer control advances the input pointer to the next record. At this point the INPUT statement is incomplete, so you should not place a semicolon after the line pointer control.

```
data perm.members;
   infile memdata;
   input Fname $ Lname $ /
```

Raw Data File Memdata

```
1---+----10---+----20
LEE ATHNOS
1215 RAINTREE CIRCLE
PHOENIX   AZ 85044
HEIDIE BAKER
1751 DIEHL ROAD
VIENNA   VA 22124
MYRON BARKER
131 DONERAIL DRIVE
ATLANTA   GA 30363
JOYCE BENEFIT
85 MAPLE AVENUE
MENLO PARK  CA 94025
```

You can use column input to read the values in the next record as one variable named Address. Then add a line pointer control to move the input pointer to the next record.

```
data perm.members;
   infile memdata;
   input Fname $ Lname $ /
      Address $ 1-20 /
```

Line Pointer Control Advanced One Record

```
1---+----10---+----20
LEE ATHNOS
1215 RAINTREE CIRCLE
PHOENIX   AZ  85044
HEIDIE BAKER
1751 DIEHL ROAD
VIENNA   VA 22124
MYRON BARKER
131 DONERAIL DRIVE
ATLANTA   GA 30363
JOYCE BENEFIT
85 MAPLE AVENUE
MENLO PARK   CA 94025
```

As you write the statements to read the values for City, notice that some of the values are longer than eight characters and contain embedded blanks. Also note that each value is followed by two consecutive blanks. To read these values, you should use modified list input with the ampersand (#38) modifier.

The values for State and the values for Zip do not begin in the same column. Therefore, you should use list input to read these values.

```
data perm.members;
   infile memdata;
   input Fname $ Lname $ /
        Address $ 1-20 /
        City #38 $10. State $ Zip $;
run;
```

Line Pointer Control Advanced Another Record

```
1---+----10---+----20
LEE ATHNOS
1215 RAINTREE CIRCLE
PHOENIX   AZ  85044
HEIDIE BAKER
1751 DIEHL ROAD
VIENNA   VA 22124
MYRON BARKER
131 DONERAIL DRIVE
ATLANTA   GA 30363
JOYCE BENEFIT
85 MAPLE AVENUE
MENLO PARK   CA 94025
```

Sequential Processing of Multiple Records in the DATA Step

Now that you've learned the basics of using the / line pointer control, let's look at the sequential processing of multiple records in the DATA step.

The values in the first record are read, and the / line pointer control moves the input pointer to the second record.

Reading the First Record of the First Observation

The values for Address are read, and the second / line pointer control advances the input pointer to the third record.

Reading the Second Record of the First Observation

The values for City, State, and Zip are read. The INPUT statement is complete.

Reading the Third Record of the First Observation

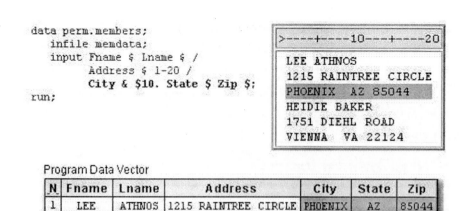

```
data perm.members;
   infile memdata;
   input Fname $ Lname $ /
         Address $ 1-20 /
         City & $10. State $ Zip $;
run;
```

```
>----+----10---+----20
LEE ATHNOS
1215 RAINTREE CIRCLE
PHOENIX  AZ 85044
HEIDIE BAKER
1751 DIEHL ROAD
VIENNA  VA 22124
```

Program Data Vector

N	Fname	Lname	Address	City	State	Zip
1	LEE	ATHNOS	1215 RAINTREE CIRCLE	PHOENIX	AZ	85044

The values in the program data vector are written to the data set as the first observation.

The Program Data Vector and the SAS Data Set Perm.Members

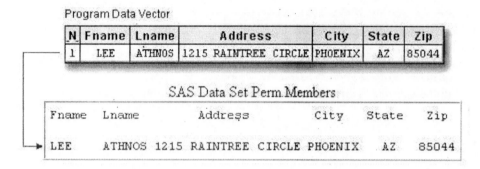

Program Data Vector

N	Fname	Lname	Address	City	State	Zip
1	LEE	ATHNOS	1215 RAINTREE CIRCLE	PHOENIX	AZ	85044

SAS Data Set Perm.Members

```
Fname    Lname         Address          City     State    Zip

LEE      ATHNOS 1215 RAINTREE CIRCLE PHOENIX     AZ      85044
```

Control returns to the top of the DATA step. The variable values are reinitialized to missing.

Reinitializing the Variable Values to Missing

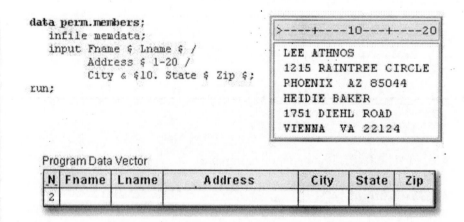

```
data perm.members;
   infile memdata;
   input Fname $ Lname $ /
         Address $ 1-20 /
         City & $10. State $ Zip $;
run;
```

```
>----+----10---+----20
LEE ATHNOS
1215 RAINTREE CIRCLE
PHOENIX  AZ 85044
HEIDIE BAKER
1751 DIEHL ROAD
VIENNA  VA 22124
```

Program Data Vector

N	Fname	Lname	Address	City	State	Zip
2					.	

During the second iteration, values for Fname and Lname are read beginning in column 1 of the fourth record.

Reading the First Record of the Second Observation

Program Data Vector

N	Fname	Lname	Address	City	State	Zip
2	HEIDIE	BAKER				

The values for Address are read. The / line pointer control advances the input pointer to the fifth record.

Reading the Second Record of the Second Observation

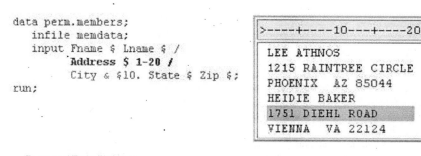

Program Data Vector

N	Fname	Lname	Address	City	State	Zip
2	HEIDIE	BAKER	1751 DIEHL ROAD			

The values for City, State, and Zip are read. The INPUT statement is complete.

Reading the Third Record of the First Observation

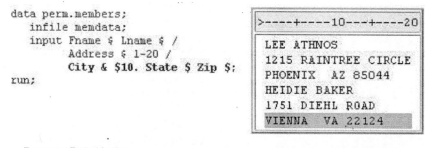

Program Data Vector

N	Fname	Lname	Address	City	State	Zip
2	HEIDIE	BAKER	1751 DIEHL ROAD	VIENNA	VA	22124

The values in the program data vector are written to the data set as the second observation.

The Program Data Vector and the SAS Data Set Perm.Members

Program Data Vector

N	Fname	Lname	Address	City	State	Zip
2	HEIDIE	BAKER	1751 DIEHL ROAD	VIENNA	VA	22124

SAS Data Set Perm.Members

```
Fname    Lname          Address        City     State    Zip

LEE      ATHNOS  1215 RAINTREE CIRCLE  PHOENIX   AZ     85044
HEIDIE   BAKER   1751 DIEHL ROAD       VIENNA    VA     22124
```

After the data set is complete, PROC PRINT output for Perm.Members shows that each observation contains the complete information for one member.

proc print data=perm.members;
run;

PROC PRINT Output of the Complete Perm.Members Data Set

Obs	Fname	Lname	Address	City	State	Zip
1	LEE	ATHNOS	1215 RAINTREE CIRCLE	PHOENIX	AZ	85044
2	HEIDIE	BAKER	1751 DIEHL ROAD	VIENNA	VA	22124
3	MYRON	BARKER	131 DONERAIL DRIVE	ATLANTA	GA	30363
4	JOYCE	BENEFIT	85 MAPLE AVENUE	MENLO PARK	CA	94025

Number of Records per Observation

Note that the raw data file must contain the same number of records for each observation.

Suppose there are only two records for the second member. Remember, the INPUT statement is set up to read three records.

data perm.members;
  infile memdata;
  input Fname $ Lname $ /
  Address $ 1-20 /
  City #38 $10. State $ Zip $;

Raw Data File Memdata

```
1---+----10---+----20
LEE ATHNOS
1215 RAINTREE CIRCLE
PHOENIX   AZ 85044
HEIDIE BAKER
1751 DIEHL ROAD
MYRON BARKER
131 DONERAIL DRIVE
ATLANTA   GA 30363
JOYCE BENEFIT
85 MAPLE AVENUE
MENLO PARK   CA 94025
```

The second member's name and address are read and assigned to corresponding variables. Then the input pointer advances to the next record, as directed by the INPUT statement, and the third member's name is read as a value for City.

The INPUT statement looks for a value for State and Zip, so the input pointer advances to the next record and reads the member's address.

The PROC PRINT output for this data set illustrates the problem.

Obs	Fname	Lname	Address	City	State	Zip
1	LEE	ATHNOS	1215 RAINTREE CIRCLE	PHOENIX	AZ	85044
2	HEIDIE	BAKER	1751 DIEHL ROAD	MYRON BARK	131	DONERAIL
3	ATLANTA GA		JOYCE BENEFIT	85 MAPLE A	MENLO	PARK

Before you write the INPUT statement, check whether the raw data file contains the same number of records for each observation. In this raw data file there are now three records for each observation.

Verifying the Number of Records for Each Observation

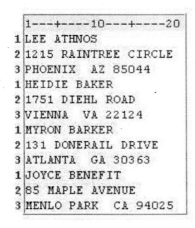
```
  1---+----10---+----20
1 LEE ATHNOS
2 1215 RAINTREE CIRCLE
3 PHOENIX   AZ 85044
1 HEIDIE BAKER
2 1751 DIEHL ROAD
3 VIENNA   VA 22124
1 MYRON BARKER
2 131 DONERAIL DRIVE
3 ATLANTA   GA 30363
1 JOYCE BENEFIT
2 85 MAPLE AVENUE
3 MENLO PARK   CA 94025
```

For more information about working with raw data files that contain missing records, see the SAS documentation.

Overview

Introduction

Sometimes raw data files contain data for several observations in one record. Data can be stored in this manner to reduce the size of the entire data file.

Each record can contain

repeating blocks of data that represent separate observations

Repeating Blocks of Data

```
1---+----10---+----20---+----30--
01APR90  68 02APR90  67 03APR90  70
04APR90  74 05APR90  72 06APR90  73
07APR90  71 08APR90  75 09APR90  76
```

an ID field followed by an equal number of repeating fields that represent separate observations

ID Field with Repeating Fields

```
1---+----10---+----20---+----30--
001 WALKING AEROBICS CYCLING
002 SWIMMING CYCLING SKIING
003 TENNIS SWIMMING AEROBICS
```

an ID field followed by a varying number of repeating fields that represent separate observations.

ID Field with Varying Number of Repeating Fields

```
1---+----10---+----20---+----30--
001 WALKING
002 SWIMMING CYCLING SKIING
003 TENNIS SWIMMING
```

This chapter shows you several ways of creating multiple observations from a single record.

Objectives

In this chapter, you learn to

create multiple observations from a single record that contains repeating blocks of data

create multiple observations from a single record that contains one ID field followed by the *same* number of repeating fields

create multiple observations from a single record that contains one ID field followed by a *varying* number of repeating fields.

Additionally, you learn to

hold the current record across iterations of the DATA step

hold the current record for the next INPUT statement

execute SAS statements based on a variable's value

explicitly write an observation to a data set

execute SAS statements while a condition is true.

Chapter 15: Processing Variables with Arrays

Which statement is *false* regarding an ARRAY statement?

It is an executable statement.

It can be used to create variables.

It must contain either all numeric or all character elements.

It must be used to define an array before the array name can be referenced.

Correct answer: a

An ARRAY statement is not an executable statement; it merely defines an array.

What belongs within the braces of this ARRAY statement?

array contrib{?} qtr1-qtr4;

quarter

quarter*

1-4

4

Correct answer: d

The value in parentheses indicates the number of elements in the array. In this case, there are four elements.

For the program below, select an iterative DO statement to process all elements in the contrib array.

```
data work.contrib;
  array contrib{4} qtr1-qtr4;
     ...
     contrib{i}=contrib{i}*1.25;
  end;
run;
```

      do i=4;

      do i=1 to 4;

      do until i=4;

      do while i le 4;

Correct answer: b

In the DO statement, you specify the index variable that represents the values of the array elements. Then specify the start and stop positions of the array elements.

What is the value of the index variable that references Jul in the statements below?

```
array quarter{4} Jan Apr Jul Oct;
do i=1 to 4;
  yeargoal=quarter{i}*1.2;
end;
```

    1

    2

    3

    4

Correct answer: c

The index value represents the position of the array element. In this case, the third element is Jul.

Which DO statement would *not* process all the elements in the factors array shown below?

array factors{*} age height weight bloodpr;

do i=1 to dim(factors);

do i=1 to dim(*);

do i=1,2,3,4;

do i=1 to 4;

Correct answer: b

To process all the elements in an array, you can either specify the array dimension or use the DIM function with the array name as the argument.

Which statement below is *false* regarding the use of arrays to create variables?

The variables are added to the program data vector during the compilation of the DATA step.

You do not need to specify the array elements in the ARRAY statement.

By default, all character variables are assigned a length of eight.

Only character variables can be created.

Correct answer: d

Either numeric or character variables can be created by an ARRAY statement.

For the first observation, what is the value of diff{i} at the end of the second iteration of the DO loop?

XisError: altImageDescription Element Should Not Be Blank.

Weight1	Weight2	Weight3
192	200	215
137	130	125
220	210	213

```
array wt{*} weight1-weight10;
array diff{9};
do i=1 to 9;
  diff{i}=wt{i+1}-wt{i};
end;
```

15

10

8

-7

Correct answer: a

At the end of the second iteration, **diff{*i*}** resolves as follows:

```
diff{2}=wt{2+1}-wt{2};
diff{2}=215-200
```

Finish the ARRAY statement below to create temporary array elements that have initial values of **9000, 9300, 9600,** and **9900**.

```
array goal{4} ... ;
```

temporary (9000 9300 9600 9900)

temporary (9000 9300 9600 9900)

temporary 9000 9300 9600 9900

(temporary) 9000 9300 9600 9900

Correct answer: a

To create temporary array elements, specify _TEMPORARY_ after the array name and dimension. Specify an initial value for each element, separated by either blanks or commas, and enclose the values in parentheses.

Based on the ARRAY statement below, select the array reference for the array element q50.

array ques{3,25} q1-q75;

ques{q50}

ques{1,50}

ques{2,25}

ques{3,0}

Correct answer: c

This two-dimensional array would consist of three rows of 25 elements. The first row would contain q1 through q25, the second row would start with q26 and end with q50, and the third row would start with q51 and end with q75.

Select the ARRAY statement that defines the array in the following program.

```
data coat;
   input category high1-high3 / low1-low3;
   array compare{2,3} high1-high3 low1-low3;
   do i=1 to 2;
     do j=1 to 3;
       compare{i,j}=round(compare{i,j}*1.12);
     end;
   end;
datalines;
5555 9 8 7 6
4 3 2 1
8888 21 12 34 64
```

```
       13 14 15 16
       ;
       run;
```

array compare{1,6} high1-high3 low1-low3;

array compare{2,3} high1-high3 low1-low3;

array compare{3,2} high1-high3 low1-low3;

array compare{3,3} high1-high3 low1-low3;

Correct answer: b

The nested DO loops indicate that the array is named compare and is a two-dimensional array that has two rows and three columns.

Creating HTML Output with a Table of Contents

Overview

So far in this chapter, you've used the BODY= specification to create an HTML file containing your procedure output. Suppose you want to create an HTML file that has a table of contents with links to the output of each specific procedure. You can do this by specifying additional files in the ODS HTML statement.

General form, ODS HTML statement to create a linked table of contents:

ODS HTML

BODY=body-file-specification
CONTENTS=contents-file-specification
FRAME=frame-file-specification;

ODS HTML CLOSE;

where

body-file-specification is the name of an HTML file that contains the procedure output.

contents-file-specification is the name of an HTML file that contains a table of contents with links to the procedure output.

frame-file-specification is the name of an HTML file that integrates the table of contents and the body file. If you specify FRAME=, you must also specify CONTENTS=.

To direct the HTML output to a specific storage location, specify the complete pathname of the HTML file in the *file-specification*.

Example

In the program below,

the BODY= specification creates data.html in the **c:\records** directory. The body file contains the results of the two procedures.

the CONTENTS= specification creates toc.html in the **c:\records** directory. The table of contents file has links to each procedure output in the body file.

the FRAME= specification creates frame.html in the **c:\records** directory. The frame file integrates the table of contents and the body file.

XisError: altImageDescription Element Should Not Be Blank.

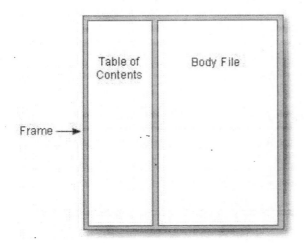

```
ods html body='c:\records\data.html'
       contents='c:\records\toc.html'
       frame='c:\records\frame.html';
proc print data=clinic.admit label;
   var id sex age height weight actlevel;
   label actlevel='Activity Level';
run;
proc print data=clinic.stress2;
   var id resthr maxhr rechr;
run;
ods html close;
```

ods html;

Viewing Frame Files

The Results window does not display links to frame files. In the Windows environment, only the body file will automatically appear in the internal browser or your preferred Web browser.

To view the frame file that integrates the body file and the table of contents, select **File ➤ Open** from within the internal browser or your preferred Web browser. Then open the frame file that you specified using FRAME=. In the example above, this file is frame.html, which is stored in the Records directory in the Windows environment.

The frame file, frame.html, is shown below.

Frame File, Frame.html

Using the Table of Contents

The table of contents created by the CONTENTS= option contains a numbered heading for each procedure that creates output. Below each heading is a link to the output for that procedure.

On some browsers, you can select a heading to contract or expand the table of contents.

Table of Contents

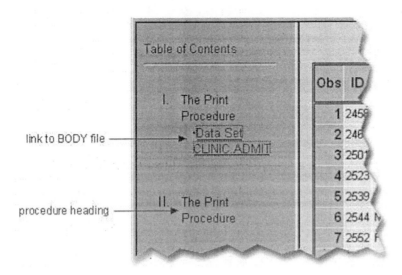

link to BODY file

procedure heading

Overview

Introduction

In previous chapters, you've seen both traditional SAS LISTING output and HTML output. HTML output is created by default in the SAS Windowing environment in the Windows and UNIX operating systems. If you are not using SAS in the SAS in the SAS Windowing environment in the Windows and UNIX operating systems, then you can set options to create HTML output. The HTML created by default is basic HTML 4.0 with default formatting.

You can use ODS to create many other types of output. You can create RTF, PDF, Excel, and many others using ODS statements. This chapter will discuss HTML output.

Using ODS, you can customize and manage HTML output by submitting programming statements. After you create HTML files, you can view them in the Results Viewer or Internet Explorer, Netscape Navigator, or any Web browser that fully supports HTML 4.0.

This chapter shows you how to create and view HTML output using ODS. You also learn how to apply styles to ODS output.

⚠ By default, all code that you submit to SAS with Enterprise Guide has ODS statements included to create HTML output.

LISTING Output versus HTML Output

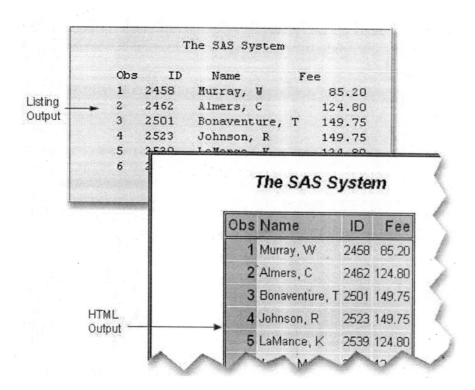

Listing Output

HTML Output

Objectives

In this chapter, you learn to

open and close ODS destinations

create a simple HTML file with the output of one or more procedures

create HTML output with a linked table of contents in a frame

use options to specify links and file paths

view HTML output

apply styles to HTML output.

Objectives

In this chapter, you learn to

determine the *n*-count, mean, standard deviation, minimum, and maximum of numeric variables using the MEANS procedure

control the number of decimal places used in PROC MEANS output

specify the variables for which to produce statistics

use the PROC SUMMARY procedure to produce the same results as the PROC MEANS procedure

describe the difference between the SUMMARY and MEANS procedures create one-way frequency tables for categorical data using the FREQ procedure

create two-way and -way crossed frequency tables

control the layout and complexity of crossed frequency tables.

Chapter Summary

Text Summary

Multiple Records per Observation

Information for one observation can be spread out over several records. You can write one INPUT statement that contains line pointer controls to specify the record(s) from which values are read.

Reading Multiple Records Sequentially

The forward slash (/) line pointer control is used to read multiple records sequentially. Each time a / pointer is encountered, the input pointer advances to the next line.

Reading Multiple Records Non-Sequentially

The #n line pointer control is used to read multiple records non-sequentially. The #n specifies the absolute number of the line to which you want to move the pointer.

Combining Line Pointer Controls

The / line pointer control and the #n line pointer control can be combined within a SAS program to read multiple records both sequentially and non-sequentially.

Syntax

LIBNAME *libref 'SAS-data-library'*;

FILENAME *fileref 'filename'*;

DATA *SAS-data-set*;

INFILE *file-specification*;
INPUT *#n variable ...*
#n @n variable ... / variable ... / variable ... ;

RUN;

PROC PRINT DATA=*SAS-data-set*;

RUN;

Sample Program

```
libname perm 'c:\records\empdata';
filename personel 'c:\records\empdata\new.dat';
data perm.emplist3;
   infile personel;
   input #2 Department $ 5-16
      #1 @16 ID $4. @1 Name $14. /
         JobCode 3. /
         Salary comma9.;
run;
proc print data=perm.emplist3;
run;
```

Points to Remember

When a file contains multiple records per observation, depending on the program, the file might need to contain the same number of records for each observation.

Because the / pointer control can move forward only, the pointer control is specified *after* the values in the current record are read.

The *#n* pointer control can read records in any order and must be specified *before* the variable names are defined.

A semicolon should be placed at the end of the *complete* INPUT statement.

SAS Libraries

So far you've learned about SAS programs. Now let's look at SAS libraries to see how SAS data sets and other SAS files are organized and stored.

How SAS Files Are Stored

Every SAS file is stored in a SAS library, which is a collection of SAS files. A SAS data library is the highest level of organization for information within SAS.

For example, in the Windows and UNIX environments, a library is typically a group of SAS files in the same folder or directory.

SAS Data Library

The table below summarizes the implementation of SAS libraries in various operating environments.

Environments and SAS Libraries

In this environment...	A SAS library is...
Windows, UNIX, OpenVMS, OS/2 (directory based-systems)	a group of SAS files that are stored in the same directory. Other files can be stored in the directory, but only the files that have SAS file extensions are recognized as part of the SAS library. 📖 For more information, see the SAS documentation for your operating environment.
z/OS (OS/390)	a specially formatted host data set in which only SAS files are stored.

Storing Files Temporarily or Permanently

Depending on the library name that you use when you create a file, you can store SAS files temporarily or permanently.

Temporary SAS Data Library

Permanent SAS Data Library

Permanent
SAS Data Library

Temporary and Permanent SAS Libraries

Temporary SAS libraries last
only for the current SAS
session.

Storing files temporarily:

If you don't specify a library name when you create a file (or if you
specify the library name Work), the file is stored in the temporary SAS
data library. When you end the session, the temporary library and all of its
files are deleted.

Permanent SAS Libraries are
available to you during
subsequent SAS sessions.

Storing files permanently:

To store files permanently in a SAS data library, you specify a library
name other than the default library name Work.
For example, by specifying the library name sasuser when you create a
file, you specify that the file is to be stored in a permanent SAS data
library until you delete it.

You can learn how to set up permanent SAS libraries in <u>Referencing Files and Setting Options</u>.

Chapter 20: Creating Multiple Observations from a Single Record

Which is true for the double trailing at sign (@@)?

It enables the next INPUT statement to read from the current record across multiple iterations
of the DATA step.

It must be the last item specified in the INPUT statement.

It is released when the input pointer moves past the end of the record.

all of the above

Correct answer: d

The double trailing at sign (@@) enables the next INPUT statement to read from the current record across multiple iterations of the DATA step. It must be the last item specified in the INPUT statement. A record that is being held by the double trailing at sign (@@) is not released until the input pointer moves past the end of the record, or until an INPUT statement that has no line-hold specifier executes.

A record that is being held by a single trailing at sign (@) is automatically released when

the input pointer moves past the end of the record.

the next iteration of the DATA step begins.

another INPUT statement that has an @ executes.

another value is read from the observation.

Correct answer: b

Unlike the double trailing at sign (@@), the single trailing at sign (@) is automatically released when control returns to the top of the DATA step for the next iteration. The trailing @ does not toggle on and off. If another INPUT statement that has a trailing @ executes, the holding effect is still on.

Which SAS program correctly creates a separate observation for each block of data?

XisError: altImageDescription Element Should Not Be Blank.

```
1---+----10---+----20---+----30---+----40---+
1001 apple 1002 banana 1003 cherry
1004 guava 1005 kiwi 1006 papaya
1007 pineapple 1008 raspberry 1009 strawberry
```

```
data perm.produce;
  infile fruit;
  input Item $ Variety : $10.;
run;
```

```
data perm.produce;
  infile fruit;
  input Item $ Variety : $10. @;
run;
```

```
data perm.produce;
  infile fruit;
  input Item $ Variety : $10. @@;
run;
```

```
data perm.produce;
   infile fruit @@;
   input Item $ Variety : $10.;
run;
```

Correct answer: c

Each record in this file contains three repeating blocks of data values for Item and Variety. The INPUT statement reads a block of values for Item and Variety, and then holds the current record by using the double-trailing at sign (@@). The values in the program data vector are written to the data set as the first observation. In the next iteration, the INPUT statement reads the next block of values for Item and Variety from the same record.

Which SAS program reads the values for ID and holds the record for each value of Quantity, so that three observations are created for each record?

XisError: altImageDescription Element Should Not Be Blank.

```
1---+----10---+----20---+----30
2101 21,208 19,047 22,890
2102 18,775 20,214 22,654
2103 19,763 22,927 21,862
```

```
data work.sales;
   infile unitsold;
   input ID $;
   do week=1 to 3;
     input Quantity : comma.;
     output;
   end;
run;
```

```
data work.sales;
   infile unitsold;
   input ID $ @@;
   do week=1 to 3;
     input Quantity : comma.;
     output;
   end;
run;
```

```
data work.sales;
   infile unitsold;
   input ID $ @;
   do week=1 to 3;
```

- 2157 -

```
    input Quantity : comma.;
    output;
  end;
run;



data work.sales;
  infile unitsold;
  input ID $ @;
  do week=1 to 3;
    input Quantity : comma. @;
    output;
  end;
run;
```

Correct answer: d

This raw data file contains an ID field followed by repeating fields. The first INPUT statement reads the values for ID and uses the @ line-hold specifier to hold the current record for the next INPUT statement in the DATA step. The second INPUT statement reads the values for Quantity. When all of the repeating fields have been read, control returns to the top of the DATA step, and the record is released.

Which SAS statement repetitively executes several statements when the value of an index variable named count ranges from 1 to 50, incremented by 5?

```
do count=1 to 50 by 5;
```

```
do while count=1 to 50 by 5;
```

```
do count=1 to 50 + 5;
```

```
do while (count=1 to 50 + 5);
```

Correct answer: a

The iterative DO statement begins the execution of a loop based on the value of an index variable. Here, the loop executes when the value of count ranges from 1 to 50, incremented by 5.

Which option below, when used in a DATA step, writes an observation to the data set after each value for Activity has been read?

```
do choice=1 to 3;
   input Activity : $10. @;
   output;
end;
run;
```

```
do choice=1 to 3;
   input Activity : $10. @;
end;
output;
run;
```

```
do choice=1 to 3;
   input Activity : $10. @;
end;
run;
```

both a and b

Correct answer: a

The OUTPUT statement must be in the loop so that each time a value for Activity is read, an observation is immediately written to the data set.

Which SAS statement repetitively executes while the value of Cholesterol is greater than **200**?

```
do cholesterol > 200;
```

```
do cholesterol gt 200;
```

```
do while (cholesterol > 200);
```

```
do while cholesterol > 200;
```

Correct answer: c

The DO WHILE statement checks for the condition that Cholesterol is greater than 200. The expression must be enclosed in parentheses. The expression is evaluated at the top of the loop before the loop executes. If the condition is true, the DO WHILE loop executes. If the expression is false the first time it is evaluated, the loop does not execute.

Which choice below is an example of a sum statement?

totalpay=1;

totalpay+1;

totalpay*1;

totalpay by 1;

Correct answer: b

The sum statement adds the result of an expression to an accumulator variable. The + sign is an essential part of the sum statement. Here, the value of TotalPay is incremented by 1.

Which program creates the SAS data set Perm.Topstore from the raw data file shown below?

XisError: altImageDescription Element Should Not Be Blank.

```
1---+----10---+----20---+----30---+
1001 77,163.19 76,804.75 74,384.27
1002 76,612.93 81,456.34 82,063.97
1003 82,185.16 79,742.33
```

XisError: altImageDescription Element Should Not Be Blank.

SAS Data Set Perm.Topstore

Store	Sales	Month
1001	77163.19	1
1001	76804.75	2
1001	74384.27	3
1002	76612.93	1
1002	81456.34	2
1002	82063.97	3
1003	82185.16	1
1003	79742.33	2

```
data perm.topstores;
  infile sales98 missover;
  input Store Sales : comma. @;
  do while (sales ne .);
    month + 1;
    output;
    input sales : comma. @;
  end;
run;



data perm.topstores;
  infile sales98 missover;
  input Store Sales : comma. @;
  do while (sales ne .);
    Month=0;
    month + 1;
    output;
    input sales : comma. @;
  end;
run;



data perm.topstores;
  infile sales98 missover;
  input Store Sales : comma.
  Month @;
  do while (sales ne .);
    month + 1;
    input sales : comma. @;
  end;
  output;
run;



data perm.topstores;
  infile sales98 missover;
  input Store Sales : comma. @;
  Month=0;
  do while (sales ne .);
    month + 1;
    output;
    input sales : comma. @;
  end;
run;
```

Correct answer: d

The first input statement reads STORE and SALES and holds the record. Month is initialized to 0. The DO loop executes while SALES is not missing. Inside the loop, month increments, an observation is output, the next SALES value is read, and the record is held. The loop stops when a missing value of SALES is read. Control returns to the top of the DATA step, the held record is released, and the input statement reads the next record.

How many observations are produced by the DATA step that reads this external file?

XisError: altImageDescription Element Should Not Be Blank.

```
1---+----10---+----20---+----30---+----40
01 CHOCOLATE VANILLA RASPBERRY
02 VANILLA PEACH
03 CHOCOLATE
04 RASPBERRY PEACH CHOCOLATE
05 STRAWBERRY VANILLA CHOCOLATE
```

```
data perm.choices;
   infile icecream missover;
   input Day $ Flavor : $10. @;
   do while (flavor ne ' ');
      output;
   input flavor : $10. @;
   end;
run;
```

3

5

12

15

Correct answer: c

This DATA step produces one observation for each repeating field. The MISSOVER option in the INFILE statement prevents SAS from reading the next record when missing values occur at the end of a record. Every observation contains one value for Flavor, paired with the corresponding value for ID. Because there are 12 values for Flavor, there are 12 observations in the data set.

Chapter Summary

Text Summary

Purpose of SAS Arrays

An array is a temporary grouping of variables under a single name. This can reduce the number of statements needed to process variables and can simplify the maintenance of DATA step programs.

Defining an Array

To group variables into an array, use an ARRAY statement that specifies the array's name; its dimension enclosed in braces, brackets, or parentheses; and the elements to include. For example: array sales{4} qtr1 qtr2 qtr3 qtr4;

Variable Lists as Array Elements

You can use a variable list to specify array elements. Depending on the form of the variable list, it can specify all numeric or all character variables, or a numbered range of variables.

Referencing Elements of an Array

When you define an array in a DATA step, a subscript is assigned to each element. During execution, you can use an array reference to perform actions on specific array elements. When used in a DO loop, for example, the index variable of the iterative DO statement can reference each element of the array.

The DIM Function

When using DO loops to process arrays, you can also use the DIM function to specify the TO clause of the iterative DO statement. When you use the DIM function, you do not have to re-specify the stop value of a DO statement if you change the dimension of the array.

Creating Variables with the ARRAY Statement

If you don't specify array elements in an ARRAY statement, SAS automatically creates variable names for you by concatenating the array name and the numbers 1, 2, 3 ... up to the array dimension. To create an array of character variables, add a dollar sign ($) after the array dimension. By default, all character variables that are created with an ARRAY statement are assigned a length of 8; however, you can specify a different length after the dollar sign.

Assigning Initial Values to Arrays

To assign initial values in an ARRAY statement, place the values in parentheses after the array elements, specifying one initial value for each array element and separating each value with a comma or blank. To assign initial values to character variables, enclose each value in quotation marks.

Creating Temporary Array Elements

You can create temporary array elements for DATA step processing without creating additional variables. Just specify _TEMPORARY_ after the array name and dimension. This is useful when the array is needed only to perform a calculation.

Multidimensional Arrays

To define a multidimensional array, specify the number of elements in each dimension, separated by a comma. For example, **array new{3,4} x1-x12;** defines a two-dimensional array, with the first dimension specifying the number of rows (3) and the second dimension specifying the number of columns (4).

Referencing Elements of a Two-Dimensional Array

Multidimensional arrays are typically used with nested DO loops. If a DO loop processes a two-dimensional array, you can reference any element within the array by specifying the two dimensions.

Rotating Data Sets

You can use arrays to rotate a data set. Rotating a data set changes variables to observations or observations to variables.

Syntax

ARRAY *array-name{dimension}* *<elements>*;

array-name(*subscript*)

DIM(*array-name*)

Sample Programs

```
data work.report(drop=i);
  set master.temps;
  array wkday{7} mon tue wed thr fri sat sun;
  do i=1 to 7;
    wkday{i}=5*(wkday{i}-32)/9;
  end;
run;


data hrd.convert(drop=i);
  set hrd.fitclass;
  array wt{6} weight1-weight6;
  do i=1 to dim(wt);
    wt{i}=wt{i}*2.2046;
  end;
run;


data hrd.diff(drop=i);
  set hrd.convert;
  array wt{6} weight1-weight6;
  array WgtDiff{5};
  do i=1 to 5;
    wgtdiff{i}=wt{i+1}-wt{i};
  end;
run;


data finance.report(drop=i);
  set finance.qsales;
  array sale{4} sales1-sales4;
  array goal{4} _temporary_ (9000 9300 9600 9900);
```

```
   array Achieved{4};
   do i=1 to 4;
     achieved{i}=100*sale{i}/goal{i};
   end;
run;


data finance.quarters(drop=i j);
  set finance.monthly;
  array m{4,3} month1-month12;
  array Qtr{4};
  do i=1 to 4;
    qtr{i}=0;
    do j=1 to 3;
      qtr{i}+m{i,j};
    end;
  end;
run;
```

Points to Remember

A SAS array exists only for the duration of the DATA step.

Do not give an array the same name as a variable in the same DATA step. Also, avoid using the name of a SAS function as an array name; the array will be correct, but you won't be able to use the function in the same DATA step, and a warning will be written to the SAS log.

You can indicate the dimension of a one-dimensional array with an asterisk (*) as long as you specify the elements of the array.

When referencing array elements, be careful not to confuse variable names with the array references.

Overview

Introduction

Now that you're familiar with the basics, you can learn how to use the SAS programming windows to edit and debug programs effectively.

SAS Programming Windows

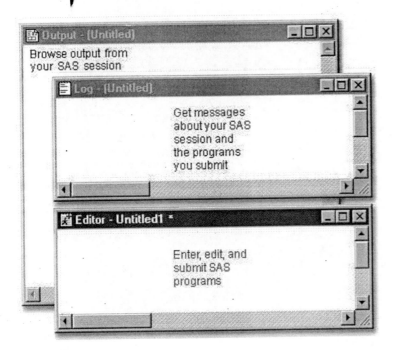

Browse output from your SAS session

Get messages about your SAS session and the programs you submit

Enter, edit, and submit SAS programs

Objectives

In this chapter you learn to

open a stored SAS program

edit SAS programs

clear SAS programming windows

interpret error messages in the SAS log

correct errors

resolve common problems.

Chapter Quiz

Select the best answer for each question. After completing the quiz, you can check your answers using the answer key in the appendix.

Which PROC PRINT step below creates the following output?

Date	On	Changed	Flight
04MAR99	232	18	219
05MAR99	160	4	219
06MAR99	163	14	219
07MAR99	241	9	219
08MAR99	183	11	219
09MAR99	211	18	219
10MAR99	167	7	219

```
proc print data=flights.laguardia noobs;
   var on changed flight;
   where on>=160;
run;
```

```
proc print data=flights.laguardia;
   var date on changed flight;
   where changed>3;
run;
```

```
proc print data=flights.laguardia label;
   id date;
   var boarded transferred flight;
   label boarded='On' transferred='Changed';
   where flight='219';
run;
```

```
proc print flights.laguardia noobs;
   id date;
   var date on changed flight;
   where flight='219';
run;
```

Which of the following PROC PRINT steps is correct if labels are not stored with the data set?

```
proc print data=allsales.totals label;
   label region8='Region 8 Yearly Totals';
```

```
run;
```

```
proc print data=allsales.totals;
   label region8='Region 8 Yearly Totals';
run;
```

```
proc print data allsales.totals label noobs;
run;
```

```
proc print allsales.totals label;
run;
```

Which of the following statements selects from a data set only those observations for which the value of the variable Style is **RANCH**, **SPLIT**, or **TWOSTORY**?

```
where style='RANCH' or 'SPLIT' or 'TWOSTORY';
```

```
where style in 'RANCH' or 'SPLIT' or 'TWOSTORY';
```

```
where style in (RANCH, SPLIT, TWOSTORY);
```

```
where style in ('RANCH','SPLIT','TWOSTORY');
```

If you want to sort your data and create a temporary data set named Calc to store the sorted data, which of the following steps should you submit?

```
proc sort data=work.calc out=finance.dividend;
run;
```

```
proc sort dividend out=calc;
   by account;
run;
```

```
proc sort data=finance.dividend out=work.calc;
    by account;
run;
```

```
proc sort from finance.dividend to calc;
    by account;
run;
```

Which options are used to create the following PROC PRINT output?

```
                                13:27 Monday, March 22, 1999

    Patient      Arterial      Heart      Cardiac      Urinary

      203           88           95          66           110

       54           83          183          95             0

      664           72          111         332            12

      210           74           97         369             0

      101           80          130         291             0
```

the DATE system option and the LABEL option in PROC PRINT

the DATE and NONUMBER system options and the DOUBLE and NOOBS options in PROC
PRINT

the DATE and NONUMBER system options and the DOUBLE option in PROC PRINT

the DATE and NONUMBER system options and the NOOBS option in PROC PRINT

Which of the following statements can you use in a PROC PRINT step to create this output?

Month	Instructors	AerClass	WalkJogRun	Swim
01	1	37	91	83
02	2	41	102	27
03	1	52	98	19
04	1	61	118	22
05	3	49	88	29
	8	240	497	180

```
var month instructors;
sum instructors aerclass walkjogrun swim;
```

```
var month;
sum instructors aerclass walkjogrun swim;
```

```
var month instructors aerclass;
sum instructors aerclass walkjogrun swim;
```

all of the above

What happens if you submit the following program?

```
proc sort data=clinic.diabetes;
run;
proc print data=clinic.diabetes;
   var age height weight pulse;
   where sex='F';
run;
```

The PROC PRINT step runs successfully, printing observations in their sorted order.

The PROC SORT step permanently sorts the input data set.

The PROC SORT step generates errors and stops processing, but the PROC PRINT step runs successfully, printing observations in their original (unsorted) order.

The PROC SORT step runs successfully, but the PROC PRINT step generates errors and stops processing.

If you submit the following program, which output does it create?

```
proc sort data=finance.loans out=work.loans;
   by months amount;
run;
proc print data=work.loans noobs;
   var months;
   sum amount payment;
   where months<360;
run;
```

Months	Amount	Payment
12	$3,500	$308.52
24	$8,700	$403.47
36	$10,000	$325.02
48	$5,000	$128.02
	$27,200	$1,165.03

Months	Amount	Payment
12	$3,500	$308.52
24	$8,700	$403.47
36	$10,000	$325.02
48	$5,000	$128.02
	27,200	1,165.03

Months	Amount	Payment
12	$3,500	$308.52
48	$5,000	$128.02
24	$8,700	$403.47
36	$10,000	$325.02
	$27,200	$1,165.03

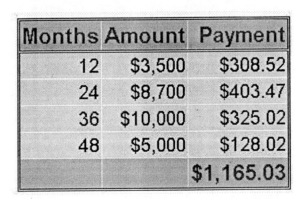

Months	Amount	Payment
12	$3,500	$308.52
24	$8,700	$403.47
36	$10,000	$325.02
48	$5,000	$128.02
		$1,165.03

Choose the statement below that selects rows in which

the amount is less than or equal to $5000

the account is 101-1092 or the rate equals 0.095.

    where amount <= 5000 and
        account='101-1092' or rate = 0.095;

    where (amount le 5000 and account='101-1092')
        or rate = 0.095;

    where amount <= 5000 and
        (account='101-1092' or rate eq 0.095);

    where amount <= 5000 or account='101-1092'
        and rate = 0.095;

What does PROC PRINT display by default?

    PROC PRINT does not create a default report; you must specify the rows and columns to be
    displayed.

    PROC PRINT displays all observations and variables in the data set. If you want an additional
    column for observation numbers, you can request it.

    PROC PRINT displays columns in the following order: a column for observation numbers, all
    character variables, and all numeric variables.

    PROC PRINT displays all observations and variables in the data set, a column for observation
    numbers on the far left, and variables in the order in which they occur in the data set.

Resolving Common Problems

Overview

In addition to correcting spelling mistakes, you might need to resolve several other types of common syntax errors. These errors include

omitting semicolons

leaving quotation marks unbalanced

specifying invalid options.

Another common problem is omitting a RUN statement at the end of a program. Although this is not technically an error, it can produce unexpected results. For the sake of convenience, we'll consider it together with syntax errors.

The table below lists these problems and their symptoms.

Identifying Problems in a SAS Program

Problem	Symptom
missing RUN statement	"PROC (or DATA) step running" at top of active window
missing semicolon	log message indicating an error in a statement that seems to be valid
unbalanced quotation marks	log message indicating that a quoted string has become too long or that a statement is ambiguous
invalid option	log message indicating that an option is invalid or not recognized

Missing RUN Statement

Each step in a SAS program is compiled and executed independently from every other step. As a step is compiled, SAS recognizes the end of the current step when it encounters

a DATA or PROC statement, which indicates the beginning of a new step

a RUN or QUIT statement, which indicates the end of the current step.

When the program below is submitted, the DATA step executes, but the PROC step does not. The PROC step does not execute because there is no following DATA or PROC step to indicate the beginning of a new step, nor is there a following RUN statement to indicate the end of the step.

```
data clinic.admitfee;
   set clinic.admit;
run;
proc print data=clinic.admitfee;
   var id name actlevel fee;
```

Because there is nothing to indicate the end of the PROC step, the PRINT procedure waits before executing, and a "PROC PRINT running" message appears at the top of the active window.

Program Window with Message

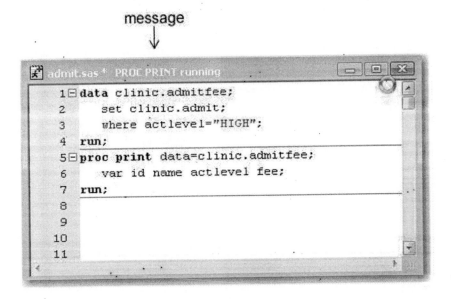

Resolving the Problem

To correct the error, submit a RUN statement to complete the PROC step.

```
run;
```

If you are using the Program Editor window, you do *not* need to recall the program to the Program Editor window.

Missing Semicolon

One of the most common errors is the omission of a semicolon at the end of a statement. The program below is missing a semicolon at the end of the PROC PRINT statement.

```
data clinic.admitfee;
  set clinic.admit;
run;
proc print data=clinic.admitfee
  var id name actlevel fee;
run;
```

When you omit a semicolon, SAS reads the statement that lacks the semicolon, plus the following statement, as one long statement. The SAS log then lists errors that relate to the combined statement, not the actual mistake (the missing semicolon).

Log Window with Error Message

Resolving the Problem

To correct the error, do the following:

Find the statement that lacks a semicolon. You can usually locate the statement that lacks the semicolon by looking at the underscored keywords in the error message and working backwards.

Add a semicolon in the appropriate location.

Resubmit the corrected program.

Check the Log window again to make sure there are no other errors.

Unbalanced Quotation Marks

Some syntax errors, such as the missing quotation mark after HIGH in the program below, cause SAS to misinterpret the statements in your program.

```
data clinic.admitfee;
```

```
   set clinic.admit;
   where actlevel='HIGH;
run;
proc print data=clinic.admitfee;
   var id name actlevel fee;
run;
```

When the program is submitted, SAS is unable to resolve the DATA step, and a "DATA STEP running" message appears at the top of the active window.

Program Editor with Message

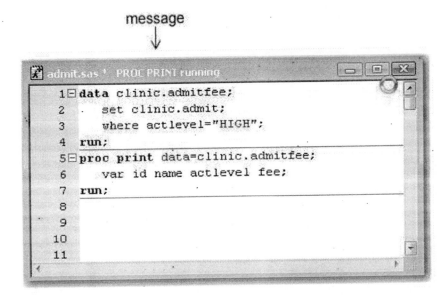

Sometimes a warning appears in the SAS log which indicates that

   a quoted string has become too long

   a statement that contains quotation marks (such as a TITLE or FOOTNOTE statement) is ambiguous due to invalid options or unquoted text.

Log with Warning Message

```
Log - (Untitled)  PROC PRINT running
93   proc print data=clinic.admitfee;
94      var id name actlevel fee;
95      title 'Patient Billing;
96      title2 'January 1998';
WARNING: The TITLE statement is ambiguous due to
         invalid options or unquoted text.
97   run;
```

When you have unbalanced quotation marks, SAS is often unable to detect the end of the statement in which it occurs. Simply adding a quotation mark and resubmitting your program usually does *not* solve the problem. SAS still considers the quotation marks to be unbalanced.

Therefore, you need to resolve the unbalanced quotation mark by canceling the submitted statements (in the Windows and UNIX operating environments) or by submitting a line of SAS code (in the z/OS operating environment) before you recall, correct, and resubmit the program.

If you do not resolve this problem when it occurs, it is likely that any subsequent programs that you submit in the current SAS session will generate errors.

Resolving the Error in the Windows Operating Environment

To resolve the error in the Windows operating environment:

Press the Ctrl and Break keys or click the Break Icon   on the toolbar.

Select **1. Cancel Submitted Statements**, and then click **OK**.

Tasking Manager Window

Select **Y to cancel submitted statements**, and then click **OK**.

Break Window

Correct the error and resubmit the program.

Resolving the Error in the UNIX Operating Environment

To resolve the error in the UNIX operating environment:

Open the Session Management window and click **Interrupt**.

Session Management Window

Select **1. Cancel Submitted Statements**, and then click **Y**.

Tasking Management Window

Correct the error and resubmit the program.

Resolving the Error in the z/OS Operating Environment

To resolve the error in the z/OS operating environment:

Submit an asterisk followed by a quotation mark, a semicolon, and a RUN statement.

```
*'; run;
```

Delete the line that contains the asterisk followed by the quotation mark, the semicolon, and the RUN statement.

Insert the missing quotation mark in the appropriate place.

Submit the corrected program.

You can also use the above method in the Windows and UNIX operating environments.

Invalid Option

An invalid option error occurs when you specify an option that is not valid in a particular statement. In the program below, the KEYLABEL option is not valid when used with the PROC PRINT statement.

```
data sasuser.admitfee;
   set clinic.admit;
   where weight>180 and (actlevel="MOD" or actlevel="LOW");
run;
proc print data=clinic.admitfee keylabel;
   label actlevel='Activity Level';
run;
```

When a SAS statement that contains an invalid option is submitted, a message appears in the Log window indicating that the option is not valid or not recognized.

Log Window with Syntax Error Message

```
Log - (Untitled)
1     data sasuser.admitfee;
2         set sasuser.admit;
3         where weight>180 and (actlevel="MOD" or actlevel="LOW");
4     run;

NOTE: There were 2 observations read from the data set SASUSER.ADMIT.
      WHERE (weight>180) and actlevel in ('LOW', 'MOD');
NOTE: The data set SASUSER.ADMITFEE has 2 observations and 9 variables.
NOTE: DATA statement used (Total process time):
      real time           0.03 seconds
      cpu time            0.03 seconds

5     proc print data=clinic.admitfee keylabel;
NOTE: Writing HTML Body file: sashtml.htm
5     proc print data=clinic.admitfee keylabel;
                                        --------
                                        22
ERROR 22-322: Syntax error, expecting one of the following: ;, (, BLANKLINE, DATA, DOUBLE,
              LABEL, N, NOOBS, OBS, ROUND, ROWS, SPLIT, STYLE, SUMLABEL, UNIFORM, WIDTH.

5     proc print data=clinic.admitfee keylabel;
                                        --------
                                        202
ERROR 202-322: The option or parameter is not recognized and will be ignored.

6         label actlevel='Activity Level';
7     run;

NOTE: The SAS System stopped processing this step because of errors.
NOTE: PROCEDURE PRINT used (Total process time):
      real time           1.54 seconds
      cpu time            0.42 seconds
```

Resolving the Problem

To correct the error:

Remove or replace the invalid option, and check your statement syntax as needed.

Resubmit the corrected program.

Check the Log window again to make sure there are no other errors.

LIBNAME Statement Options

There are several options that you can use with the LIBNAME statement to control how SAS interacts with the Excel data. The general form of the SAS/ACCESS LIBNAME statement (with options) is as follows:

libname libref 'location-of-Excel-workbook' <options>;

Example:

libname doctors 'c:\clinicNotes\addresses.xlsx' mixed=yes;

DBMAX_TEXT=n

indicates the length of the longest character string where n is any integer between 256 and 32,767 inclusive. Any character string with a length greater than this value is truncated. The default is 1024.

GETNAMES=YES|NO

determines whether SAS will use the first row of data in an Excel worksheet or range as column names.
YES specifies to use the first row of data in an Excel worksheet or range as column names.
NO specifies not to use the first row of data in an Excel worksheet or range as column names. SAS generates and uses the variable names F1, F2, F3, and so on.
The default is YES.

MIXED=YES|NO

Specifies whether to import data with both character and numeric values and convert all data to character.
YES specifies that all data values will be converted to character.
NO specifies that numeric data will be missing when a character type is assigned. Character data will be missing when a numeric data type is assigned.
The default is NO.

SCANTEXT=YES|NO

specifies whether to read the entire data column and use the length of the longest string found as the SAS column width.
YES scans the entire data column and uses the longest string value to determine the SAS column width.
NO does not scan the column and defaults to a width of 255.
The default is YES.

SCANTIME=YES|NO

specifies whether to scan all row values in a date/time column and automatically determine the TIME. format if only time values exist.
YES specifies that a column with only time values be assigned the TIME8. format.
NO specifies that a column with only time values be assigned the DATE9. format.
The default is NO.

USEDATE=YES|NO

specifies whether to use the DATE9. format for date/time values in Excel workbooks.
YES specifies that date/time values be assigned the DATE9. format.
NO specifies that date/time values be assigned the DATETIME. format.
The default is YES.

Chapter Summary

Text Summary

Raw Data Files

A raw data file is an external file whose records contain data values that are organized in fields. The raw data files in this chapter contain fixed fields.

Steps to Create a SAS Data Set

You need to follow several steps to create a SAS data set using raw data. You need to

reference the raw data file to be read

name the SAS data set

identify the location of the raw data

describe the data values to be read.

Referencing a SAS Library

To begin your program, you might need to use a LIBNAME statement to reference the SAS library in which your data set will be stored.

Writing a DATA Step Program

The DATA statement indicates the beginning of the DATA step and names the SAS data set(s) to be created.

Next, you specify the raw data file by using the INFILE statement. The OBS= option in the INFILE statement enables you to process a specified number of observations.

This chapter teaches column input, the most simple input style. Column input specifies actual column locations for data values. The INPUT statement describes the raw data to be read and placed into the SAS data set.

Submitting the Program

When you submit the program, you can use the OBS= option with the INFILE statement to verify that the correct data is being read before reading the entire data file.

After you submit the program, view the log to check the DATA step processing. You can then print the data set by using the PROC PRINT procedure.

Once you've checked the log and verified your data, you can modify the DATA step to read the entire raw data file by removing the OBS= option from the INFILE statement.

If you are working with a raw data file that contains invalid data, the DATA step continues to execute. Unlike syntax errors, invalid data errors do not cause SAS to stop processing a program. If you have a way to edit the invalid data, it's best to correct the problem and rerun the DATA step.

Creating and Modifying Variables

To modify existing values or to create new variables, you can use an assignment statement in any DATA step. Within assignment statements, you can specify any SAS expression.

You can use date constants to assign dates in assignment statements. You can also use SAS time constants and SAS datetime constants in assignment statements.

Subsetting Data

To process only observations that meet a specified condition, use a subsetting IF statement in the DATA step.

Reading Instream Data

To read instream data lines instead of an external file, use a DATALINES statement, a CARDS statement, or a LINES statement and enter data directly in your SAS program. Omit the RUN at the end of the DATA step.

Creating a Raw Data File

When the goal of your SAS program is to create a raw data file and not a SAS data set, it is inefficient to list a data set name in the DATA statement. Instead use the keyword _NULL_, which allows the power of the DATA step without actually creating a SAS data set. A SET statement specifies the SAS data set that you want to read from.

You can use the FILE and PUT statements to write out the observations from a SAS data set to a raw data file just as you used the INFILE and INPUT statements to create a SAS data set. These two sets of statements work almost identically.

Microsoft Excel Files

You can read Excel worksheets by using the SAS/ACCESS LIBNAME statement.

Steps to Create a SAS Data Set from Excel Data

You need to follow several steps to create a SAS data set using Excel. You need to

    provide a name for the new SAS data set

    provide the location or name of the libref and Excel worksheet

Referencing an Excel Workbook

To begin your program, you need to use a LIBNAME statement to reference the Excel workbook.

Writing a DATA Step Program

The DATA statement indicates the beginning of the DATA step and names the SAS data set(s) to be created.

Next, you specify the Excel worksheet to be read by using the SET statement. You must use a SAS name literal since SAS uses the special character ($) to name Excel worksheets.

Submitting the Program

When you submit the program, you can use the CONTENTS procedure to explore the new library and contents.

After you submit the program, view the log to check the DATA step processing. You can then print the data sets created from the Excel worksheets by using the PROC PRINT procedure.

Once you've checked the log and verified your data, you can modify the DATA step along with the WHERE statement to subset parts of the data as needed.

Syntax

Reading Data from a Raw File or Reading Instream Data

LIBNAME *libref 'SAS-data-library'*;

FILENAME *fileref 'filename'*;

DATA *SAS-data-set*;

INFILE *file-specification<OBS=n>*;
INPUT *variable <$> startcol-endcol...*;
IF *expression*;
variable=expression;

DATALINES;

instream data goes here if used

;

RUN; /* *not used with the DATALINES statement* */

PROC PRINT DATA= *SAS-data set*;

RUN;

Creating a Raw Data File

LIBNAME *libref 'SAS-data-library'*;

DATA _NULL_;

SET *SAS-data-set;*

FILE *file-specification;*
PUT *variable startcol-endcol...*;

RUN;

Reading Data from an Excel Workbook

LIBNAME *libref '<location-of-Excel-workbook>'*;

PROC CONTENTS DATA= *libref._ALL_;*

DATA *SAS-data-set;*

SET *libref.'worksheet_name$'n;*
WHERE *where-expression;*

RUN;

PROC PRINT DATA= *SAS-data set*;

RUN;

Sample Programs

Reading Data from an External File

```
libname clinic 'c:\bethesda\patients\admit';
filename admit 'c:\clinic\patients\admit.dat';
data clinic.admittan;
   infile admit obs=5;
   input ID $ 1-4 Name $ 6-25 RestHR 27-29 MaxHR 31-33
      RecHR 35-37 TimeMin 39-40 TimeSec 42-43
      Tolerance $ 45;
   if tolerance='D';
   TotalTime=(timemin*60)+timesec;
run;
proc print data=clinic.admittan;
run;
```

Reading Instream Data

```
libname clinic 'c:\bethesda\patients\admit';
data clinic.group1;
   input ID $ 1-4 Name $ 6-25 RestHR 27-29 MaxHR 31-33
        RecHR 35-37 TimeMin 39-40 TimeSec 42-43
        Tolerance $ 45;
   if tolerance='D';
   TotalTime=(timemin*60)+timesec;
datalines;
2458 Murray, W          72  185 128 12 38 D
2462 Almers, C          68  171 133 10  5 I
2501 Bonaventure, T     78  177 139 11 13 I
2523 Johnson, R         69  162 114  9 42 S
2539 LaMance, K         75  168 141 11 46 D
2544 Jones, M           79  187 136 12 26 N
2595 Warren, C          77  170 136 12 10 S
;
proc print data=clinic.group1;
run;
```

Reading Excel Data

```
libname sasuser 'c:\users\admit.xlsx' mixed=yes;
proc contents data=sasuser._all_;
run;
proc print data=sasuser.'worksheet1$'n;
run;
```

Creating an Excel Worksheet

```
libname clinic 'c:\Users\mylaptop\admitxl.xlsx' mixed=yes;
data clinic.admit;
   set work.admit;
run;
```

Points to Remember

LIBNAME and FILENAME statements are global. Librefs and filerefs remain in effect until you change them, cancel them, or end your SAS session.

For each field of raw data that you read into your SAS data set, you *must* specify the following in the INPUT statement: a valid SAS variable name, a type (character or numeric), a starting column, and if necessary, an ending column.

When you use column input, you can read any or all fields from the raw data file, read the fields in any order, and specify only the starting column for variables whose values occupy only one column.

Column input is appropriate only in some situations. When you use column input, your data *must* be standard character and numeric values, and these values *must* be in fixed fields. That is, values for a particular variable must be in the same location in all records.